To Peggy
with lo

ECHOES

Sunny Serafino

a novel by

SUNNY SERAFINO

InstantPublisher.com
P O Box 985
Collierville TN 38027

ISBN: 1-59196-331-1

This book is a work of fiction. Names, characters and incidents are either the products of the author's imagination or are used fictitiously. Any resemblance to actual events locales, or persons, living or dead, is entirely coincidental.

Dedications and Acknowledgments

This book is dedicated to all those who courageously meet and triumph over adversity with perseverance and faith. It is also dedicated to all those who hold the sanctity of family above petty differences.

I have so many people to thank it would be impossible to name them all because they have contributed along the way. I thank my parents, Charles and Doris Allen, who are gone but not forgotten, for the values they taught me and examples they provided me. I thank my friends who have steadfastly encouraged and helped me, especially Bette Crosby, Dot Pansius, and Peg Bendicksen. Special thanks also go the faithful members of Script Teasers and Morningside Writer's Group (you know who you are), and last but certainly not least, I thank my husband, Lenny. My efforts would be all for nothing without your encouragement and love.

Also by Sunny Serafino

Nobody's Child

Shadows in the Heart

Pure Gold

CHAPTER ONE

Lily Hoffmann pressed her foot on the accelerator. She had a one o'clock appointment with Doctor Willistein. It was twenty minutes to one, and she was on the wrong side of the railroad tracks when she heard the mournful whistle of a freight train sound for the crossing ahead. Too late, the blinking red lights of the gates lowered in front of her.

Drumming her fingers on the wheel, she sighed audibly and watched as the endless chain of freight cars rattled across the road in front of her. She hated to be late, not that her doctor wouldn't understand. He'd been the family doctor for thirty years. Doctor Bob's office had been on the south side of the city since he began his practice. He hadn't followed the other specialists when they moved to the plush North Eagleton Medical Complex next to the new hospital.

What's so urgent about this appointment anyhow? She remembered his strange telephone call yesterday, calling her himself instead of having Shirley do it. "Please have George come with you," he'd said.

What nonsense. As if George would miss a half day's work to hold her hand in the doctor's office. Hadn't she been through test after test over the past months? She hadn't needed George with her then and she didn't need him now. He'd just mutter about more foolish tests—a lot of fuss over nothing.

She was pretty sure what the doctor was going to say. "Lily, you need a rest, a change of scene. You're run down after caring for your mother during her illness last year," that's what he'd say. Well, she'd be the first to agree. Last year had been grueling, watching her widowed mother's life slip away after a stroke. So far, this winter hadn't been any picnic either with snowfall after snowfall, the big ice storm, and George coming down with the flu.

The thought of a prescribed vacation sounded great. George would have to listen if Doctor Willistein suggested it. A vacation in Florida maybe? They could visit Patty, they hadn't seen her in two years. *Well, let's not celebrate miracles before they happen. A trip anywhere would do. February is such a dreary month.*

She was surprised to find no one in the waiting room. *No patients? In February? How strange.* Usually it was filled, especially during the winter months. Lily signed the sheet in front of the opaque window and turned to sit in one of the familiar worn chairs that lined the walls of the room.

"Hi, Missus Hoffmann," Shirley called as she slid the window open. "Doctor Bob's waiting for you in his office."

"Hi yourself, Shirley. Where is everyone? Nobody sick anymore?" Lily sounded flippant but her stomach twinged and she wished she'd taken time to eat lunch. She'd reasoned herself out of lunch because she ate breakfast so late. This morning after George left for work, she'd slipped back into bed. Lately she was so tired. She needed a change, a real vacation. That's what she needed, not more tests.

He sat at his cluttered desk in the small office and rose as she entered.

"Don't tell me I need more tests because I'm not taking them."

"Nope. No more tests." He reached forward to take her hand, more in a friendly grasp than a handshake. "I have the reports from all the procedures you've done over the past month. Sit down, Lil. Where's George?" he asked, looking at the door behind her. Robert M. Willistein, M.D. had been a personal friend of George and Lillian Hoffmann for over thirty years. Face to face, it was Bob and Lil.

She sat in one of the chairs that faced his desk. "He's swamped at work and couldn't take the time off. Besides, I don't need him to hold my hand." Again, she joked but the words sounded forced and her stomach contracted.

"I wish he was here with you, Lil." He picked up a stack of papers, charts and x-rays, slid two of the x-rays into the view box next to his desk, but didn't turn it on.

His leather chair grumbled as he lowered himself into the curves and grooves his body had formed over the years. "How are you feeling?"

"Tired and grumpy."

"Grumpy?"

"Well, I groused all the way over here because I'm not only tired, I'm tired of tests and doctors. Present company excluded." Her smile was forced.

"No more tests, Lil."

"Well then, what? A vacation? More vitamins?" She smiled.

"It's not good." His hands trembled as he reached for some charts in a folder on his desk.

Lily sucked icy air between clenched teeth. Her voice stuttered. "What do you mean *not good*."

"It's back."

"Back? What's back—Oh, God, no. The cancer?" Her hands formed tight claws around the arms of the chair. "No, it can't be. It's almost five years. You said…"

"I said there were no guarantees, Lil. Doctor Schwartz agreed."

"He said he got it all. He said if I was cancer-free for five years…" her voice was muffled by sobs that filled her throat. She drew in a stuttering breath, "Wait. I had a mammogram last fall. There was nothing. Nothing."

"It isn't breast cancer this time, Lil."

She looked from the still dark x-ray viewer to his face and then down to the papers visibly shaking in his trembling hands. "What then?"

He flipped on the switch and light glowed behind the x-rays caught in the clips. "You can see these dark patches in your lungs, Lil. After getting the all clear on the mammogram report, we started checking everything."

"Well, what does all that mean?" she asked, pointing a shaking finger at the glowing x-rays. "Chemo? For God's sake, say something. What can we do?"

Doctor Bob leaned back in his chair and it creaked with the weight shift. He dropped the papers on his desk and folded his hands on top of the pile. "Do you remember after you had the mastectomy, Doctor Schwartz and I went over the possible procedures you could take at that time? He recommended chemotherapy, maybe radiation, but he told you it was your decision whether you wanted to follow those procedures."

"And I said no. George said no." She was sobbing openly now. "George didn't want to put me through any more after the surgery. I didn't…"

"It was your choice and I didn't disagree," he said quietly. "Lily there is no one to blame, not you, not George, not the doctors. This just happened. There are never any guarantees in medicine; it isn't an exact science. You know I've said that before."

Lily stared at him in disbelief. "This can't be happening."

"I know Doctor Schwartz said he thought he'd gotten it all, Lily. Lymph nodes, glands, everything, but he did warn that without chemo or radiation the cancer might metastasize—might return—not necessarily in the other breast—maybe somewhere else. It usually happens within five years of surgery. Usually—but not always."

"But it was four and a half years ago! Five years and I'd be safe. There has to be something I can do. Surgery? Treatments? Drugs?" She was grasping at straws.

"I'm sorry, Lily. So sorry." He handed her a single sheet of paper; she didn't look at it, instead focusing on his eyes beneath the heavy, drawn eyebrows.

"Well, what then?"

"The results of the scans show both lungs are involved," he said pointing to the now-bright x-ray.

Her frown deepened. *This can't be happening. Cancer? Lungs? I'm worn out.* Aloud she repeated her thoughts. "Cancer? Lungs? I don't understand. I'm just tired."

He rose and came around the desk, squatting down beside her chair. "No treatments, Lil. It's too far along, too late. I'm so very sorry." His eyes filled with tears and the hand that took hers from her lap was icy cold."

"You mean…" she looked down at the paper in her lap where she'd left it, then raised her eyes to the x-ray gleaming like a beacon on the wall. "What's too late?"

"It's terminal." He forced the words from his frozen lips. "That's why I wanted George here with you, but I couldn't delay telling you, my dear."

"I'm going to die?"

He answered, and although she watched his lips move, she didn't hear what he said. Was he out of his mind? This was ridiculous.

"No. You're wrong. There's some mistake. I don't give a damn what those tests show," she shouted pushing the papers back across the desk. "I'm a little run down. I need a rest, a change of scene, stronger vitamins. There's nothing wrong with me." Her voice weakened with each word. "This isn't fair. I'm not ready to die."

Bob Willistein patted her shoulder, walked back to his chair, flipping the light off as he sat. "This is the part of my job I hate," he whispered. "You're right. It isn't fair, but the diagnosis has been confirmed by the tests," his arm swung helplessly across the papers scattered across the desk. "I've sent all the reports to Doctor Schwartz. If you want to make an appointment with him…"

The office was too quiet. Everything seemed wrong. Was he telling her she was tired because she was dying? Was she losing weight because the dark shadows on the x-rays of her lungs were cancer? There was no cure, no treatment, no hope?

"It can't be. Somewhere there's an error."

"There's no mistake Lily. That's why I ran all the tests, to confirm what the first ones showed."

"You didn't tell me about the first tests."

"I wanted to be absolutely sure before I talked with you."

"Well, you're wrong," she said, her chin trembling with emotion. She stood but the office was too cramped for her to pace. Trapped, she turned her back to the doctor. She didn't want to look at him. The wall facing his desk was covered with pictures of his extended family of patients. George and the kids were there; so were many of her friends. Her eyes blurred, preventing her from picking out those she knew.

He rose and came to her, putting one arm around her shoulders. "It wasn't easy for me to tell you, Lil. I've known you for over thirty years, delivered your three children. You're family. Don't you think I'd make damn sure before I made a statement like this? You have cancer. It's too advanced for treatment. Maybe if we'd found it sooner…"

"I was taking care of my mother."

"I know."

"This isn't happening. No. It can't be."

He spoke softly, "You can get another opinion, see another doctor. I'll make arrangements for you if that's what you want to do."

"I don't know what I want to do." The room shrank around them, turning unaccountably cold. She felt faint, her mind concentrating on the tightness in her chest as if she were suddenly breathing very thin air.

He sensed her distress and eased her back into the chair. No matter how many times he had to deal with death, it never became easy. "Do you want to lie down? I can have Shirley put you in one of the examining rooms and stay with you for a while."

She shook her head, drawing in a deep gulp of air as if that would lift the ache in her chest.

"Shall I call George?"

Lily stiffened. "No. Don't call George. I don't want him to know yet. There's too much to think about. Too much…" she paused. She didn't finish the sentence because she didn't know *what* she had to think about, only that there was a *lot* to think about. Softly she asked, "If you are right about this…how long?"

His voice broke when he answered her question. "Possibly three to six months. There's no way to be certain, Lily.

He crowded into the chair next to her. They talked in low voices, remembering the past. The examining rooms along the hallway remained empty and silent. Nothing was the way it should be. There was no mention of the future. What was the future?

#

After she left his office, she didn't go home. Something compelled her to keep driving when she reached the intersection that led to their house on Mountainview Terrace. Instead of turning left, she headed for the park downtown.

The sky was gray with smoky February clouds scudding over the hills that rose from both sides of the river. A few hearty souls walked along the concrete paths. Lily parked the car and stepped over a low fence that separated the macadam from the winter-burned lawn. She walked toward the picnic area and sat on a bench, plunging her hands into her pockets. It was cold and damp but she was too numb to notice. From the bench, through the bare branches, she saw the empty playground she had visited so often when her children were young. She imagined their shouts of laughter as they urged her to push them higher on the swings, catch them as they careened down the sliding board, or balance them on the seesaws.

Her eyes misted as she watched a young mother pushing a baby carriage and holding the hand of a little boy about four-years-old. How many times had she brought her children here? Michael had been four once, holding on to the carriage as she pushed Debra.

The mother and child paused when they came to her bench.

"Rotten day, ain't it?" the young woman said.

Lily fought to speak. "Kind of cold and cloudy. But you're smart bringing the children out for a walk. I used to bring my kids here when they were small."

"Yeah, well," she said, shrugging. "Come on Kevin. Let's go home. It's too cold to stay and play." The little boy hesitated a minute, looking into Lily's face as if he wanted to say something. Did he read her distress? Children are so perceptive sometimes. Instead, he put his hand on the side of the carriage.

"Have a nice day," the young woman said as she turned and went toward the west exit. Lily was alone again.

Angrily wiping her eyes, she rose and walked along the path toward High Street. On the busy street she wasn't alone, but there was no comfort in the crowd of people hurrying along the brick sidewalks. *Oh, God. Is that Irene Miller?* She didn't want to meet anyone she knew because she wouldn't be capable of small talk. She turned quickly to look in the shop windows, as if she really cared what they were displaying. When she noticed her reflection, she was stunned. Who was that withered old woman who stared back at her? It wasn't long ago that she and Kate decided they both looked much too young to have to claim all the years they had amassed. She raised her shoulders and turned to go back to her car.

Kate. She should tell her. But not now. Lily buried her fear and confusion deep within herself. No, not yet. She had to think, sort through the emotions that were weaving a tight, impenetrable, muffler around her heart.

#

At home she cried. Walking through the rooms, she talked to herself. *How could this happen? Why me? Why now?* There were things she'd never get to do. The things she'd saved for *someday*.

Over a solitary cup of coffee in the kitchen, she tried to remember what Bob had said. The words were blurred by her confusion. *Was he right when he said three to six months? I can't remember what else he said. What happens next?* She was afraid of making mistakes in the time she had left. Lily knew if she told George, he'd cry. He was a hard man and didn't cry easily but he'd cry if he knew she was dying. How did a mother tell her children she was dying? She didn't want pity, she wanted…

What did she want? Banging her closed fist on the tabletop, she knew what she wanted. She wanted this to be a big mistake. She wanted the phone to ring and Bob to tell her it wasn't true, the tests were wrong.

The house remained quiet; the telephone didn't ring.

What would happen to the kids and George? For thirty-five years she'd been Missus George Hoffmann, wife and mother. Years of trying to please a discontented man, making ends meet, finding excuses for the children when they angered their father. Not easy, but there were good times. Birthday parties, vacations, Christmas. When the kids were little the conflicts were smaller and the battles less frequent. The arguments and distance between them increased as they grew.

Lily sat at the kitchen table. Everything was the same and yet nothing was the same. She looked around the room, her eyes falling on her collection of salt and pepper shakers lined up on a shelf George built for her, even though he considered the collection a waste of time and money. The clock ticked loudly in the quiet room. George would be home in an hour. He'd expect dinner to be ready as it always was. Reluctantly she rose, blew her nose again and washed her hands at the sink. Her stomach rolled as she thought of food. *Stop it. You have to think this out and you can't be weeping and puking all over the place. You have to think.* Sadly, all Lily could think about was her own death. Her hands shook as she put the potatoes on to boil.

#

"What's the matter with you?" George pushed his chair back from the table. "You've dropped everything you touched. You haven't said three words since I've been home, and you didn't eat a thing. Don't tell me you're on some damn fool diet again. You're getting skinny."

Lily didn't answer, just picked up the dirty dishes and stacked them in the dishwasher.

"You go somewhere today?" George spoke over his shoulder as he went into the living room.

Lily's heart thudded to a stop in her chest. "Why?"

"Saw the car was moved."

A deep, long breath escaped her lips as she put the leftovers in the refrigerator. "I drove downtown for a while. Didn't buy anything." She hadn't told George about the appointment this afternoon. Yesterday she'd thought it better to avoid the subject of doctors and tests; tonight she was very glad she'd made that decision.

Lily heard his recliner creak as he adjusted it. She hurried through and sat in her own matching chair. Next to her was a basket that held her latest needlework project. Automatically she reached for the embroidery hoop then quickly withdrew her hand. She wasn't steady enough to thread a needle; her concentration was muddled.

George leaned his head back and closed his eyes, fingers automatically reaching for the remote control. Something was wrong. Lily looked like she might have been crying and he hadn't done anything to make her cry. Had she heard from one of the kids? "Everything okay?" he asked.

"Sure. Why?"

"You look different."

"Different? How?" Lily twisted her hands, keeping them out of sight.

"How should I know? You look different, like something's bothering you." He pressed the button and the television came to life. Commercial after commercial flipped across the screen as he thumped his chair into a more upright position, a finger firmly pressing the channel selection button. George was proud of the cable hookup. He was also very good at ignoring any subject that didn't coincide with his outlook or feelings.

Lily sighed. "Think I'll go up to bed and read for a while. I'm a little tired."

George grunted, absorbed in choosing a television program to watch. "You're always tired lately," he said.

She rose and started to climb the stairs. *Always tired.* Halfway up the flight of carpeted steps she turned and looked at George. The light from his reading lamp shone through the thin strands of hair on the top of his head. His glasses had slipped down his nose and he leaned forward, watching the images intently.

She loved him. They'd met thirty-five years ago at a dance in the basement of Sacred Heart Church. George Hoffman, older than she, wasn't a regular but she was attracted to him immediately. He'd stood at the back of the room, separated from the groups of friends gathered in tight little circles while the records spun on the turntable and Sister Mary John fiddled with the volume. Lily sat on one of the folding chairs along the wall with her best friend, Kate O'Donald. George asked Lily to dance. He was a poor dancer but she felt special in his arms.

He told her he only came to the dance because his brothers had dared him. His family didn't belong to Sacred Heart; they were Lutherans. They lived on the south side of town and he and his father and two brothers all worked for the foundry. She told him she was an only child, that her father and mother had a little grocery store in the Briar Hill section of town. She remembered he grunted something about only rich people lived in Briar Hill.

She loved him now and she'd always love him. The trouble was she didn't want to think about always. How long was always?

Lily stopped at the top of the stairs. She felt the strange breathlessness the exertion brought. Up until this afternoon she thought the shortness of breath was because she was out of shape. She needed to exercise more, promising herself when spring came, she and Kate would start going for long walks.

The doors stood open to the three empty bedrooms that had belonged to her children for so many years. She liked to leave the doors open so that as she passed she could relive the memories they held. Tonight she closed the doors quietly, not wanting reminders of the past.

She hurried to the room she and George had shared for thirty-five years. The past wasn't what she wanted to think about tonight and yet everywhere she looked it pressed on her like a humid summer afternoon just before a storm. The house was such a big part of her life but she'd never really thought about it until today. Now everything seemed very precious, the wallpaper she and George had hung themselves in the upper hall; the glass doorknobs on the doors, the pantry George had built for her. Eerily she remembered voices calling from room to room.

As she crossed their bedroom directly over the living room, the floor squeaked as it always did. She caught sight of her reflection in the mirror and stopped to stare. The same face she'd been looking at for over fifty-seven years stared back, but it seemed paler, more lined tonight. Maybe she'd start wearing a little makeup.

Seated at her ancient dressing table, she looked at the framed photographs of their three children and wiped the tears that filled her eyes. How had she let them slip away from her? And, more importantly, why had she wasted so much precious time?

Lost in thought, Lily wrenched herself back to the present. She drew in a stuttering breath. Tomorrow she'd call Kate.

CHAPTER TWO

Lily and her best friend, Katherine Elizabeth Agnes O'Donald, had attended the same parochial schools from first grade through graduation. Never married, Kate was the O'Donald family mainstay to her two sisters, seven brothers, and the nieces and nephews who increased in number each year. Once, right after graduation, it was rumored Kate was going to enter a convent and become a nun, but someone in the O'Donald family always needed her, so she remained in Eagleton, spreading her charity closer to home.

Lily twisted the cord on the kitchen wall telephone, listening to the mechanical buzz after she dialed Kate's number. She bit her lip. It wasn't going to be easy talking to Kate without going to pieces. They'd shared their lives for so long, the established bond made it impossible for them to keep secrets from each other. Kate was the sister Lily never had, and Kate admitted that she was closer to Lily than either of her own sisters.

"Hi," Kate said cheerfully. "I knew it was you."

"You did, huh? Telepathy turned on?"

"It's quarter after eight. Who else would call me this early?"

Lily didn't reply and sensing tension, Kate asked, "What's up?"

"Nothing. Just needed to talk."

"I'm coming over."

"No! Wait!"

"Never mind 'No, wait,' I'm coming over. Put the kettle on. We'll have tea." Kate hung up before Lily could say another word.

Lily had wanted to talk to Kate without having to look into her eyes. She clunked the phone into the cradle on the wall and put the kettle on. Sliding into a chair at the kitchen table she waited.

#

Kate peered through the window between the ruffled curtains before stepping inside. She didn't need an invitation. Standing on the little rug inside the door, she studied Lily. From the time they shared the same colored chalk in first grade, she'd shared Lily's life; listening to her romantic interests, aspirations of becoming an actress, and then a teacher. Kate watched her fall in love with George and forget everything else she'd planned for her future. At the wedding, as the Maid of Honor, she'd caught Lily's bouquet because Lily tossed it to her.

"You okay?" she asked softly.

"No. I told you not to come." Lily's voice was tight and tense, yet weak.

"Why? Something's wrong, I know it. You've never held back before. Have I done something?"

Lily shook her head, raising tear-filled eyes to greet Kate. Her lips trembled and she looked away. "It's something I don't know how to tell you. I can't tell you or George. Kate, I'm afraid. " She covered her face with her hands and her shoulders heaved rhythmically with sobs seething from deep within her. For the first time, the full weight of her lonely burden descended upon her.

The sound of weeping dominated the quiet room. Kate gently rubbed Lily's shoulders. It wasn't time for words. Not yet. When some of the grief subsided, Kate sat next to Lily, holding her hands. Kate's cheeks, too, were wet with tears, not for the grief that was so devastating to Lily, because she didn't know what that was yet. She cried because she shared Lily's agony, whatever it was.

"I'm sorry," Lily said, her breath coming in gasps.

"You have to tell me."

"I know."

Rain started to beat against the kitchen windows, diverting their attention for a moment.

"What did you mean you *can't* tell me or George? Whatever the secret is, did you think you could fool me?" Kate watched Lily's face become even paler, then flush. "Tell me. Whatever it is, for God's sake tell me. You know we've never kept anything from each other. Never!" Kate's chest tightened as she waited for Lily to speak. She had a feeling this was more serious than some of the antics one of the kids had pulled.

"I don't know how to start. I know I have to tell someone and I can't tell George. Not yet." She hesitated, "Oh, Kate, it's not what's happening, it's trying to figure out what to do about it."

"For God's holy sake, Lily, stop rambling and speak up. There hasn't been anything in the last fifty years we haven't shared."

Lily shivered in the warm kitchen. "It's back. The cancer's back and I'm dying," she whispered.

The soft-spoken words shifted Kate as if an earth tremor had moved the ground beneath her. Her fingers automatically made the sign of the cross; she paled and whispered, "In the name of our God—dying? Lily, what are you talking about?"

"I'm afraid to die, Kate, I'm scared to death." The unfortunate conflicting choice of words was not lost on either of them.

"Now wait a minute. How do you know you're dying?"

"Doctor Bob. You know—all those tests," she shrugged.

"But you said the mammogram was normal."

"It is. But the cancer is back."

"Tell me," Kate said, sliding forward to the edge of her chair.

Again Lily started to cry, softly this time, her sobbing distorting her voice. "It's metastasized; it's lung cancer. Inoperable. It's too far gone, terminal. There's nothing to do, no hope."

"There's no such thing as no hope," Kate said, bolting out of her chair, "does George…oh my God—you haven't told George?"

Lily shook her head, fumbling in her pocket for her handkerchief.

Kate moved to her side. "You have to tell me everything now."

"This is the first time I've cried. Really cried."

"How long have you known?"

"I saw Doctor Bob yesterday afternoon."

"And you didn't come right over and talk to me?"

"It's not like sharing a secret. Not like sharing a *happy* secret. I had to get it straight in my mind before I told you. There's so much to think about. When *do* I tell George? I know I have to tell him. Still, is any good served by telling him right now?"

"How long does the doctor give you?"

"Three to six months."

"No! Oh, no," Kate's shoulders drew up in a protective arch, head bowed, tears flowing freely, her hands clasped across her chest. She stood at the sink, raised her head and stared out the window. The bare branches of the oak tree glistened as the rain painted them gunmetal gray. "That's not enough time," she whispered.

"We never have enough time. You don't think about it until you know it's ending."

Kate drew her hands into tight fists; she'd helped members of her own family through the last days of life; her mother and father, several aunts and uncles, and once a six-month-old nephew. Death was never easy and yet she'd found the strength before. Why did she feel so helpless now? Why did Lily have to know in advance her life was ending?

"Now wait a minute. What about another opinion? A new drug? They're always doing research. This is what—five years now? For God's sake, you can't accept this without doing anything?

I can't accept it," her brows folded into a tight line across her forehead.

"He mentioned another opinion. I said, I don't think so. What's the use?"

"The use? Maybe there's something he didn't find, didn't explore."

"Like what?"

"I don't know. You can't just say 'okay, I'm dying' and sit and wait." Kate paced the room. Her long strides took her back and forth for several moments. She turned and without speaking, they met and encircled each other with trembling arms, hands ineptly patting the other's back, like mothers soothing a hurt child.

Breaking away and wiping her eyes, Kate drew herself up to her full height. Four inches taller than Lily and normally many pounds lighter, she had always appeared to be the stronger. "What about the kids?"

"I can't tell them either. Not yet. I cried when I came home yesterday. Then I tried to think, but I didn't know what to think about."

Kate noticed how thin and pale Lily looked this morning. Had she missed these signs? What kind of a friend would miss those things? Smothered by the emotional tension in the room, she walked to the window. "This is too much to take in all at once. I want to help you and I don't know how. I want to change things, make them right, wake up from this nightmare." She turned to look at her long time friend. "You're thin. I should have noticed."

"I thought being tired all the time and losing weight was a sign of old age." Lily's attempt at humor failed.

"You're not old."

"I know."

"What did you think about; what did you decide?"

Lily ran her hands through her graying hair. "I don't know. Maybe I should talk to George first. But then again, maybe I should wait."

Kate stared at Lily but didn't speak.

"Oh. You're right. I can't worry about things happening too fast, can I?"

Kate took the simmering kettle from the stove and poured hot water into the teapot. "Sit down. We'll have tea. Remember when we were little we had tea parties? Tea was my mother's cure for everything; a headache, a bad grade, a pimple? Irish medicine my Da used to say."

They sat next to each other at the worn kitchen table, stirring the tea in thick mugs and spoke softly about inconsequential things, then Kate asked, "What do you want me to do?"

Lily shrugged. "What is there to do?"

"You have to tell George and the kids. You can't wait until…"

Lily tightened her lips. "I know. Not yet though. I want to be able to talk without bawling like a banshee."

"What about another opinion? Want me to go with you to a doctor?"

"I don't think so. I'll think about it." *But I can't take too long*, she finished silently.

"I'm going to call Mercy House. There's always someone who can take my usual Thursday for me."

"No. Don't change your plans. You're needed there."

"I'm needed here now. I can't leave you alone."

"I need to be alone. I have to think things through. Go. I'll call you if I need you."

"Promise?"

"Promise. I'll call you later."

Kate stood and pulled her coat from the back of the chair. "I still don't like leaving you."

"Go," Lily said, making a shooing motion with a trembling hand. "I'll see you tomorrow." She tried to smile.

"You going to the library tomorrow?"

Lily grinned weakly. "Why not? Nothing's changed, has it? At least not yet."

Every Friday during the winter months, Lily and Kate went to the library and then to Scarlette's for lunch. It was a ritual they had observed for years.

Kate opened her arms and Lily moved into them. This wasn't the first time they'd shared tears and faced problems. "Let me help."

Lily nodded. "Don't tell George. Not yet."

"I won't, but I think you're wrong. If it were him, you'd want to know wouldn't you?"

"If it were him, I'd know."

Neither said anything for several moments. Kate had never been a wife or mother but she sensed the feelings Lily had right now. Some women were the caregivers of the world, knowing instinctively when and where the hurt lay.

There was no sound inside the warm kitchen except the soft pelting of rain against the windows. Lily turned to Kate and said, "You know, you were wrong before when you said you always told me everything. You didn't."

"I did, too."

"No, you didn't."

"When didn't I tell you everything?"

"After graduation when there was talk that you'd go away to the convent."

They stood a foot apart and stared at each other. "I started that rumor to look important. I was mad at you for spending so much time with George." Kate waited expectantly for Lily's reaction.

Suddenly they were both laughing. "You dope," Lily choked. "George never took your place in my life. That love was different."

"I know," Kate said. "But I was a dope then."

The laughter melted the emotional ice. It would be okay now. This was women's business. Together they'd handle the crisis.

CHAPTER THREE

Lily lay on a couch in the living room, one arm across her brow. Usually chilly these days, she pulled the crocheted afghan across her. The room was dim because she hadn't yet opened the drapes. Pain pulsed at her temples and pressed against the backs of her eyes. She sighed and looked at her watch through carefully controlled slits.

Darn. Almost ten o'clock. Kate will be here in a few minutes. She allowed a small moan to escape as she swung her legs over the side of the couch and thrust her feet to the floor. The room tilted, she swayed at her sudden change of position and stumbled into the kitchen.

At the sink, she looked through the sunlit windowpanes. *Nothing's changed and nothing's the same. Do I order plants for those empty flowerbeds?* She heard the door open and turned to see Kate entering.

"Hi. How're you doing? Ready to go?"

"Of course, I'm ready to go. It's Friday, isn't it? It's library day. How am I? I've got a screaming, thumping headache."

"You've had a headache for two weeks. What did Doctor Bob say when you called him?"

"He said it wasn't associated with my problem. Problem!" Lily huffed. "He said it was stress and he wants me to take tranquilizers. Called in a prescription."

"Did you pick it up?" Kate shrugged out of her coat, and draped it over a chair. "Can we get it later?"

"No. It probably won't help." Lily turned her back and stared through the window. "Why do I keep looking out this stupid window? Everything's the same, but it's not. Same tree, same yard. For the first time in weeks the sky is blue and I don't give a damn."

Kate picked up the kettle and, elbowing Lily aside, filled it at the sink. "You just feel blue this morning. Let's have a cuppa before we go out. We'll have lunch at Scarlette's today, okay?"

"Will you stop being so damn cheerful and practical? Who the hell are you to tell me how I feel. You don't understand. I walk around this house hour after hour, day after day, looking into closets and rooms, touching things and remembering. Everything I see or touch reminds me of the life I'm losing. I remember happy times when the kids were little…"

"Well, maybe you'd feel better if you stop feeling so darn sorry for yourself."

"Sorry for myself? You think that's what this is all about? I thought if anyone would understand, you would. I thought you were my friend."

Kate heard the sob at the end of Lily's words, but she didn't turn around. Instead she reached for the mugs in the cupboard next to the stove. "I *do* understand—or at least I think I do. No one really knows about anything unless they've lived through it. I'm living through this with you. And, I *am* your friend. Always *have* been and always *will* be."

"There's so much *to do*, to think about. I can't get started because I don't know *what* to do first. Where do I begin?" Lily stormed around the kitchen, her fists clenched at her side.

Kate turned to face her. "Make a start. You won't solve anything by hiding in dim rooms; by making yourself more uncomfortable than you should be because you can't come to grips with things. Do something positive instead of moaning about what to do. Get another opinion if it will ease your mind. Don't, if you think it's useless, but make a decision. Get the tranquilizers if they'll help calm you. Talk to someone other than me, if you think it'll help."

They stared at each other, then Lily moved to the chair next to the window and sat at the battered old table, her trembling fingers traced the scratches. "Michael made these when he built his model airplanes." The water hissed in the kettle. She spun the lazy Susan in the center of the table. "Patty use to call this a 'daisy Susan' until someone corrected her."

"They're good memories, Lil."

"Every corner of this house is a reminder of the past, Kate. I'm not ready to leave all this and yet I know exactly when it's all going to end."

"No, you don't, not exactly. They may be wrong. No one but God knows when. In some ways, you may be lucky."

Lily looked up sharply. Her red-rimmed eyes were sunken, her cheeks pale. "Lucky?"

Kate shrugged her shoulders. "You could walk in front of a truck and suddenly be gone. No time to make plans, no time to think about what legacy you'd like to leave."

"Ha," Lily snapped. "A truck would be welcome."

"You don't mean that."

Lily lowered her head and closed her eyes. "No, I don't mean that." She looked up, tears filling her eyes. "I know you're trying to help. I'm sorry I'm being so bitchy today."

"Don't be sorry. Be as bitchy as you like. I'm glad you're getting mad. It's good for you to talk about what's bothering you. Let it out. If you want to yell at me go ahead. But don't be surprised if I yell back."

"You're a good friend."

Kate filled the teapot, then moved behind Lily and massaged her shoulders and neck, sensing the tension beneath her fingers. "Headache any better?"

Lily shook her head.

"You look terrible."

"Thanks."

"Did you eat anything yet?"

Again Lily shook her head, indicating that she hadn't.

"That's crazy. You're getting thinner and thinner. I saw you sway when you turned away from the sink. You'll be falling down from starvation soon; then George will wonder what's really wrong with you. I saw him looking at you when we were in the kitchen together the other night. He knows something's up. When are you going to tell him?"

Lily sighed. "Soon. I have to get things straight in my mind first and we're back to square one, aren't we? What do I do Kate? What's first?"

Kate poured the tea and they both watched the ritual, glad for the diversion. She sat across from Lily. "It's up to you. What do you really want to do? Want to get away for a while? Want to talk to the kids? Father Gainer? Doctor Bob again?"

"No. I have you to talk to. And to yell at." Lily smiled for the first time today. "I've done so much thinking my brain is addled. But," she hesitated, "I know one thing I want to do, but it might not be possible."

"What's that?" Kate asked, perking up at the first sign that Lily was moving toward something positive.

"I want to see the kids. I mean I want them to come home and be together—together like family again, like friends; one more time. Once more before…" She struggled to swallow.

"Well then, make it happen. If that's what you want call them and tell them you want them home. Tell them about…"

"No," Lily said sharply. "I don't want them to come home out of pity. I want them to *want* to come home."

"You might not be able to make them *want* to come home, Lil," Kate said softly.

Lily stirred her tea and stared out the window. Kate was right. How could she make them *want* to come home? They were so separated. Separated for too long by both distance and disinterest in each other. How had this all happened? She looked up. "Well, it's what I want. Somehow I'll make it happen."

Kate reached across the scarred table and touched the back of her friend's cold, thin hand. "I'll help. If you want it bad enough, it'll happen."

"Pollyanna," Lily whispered through her tears.

#

Later that day, Lily wandered aimlessly through the rooms of her home once again. This time, however, her feet didn't seem so reluctant to retrace the patterns she'd followed so many times recently. Her headache was reduced to a mere reminder. *Maybe it was the talk with Kate, or lunch*, she thought, remembering the creamy soup and the chicken salad, followed by an expensive dessert at Scarlette's. Even though she'd pushed most of it around the plate, it was more food than she'd consumed in a while.

She paused at the top of the stairs and waited for her breathing to become less stressed. The open door directly across the landing beckoned and she moved quietly into the room that Michael had occupied for nineteen years. The same brown and gold patterned drapes hung at the windows. A well-worn carpet covered the center of the room, framed by polished hardwood floor. The walls were painted cream and formed a cool, clean background.

The room was so like him, neat, orderly, reflecting his sense of pride in accomplishments. She smiled as she walked slowly past the shelves filled with displays of his hobbies that covered two entire walls. George had built the shelves, adding to them as the collections grew and changed over the years. The oldest treasures, an entire battalion of toy soldiers, complete with cavalry and enemy Indians, were in a glass showcase, relegated to a place of honor, put away so long ago, but still cherished. Model airplanes, cars, and boats, all carefully, painstakingly, created from kits that were Christmas and birthday presents, lined other shelves and dangled from the ceiling. *He was so patient, fiddling with the tiny plastic and wooden pieces. The house always smelled of glue.*

She stood next to his desk, uncluttered, everything in its proper place. She touched his calculator and an old typewriter he used for high school assignments. A smaller shelf held some of his oldest books, the rest he'd taken with him when he left for college and then moved on to his new life in New York.

Michael's life had been orderly and purposeful, but George had been disappointed. His son didn't excel in sports in school and maintain a rough and tumble relationship with his male friends. For years he tried to push Michael into Little League groups, swimming meets, and wrestling lessons. "The damned kid's going to grow up to be a sissy," he'd growled.

Michael had tried to please his father, occasionally accompanying him on fishing trips, but the thrill of hooking a fish and fighting him to the shore or over the side of a boat wasn't there. He'd confessed to his mother that he hated the smell of fish and bait, hated the slimy feel of both. After a few years, he'd given up trying to be someone he wasn't and George watched his son thrill over mathematical accomplishments as if they were a bases-loaded home run. George didn't give up easily though, and she remembered the arguments about high school sports and finally Michael's career choice as an investment broker in New York.

"Business management and finance," George had sputtered when he found out what subjects Michael was taking in college. "What's wrong with working in the foundry like I did; like my grandfather did, and my uncles and cousins do?"

Lily was torn between her son and husband. She understood both sides, or thought she did. They were just different and George resented the differences. *He was a good father, though. Even if he did grumble about their 'high falutin' education, he provided well, and always paid their college expenses over and above the scholarships they earned. They shouldn't have become enemies.*

She paused at the door as if taking stock of the contents. What would happen to these treasures? Shortly after Michael and Simone had purchased the brownstone home in New York, she'd asked him if he wanted any of these things. "Not now," he'd answered quietly. "But don't get rid of them."

The next room belonged to Debra. The soft rose-colored walls, gave the room a warm glow even on dark days. Fluffy sheer white curtains covered the lone window and the windowsill held small china animals she'd begun to collect. For years she'd insisted she wanted to become a veterinarian when she grew up but changed her mind when Kate's old dog became ill and had to be euthanized. Like Michael, she possessed an orderly, analytical mind. Debbie loved to draw and her pictures were usually neat geometrical designs or detailed pen and ink scenes. Lily ran her hand over the drawing table George had made for his daughter for Christmas one year. In college she'd chosen a vocation in architecture. *Not a real surprise*, Lily mused, except George thought it was unnecessary for a girl to even have a career. "A waste of time and money, if you ask me," he said to his sullen daughter. "You'll get married and have kids like every other girl."

Stuffed toys and dolls lay against the ruffled pillows on the poster bed and Lily knew there was a cardboard carton in the corner of the closet that held the remaining menagerie. Debbie spent one week each summer in Eagleton, moving back into her old room, blending quietly into the household. *She was always so quiet. No, not really. As a little girl she was all ruffles and giggles.* Lily remembered Michael and Debra laughing loudly and rolling in a tangled mass on the living room floor, holding mock battles between the legs of the dining room furniture. George had laughed at them then when he came home from work. When had that changed?

It wasn't until Debbie was a teenager that she began to recede into herself. Her friends were quiet and studious, and George confessed to Lily he didn't understand girls. Before Lily, the only woman in his life was his mother. Lily remembered the grim, cold, foreign woman who was her mother-in-law for a short time before dying suddenly one winter less than two years after she and George were married. She shivered as she remembered.

Lily stood in the doorway to Debra's room a long time before moving to the third door. Patty's room.

I think George was disappointed that our third child was another girl. He was already grumbling about Michael's lack of interest in sports and outdoor activities at the age of eight. Debbie was five and had established herself as the little queen of the household. Did they resent a new baby? Had that made them estranged from their little sister?

Lily stepped into the room. Plain white walls, straight sheer white curtains, green shag scatter rugs in front of the bureau and at the side of the twin bed, gave no indication of the former occupant's personality. Even her bedspread was white chenille. Stark and bare, it reflected Patty's lack of involvement in the family and her youth. No reminders of her interests. She'd excelled in many things, but briefly. After she won the city championship trophy in softball, Lily had hoped George's dream of having an athlete in the family might have been fulfilled. But the thought didn't last long because the next season Patty left the team. Lily cut out and saved her daughter's rave notices for a performance in a high school play but nothing could convince her to try out for another part the next year.

Hidden in the closet, Patty had a small collection of one-time awards because she never again attempted to repeat her achievements. Her last three years in high school had been uneventful, her report card evidencing just enough effort to receive moderate grades. Comments from teachers were always the same. "Patty could do better if she applied herself to her studies."

Lily walked around the room, barren of reminders of her youngest daughter. No toys, no books, no collections. Nothing seemed important enough for Patty to keep. Her life now reflected the same attitude, moving from place to place, not making permanent friendships, or at least none the family knew of. Lily shuddered and left the room, moving down the hall to her bedroom.

Sitting on the side of the bed, she tried to reflect on the events of this day. *Nothing's changed*, she thought and then corrected herself. *Yes, I've changed. Kate's right, I don't have time to feel sorry for myself. It won't change anything. But I have a plan—well not exactly a plan, more like a goal. The kids have to come home for one last weekend together.*

She lay back across the bed, tired but more at ease than she'd been for weeks. *I'll rest for an hour and then make dinner.* Even the thought of food wasn't so unpleasant. She smiled and closed her eyes.

CHAPTER FOUR

The funny thing about plans is that sometimes something pops into your head and there it is all laid out in your mind like a road map. Then again, there are times you know what you *want* to do but haven't *any* idea how to accomplish the thing. Lily knew very well what she wanted, but the path was muddied, the chart unreadable. Dozens of possibilities circled in her mind. She just didn't have the right map—yet.

The morning was bright, brighter than any so far this spring and nice enough for her to walk the length of the back yard. She noticed things looked a bit greener, yet there were no buds forming anywhere on the shrubs or trees. It was too early in March to see that. In the front yard, the tulips and crocuses had poked through the wet earth, but here in the back there was no change. Still, it looked brighter, newer.

She climbed the steps to the kitchen door, turned and looked across the fence at the woods behind the alley that ran along the back of all the properties on Mountainview Terrace. Bare limbs and twigs moved in the soft breeze and the pines, scattered through the trees, stood out in startling green. "Green's my favorite color," she murmured as she reached for the doorknob. Why? She shrugged. "Because it holds promise." *A good sign,* she thought.

Shivering slightly she entered the warm kitchen. A pad of paper and a pen lay on the table where she'd left them earlier. For the past week she'd been composing a letter to the kids; a letter strong enough to entice them to visit and yet not threatening enough to make them worry. It had taken her days to decide on a letter. At first she thought she'd call each of them but they might read something in her voice, triggering worry. No, she'd better write and then maybe follow it up with a telephone call, at least to Michael and Debbie. No telling how she would contact Patty.

The telephone rang before she could sit at the table. Lily crossed the room and took the receiver off the wall. "Hello."

"Hi, it's Kate. Just checking on you. Need anything? I'm going to the grocery store."

"No thanks. You know, Kate, you don't *have* to call me every day."

"I know I don't *have* to. Don't we usually talk almost every day? Haven't we done that for years?"

"I know. I'm more conscious of your attention lately." Lily twisted the telephone cord.

"Nuts. Don't think I'm babying you because I'm not."

Lily smiled. Kate had called almost every day during the last thirty years but not like clockwork. For the past three weeks she'd called every morning between eight thirty and nine o'clock.

"What are you doing?" Kate asked

"I'm still working on *the letter*," Lily answered, emphasizing the words. "I think it's done. I've revised it and rewritten it enough and I'm sick of it. It goes into the mail today."

"Good. Have you changed it much since the last time I saw it?"

"No. Pretty much the same."

"I thought it was good. You said just enough, dwelling on the family reunion and things like that."

"I hope it works."

"It will, and don't call me a Pollyanna again. I have a good feeling about this."

"I hope you're right." For several seconds no one spoke, then Lily said, "Well, get going on your chores. I'm going to start to sort through some of that junk we have stored in the basement."

"Lil, have you decided when you're going to talk to George?"

Lily bit her bottom lip. "I've thought about that a lot, too. You're right. I have to tell him. Just can't decide whether to get an ally to help me or not."

"Me?"

"No, thanks, but I think if anyone needs to be involved it should be Doctor Bob. The man thing, you know?"

"Sure. Well, call me if you need anything."

"I will."

They hung up. Lily remained standing in the doorway to the dining room. She took a deep breath, trying to expand lungs that seemed heavier and heavier as the days passed. "Oh, for heaven's sake. Stop imagining things," she muttered. Sitting at the table, she picked up her pen and a clean sheet of paper and started to write the first of the three letters she'd mail later today.

#

Every Thursday night for as long as he could remember, George Hoffmann met Art Yount, Bud Mangione and Norm Stromeir at the Eagleton Lanes. Back when they all worked swing shifts at the foundry they weren't always able to play in the same league. Ever since their length of service earned them the privilege of steady day work, they bowled together in the foundry's Thursday night league. They left work together, ate dinner at the bar at the lanes, bowled three games, and then stayed for a beer or two. Tonight they sat at a table near the bar.

Art tipped his glass back and drained the last drops of amber liquid. "Gotta go. The old lady will be standing on the porch if I get home late again. She's getting to be a real nag about Thursday nights. Like it was something new or something."

"What's she think you're doing? You're too damn old to get into trouble." Norm hit Art on the arm.

"Right. Too damn old. But we can still kick butt on the lanes, right?" Art stood and tapped the hands raised in farewell. "See ya tomorrow."

Bud slid some money under the ashtray in the center of the table. "Wait Art. I'll walk out to the parking lot with you. Take care of the check will you, George?" He touched the remaining two men on the shoulder and followed Art through the smoky room to the door leading outside.

For several minutes neither George nor Norm spoke, listening to the noisy crowd at the bar.

"We rolled a couple of good games tonight," Norm said. "I let you guys down for a couple of frames on that last game though. Getting old I guess."

"Old hell. You're younger than I am." George twisted his glass on the tabletop.

"What—by two months?"

"Yeah." George and Norm had been friends since childhood, both dropping out of school in the tenth grade to work in the foundry with their fathers.

Norm watched George play with the empty glass. "Want another beer?"

"Nah." Still, he made no move to leave.

"Something wrong?" Norm sensed a strange uneasiness in George tonight.

"Nah. I was thinking about what Art said before he left."

"What about?" Norm furrowed his brow. His face was thin and angular and he looked like a puzzled fox.

"Saying his wife would be mad if he got home late. Guess the girls are getting along. They get strange when they age. Not like us." He smiled weakly. "We don't change."

Now Norm knew there was something wrong. This wasn't like George. "What's up, Georgie? Something wrong with Lil?"

"Nah. Nothing's wrong with her. She's complaining all the time lately about being tired. She's losing weight and moping around the house. You know how she always had projects going, doing something with needles or a hot glue gun.

Nothing since Christmas. I don't even hear her and Kate planning anything."

Norm studied George who avoided eye contact by concentrating on the pattern of wet circles he was making on the tabletop with his empty glass.

"Maybe it's the long winter. Grace has been complaining about being cooped up in the house for so long."

George shrugged. "Usually Lil keeps busy. Something's different and I can't figure it out."

At the next table Mick Falcone overheard part of the conversation and turned his chair around to join George and Norm. Known for drinking too much and getting loud, the men he'd bowled with had left a while ago and he'd continued to drink by himself. "You know what," he interrupted. "Sounds like your wife has found a boyfriend, old George. Maybe she's feeling guilty about running around on you. Maybe some young guy's tiring her out." His grin was wet and lopsided and his eyes squinted as the smoke from the cigarette he held between his teeth curled up across his face.

"Shut your mouth, Falcone," Norm said, putting his hand on George who had angrily pushed his chair back from the table and stood facing the adversary, face beet red, fists raised in front of him.

Norm put both hands on George's raised arm and said, "He's drunk, Georgie." He turned to Mick, wedging himself between the two men who'd both come up out of their seats and stood facing each other. "What the hell's wrong with you. You're drunk. Get the hell out of here before you cause some real trouble and get thrown out."

"You shut your goddamned mouth, you slime ball. You ever say anything about my wife again and I'll beat the shit out of you," George threatened Mick across Norm's left shoulder.

By this time, several men from nearby tables had turned to watch the scene.

Mick was weaving from side to side a few feet from George's still clenched fists. "Shit, George, you know I was only kiddin'. You know me better'n that." He pulled the cigarette from his lips and ground it out in the ashtray without breaking eye contact with George.

"I know you're a damned drunk with a foul mouth and a filthy mind," George growled. "You're lucky I don't beat pathetic drunks or you'd be a bloody mess by now. Get the hell out of here."

The bartender had come around the end of the bar and stood a few feet away. "Trouble George? Norm?"

"No. It's okay, Sam," Norm said. "Mick's leaving."

Wordlessly, Mick turned and moved slowly through the path that had been opened for him by the men standing in the room. A blast of cold air rushed into the room as the door closed behind him. Within moments the volume of talk and laughter resumed. George and Norm sat at their table.

"Wanna go?" Norm asked.

"Sure," George said, pulling some money from his pocket and taking Bud's money from under the ashtray. "I'll get yours tonight."

"You don't have to do that. We always pay our own." Norm was embarrassed by the sudden gesture of benevolence as he watched George go to the bar and settle the check.

They walked through the bowling alley to the rear of the building. Before pushing the door to the parking lot open, Norm pulled on George's arm. "He's crazy you know. Don't let him get to you."

"I know he is. Damn drunk. They should throw him out of the leagues."

The two friends stood in the dimly lit hallway for a moment. Norm put his hand on the push bar that opened the big metal door. "There's nothing to what he said. Lil wouldn't do anything like that. You know that."

"Yeah, I know. It's none of his damned business and I shouldn't 'a said anything about it anyhow. She'll be fine. You're probably right; it's just the long winter."

"That's probably it."

They walked across the parking lot, the overhead lights glowing dimly on the roofs and hoods of the few remaining cars parked there.

"See ya tomorrow," Norm called as he got into his car.

George watched him start his car, switch the lights on, and pull away before he turned the key in his ignition. He sat in the cold car, listening to the engine and thought about Lily. Tired all the time, moping around the house, losing weight. He knew Mick was wrong. He didn't know *what* the problem was; he just knew something wasn't right.

He drove automatically, unaware of time until he pulled into the alley behind the house. The night air was cold and damp as he opened the overhead door and drove into the crowded garage.

George walked up the path to the kitchen door. Shivering, he stopped. His eyes searched the house, noting the small glow of light from the kitchen where Lily had left the light on over the stove. *She's in bed— asleep. When was the last time we made love?* He couldn't answer his own question. Again a nagging uncertainty ran through his head. Something was wrong.

CHAPTER FIVE

"Are you crazy? Just sorting through all the stuff you have stored in the attic, basement and garage would take six months." Kate's hand quickly covered her mouth. "Oh, Lily, I'm sorry. That was mean. I wasn't thinking."

They sat on the bottom steps of the basement stairs looking at two small boxes Lily had packed yesterday. It had taken her an hour and she'd been exhausted when she climbed the stairs to rest.

"Oh, shut up. You can make references to time. It doesn't bother me. I know I don't have a lot of time left. Damn! I wish I knew how much there really was."

Kate, who was sitting two steps higher than Lily, reached down and patted her back. "I'm sorry anyhow, I wasn't thinking when I blurted that out. I always was tactful, wasn't I? But, you can't go pawing through thirty-some years of stuff, it's a big job."

"I know. I thought with your help and George's, when I tell him, we'd be able to sort out some of the stuff the kids might want."

"Lil, there's no hurry to do that and it's morbid. Let them worry about that on their *own* time. Besides, George will be here. There are more important things for you to think about and do. And one of the best things for you to do now is to get as much rest as possible and think about your reunion. Have you heard anything?"

"Of course not. I only mailed the letters three days ago. They might not have even gotten them yet. I wonder…"

"Wonder what?"

"Oh, I wonder what their first reaction was, or will be."

"Let's go upstairs," Kate said standing. "If you really want some of this stuff sorted and packed, I'll come over every afternoon and do it. You can supervise."

"No. You're right. It was a dumb idea. I felt like doing something. Something meaningful."

They automatically sat at the kitchen table where most of their visiting had been done over the years.

"You haven't said anything, but I know you're wondering about George. I haven't told him yet, but I did call Doctor Bob."

"What did he say?"

"He said he'd be glad to be with us when I tell George. He offered to tell him himself. Said we could come to the office either together, or he'd see George alone. He even offered to come to the house some night after work."

"That was nice of him. What did you decide?"

"Me? Decide? You must be kidding. You know I can't make a decision without stalling and putting things off. I said I'd call him by the end of the week."

"Well, did you think about whether you want to be in the office or at home?"

"Maybe we should take advantage of his offer to see him here. George might be more comfortable here than in the office. But then again, maybe it would be better if we were alone and I told him myself."

"Just *do* it, Lil. Nothing's going to be gained by putting this off. He should know. He'll be able to help you."

Lily bit her lip, fighting tears, her fingers twisted together. "Maybe I should have told him the day I found out. It might have been easier than thinking about it for a month. I've cheated him out of a month. Will it make any difference?" Tears slid down her cheeks and Kate covered one of Lily's hands with hers while handing her a tissue.

"You never cheated anyone in your life, especially George—or your kids. Go lay down for a while—you look tired. Want me to stay down here until you've rested?"

"No, thanks. I'll lay on the couch in the living room. Call me tomorrow. And don't worry about me. I'll be fine. I was doing so well until I started messing around with that junk in the basement. You're right. I must be crazy." She wiped her eyes with a tissue and tried to smile.

Kate rose and went to the back door. With her hand on the knob she turned. "Okay, I'll go, but promise me you won't do dumb things again like messing around in a dusty basement or attic. And promise me you'll call me the minute you hear from any of the kids."

"I promise."

Kate closed the door softly. Her eyes filled with tears as she walked down the path to the back gate and her car parked in the alleyway. "Stop that you ninny. This isn't going to get easier," she whispered to herself as she hurried to her car.

#

George wiped the gravy from his plate with a piece of bread. Lily had made his favorite dinner tonight, Swiss steak, mashed potatoes, tiny peas and lots of gravy. He noticed she ate very little, taking a small portion of everything on her plate and moving it around a lot before resting her fork across the food that remained on the plate. He'd also noticed her hands trembling when she removed the dishes.

"Want dessert now or later?" she asked, rinsing the plates at the sink.

"Later, I guess. What did you make?"

"Baked apples, but they're kind of hot now. They'd be better a little cooler. You could have ice cream with them."

"Sounds good. Let's have them later with a cup of coffee." He rose, watching her working at the sink just as she had for over thirty years. "Need help?"

She spun around to look at him. He never offered to help. At least not since the children had been assigned after-dinner chores years and years ago. After they'd left, he never thought to resume the ritual of helping to clear the table as he had when they were first married. He looked different tonight, too. Like he was trying to please her or make amends for something.

"I'm fine. You go sit down; you've worked hard today. I'll be right in."

She watched him disappear through the dimly lit dining room and heard his chair creek as he settled into the recliner, turning on the television. That was more like it. Normal. Sounds of the evening news reached her as she filled the coffee pot and put out cups, saucers and dessert plates.

When Lily left the kitchen she knew that tonight she'd tell George. She didn't know how she would do it, she didn't have any planned speech ready, but she knew she would tell him tonight. Strangely, she felt calmer than she thought she would. An unexplainable peace went with her as she crossed the dim dining room and settled into her chair on the other side of the lamp table that separated them.

"I wrote to the kids," Lily said, game show contestants shouting wildly in the background.

"Huh?" George contemplated turning the volume down.

"I said, I wrote to the kids."

He looked at his wife. Her needlework lay in her lap and she was staring blankly across the room. He pressed the mute button. The contestants became mimes, exchanging puzzled frowns for euphoric smiles.

"How come?"

"I wanted to invite them to come for a visit. In April. A weekend at the end of April."

"All of them?"

"Yes."

"All of them together?"

"Yes."

"What for?"

"Because I want to see them. They haven't been home here together in years. It's time."

"They won't come. Not in April. Mike and Debbie won't be getting any vacation time in April and who knows where Patty is."

"She's in Tampa. Remember her card?" Lily didn't look at him, keeping her eyes on the television screen, watching the wheel spin, the mute hands clap, the silent shouts of encouragement.

George leaned forward in his chair. *Now what's up?* "Even if she gets your letter, which is doubtful, why would she want to come north in April? Doesn't make sense, Lil. Why do you want them here anyhow? I mean, why now all of a sudden. Deb comes every summer. Mike hasn't been here since last Thanksgiving and that was for about four hours."

Lily swallowed with difficulty. Suddenly the words she wanted to say had become uncomfortable lumps in her throat. She felt as if she were panting instead of breathing.

"Because it's important to me, George. Because…"

He waited. She turned to look at him and he saw tears in her eyes. "Jesus, Lily. What the hell is it? You're acting crazier and crazier. Ever since Christmas."

"I'm sorry. This isn't easy. I have to tell you something and I thought I knew how to do it and now everything's all mixed up in my brain. I know I have to do it. It's not fair to you…"

"For God's sake, what the hell are you talking about?" George flipped the lever on the chair and snapped forward.

In slow motion Lily put her needlework back into the basket at her side. She remained bent forward slightly, her hands twisting in her lap. "I've been so tired lately."

"I know."

"Well, remember I went to Doctor Bob and he's been running some tests?"

"Yeah."

They waited, daring the other to speak. The room was too quiet.

"A month ago I got the results."

"And?"

Lily brought one hand to her face, covering her mouth as if to suppress the words and the sobs that threatened to escape. "Oh, Lord, this is so hard." Her hand muffled her voice, and emotion shook her body. She turned and looked directly into her husband's puzzled eyes. "The news was bad, George. Bad."

"What do you mean bad?"

Without lowering her eyes she said, "It's back, George. The cancer's back."

George catapulted himself from his chair. "Cancer? That's crazy, it can't be. You had the surgery. It was all over five years ago."

"Four and a half. But it's back, and this time in my lungs. Doctor Bob says…"

"What? He says what?"

"He says it's inoperable. Terminal. I'm sorry." She raised her head, stretching her thin neck to its limit, tears streaming silently down her cheeks, a small keening sound coming from deep within her heart. "I'm so sorry," she repeated in a whisper.

"Now wait a minute," he said, shuffling a few steps closer. "This can't be right. They can't be right. You had the surgery."

"I know but Bob says it metastasized, spread to another place. Don't you remember after the surgery Doctor Schwartz said that if I didn't have the chemo, it might."

"Might!" George shouted. "Might. Now it has? Was it because I said no to that chemo crap? I didn't want you going through any more after the surgery. You'd been through enough!" His words echoed in the room.

"It's not your fault—not mine—not the doctor's. It just happened. There's nothing anyone can do. I'm dying, George."

The words entered George's ears but somewhere between the auditory canal and his brain they became confused. What was she saying? His mouth hung open, his chest tightened and his breathing all but stopped.

Suddenly the loss of weight, the increasing tiredness, and lack of interest in anything that usually occupied her was becoming clear, as if her words finally parted the thick fog in his head and some sense—not a lot—but some sense filtered through.

"Dying?" he whispered. "No. Lily there must be a mistake." He knelt by her chair, awkwardly reached for her hands and felt icy skin stretched over thin bones no longer padded with flesh. How could he have been so blind? Why hadn't he questioned her earlier about all those damned doctor visits and tests? For the briefest moment he remembered his vague doubts of a few days ago. How could he have been so stupid?

"There's no mistake. He took all the tests he possibly could. They all said the same thing."

"Another opinion. Lily you—we—can't just accept this. How long have you known?

"A month," she whispered.

"A month? Why didn't you tell me?"

She leaned forward and he twisted to take her in his arms as he crouched on the floor in front of her chair. He felt her body quiver with the sobs that began to rise uncontrollably and his tears fell into her hair. His fingers patted her back, his throat closed. There were no words.

Several minutes later he struggled to his feet, tugging her with him. "Here," he said, leading her to the couch. "Here, let's sit here."

She followed blindly and they sat as two lovers had so many years ago. She nestled into his side, his arm protectively around her shoulders. Her sobs diminished to quiet weeping. Her chest ached but she knew it was only emotion and not further signs of the disease that engulfed her lungs.

"I'm so sorry," she stuttered weakly.

"Sorry, hell. Sorry for what?"

"That I didn't tell you sooner. It was too hard. I didn't want to believe it at first, and then I was angry, and then I didn't know what to do?" He squeezed her shoulder.

During the quiet few minutes on the couch George had given his thoughts free reign. Why? She'd known a month? Kept it to herself? Good God! There had to be an explanation. There had to be something they could do.

"Tell me again. Tell me what Bob said."

She remained at his side, her right arm pinched between them, her left arm stretching across his body, fingers clenching his shirt. "He said it's from the cancer four years ago. Four and a half years ago. But this time it's in my lungs—both lungs." She pulled air inside, trying to smother the pulsing in her chest. "It's terminal."

The word burned into his heart. Terminal. That's what happened to others, not his wife. His eyes still burned from the unaccustomed tears that had flushed them. Terminal means the end is... When? Suddenly the impact of that devastating word hit him. How long until terminal? He twisted to look at her face buried against his chest. "How long?" It hurt to put the thought into spoken words.

She pulled her head back and looked into his eyes, strangely glazed and red. "He said three to six months. He could be wrong. It could be longer." Or shorter, they both finished silently.

"Now wait. We can get another opinion. There are experts. In New York. Maybe Michael knows someone. Someone who's a real expert."

"No." Lily sat up sharply. "No. I don't want the children to know. I want them to come for a visit so that we can all be together at least one more time. I need this, George. I need this." Again soft sobs threatened. "I need to see them all together," she whispered. "I want them to be friends."

"Well, we can still get an expert. Bob's okay. We've always had him. Colds, sickness. Little sicknesses. This is different. Maybe he's wrong. Or maybe there are things we can do. I've heard of weird new treatments."

"If you really want to get someone else, we will. But I think he's right. Somehow, deep down inside me, I feel he's right."

They remained where they were, bodies closer than they had been in a long time. *How long*,

George wondered. *How long has it been since I held her?* Deep feelings of spousal neglect stirred within him.

"We'll think about it, Lil. I can't believe you didn't tell me for a whole month. Jesus," he sounded angry now, "Jesus, why would you keep this to yourself?"

"I did tell Kate." She felt him stiffen. She'd never known him to be jealous of the time she spent with Kate. Now she worried, *will he be angry that I confided in Kate before I told him?* "I needed someone—I needed a woman to cry with, honey. Please don't be upset with me." She waited for his response.

"I'm not upset with you. You're right. Maybe another woman can help more. I sure can't think of the right things to say or do. What *can* I do?" He turned to her again, waiting for words of wisdom.

She shrugged her shoulders and moved away slightly. "What is there to do? If you want, we can get another opinion. Maybe you want to talk to Doctor Bob. I've come to the point where I have to take it one day at a time. At first my head was filled with *plans*. Plans about what I should do before I go." Her voice broke and she took a deeper breath. "Plans about what and when to tell you. I feel guilty about waiting a month. You were cheated out of a month but I guess not really. We were together like always and maybe I needed that time to come to grips with things. Maybe I should be asking you what *I* can do to help you."

"Oh, for Christ's sake, Lily," he said, again fighting tears. "If you aren't something. Worrying about what you can do for me. Haven't you given me a lifetime of…" He was at a loss for words.

What had she given him? He was right to stop there. She'd given him a lifetime, period. This time he couldn't stop the tears and they flowed down his cheeks, his thumb stemming them away.

Together they sat in the quiet, comfortable, familiar room. After several minutes George pulled his arm from around her shoulders, stood and pressed the button on the remote control, extinguishing the commercial that had been running silently across the screen. "I'll plug in the coffee pot. We can have coffee, okay?"

She nodded. Things *were* going to be different. Already George was making coffee. A minuscule smile tugged at the corners of her lips. They'd been together for a long time. They'd still be together for a long time. Forever didn't have earthly boundaries.

CHAPTER SIX

She knew someone was watching her before her eyes were open. In the dim early light of morning Lily looked up into George's face. He stood next to her side of the bed.

"Good morning," he whispered. "Sorry. Did I wake you?"

She looked at the clock. "It's seven-thirty. I should have been up half an hour ago." She pushed the covers back.

"No. You stay in bed. I can get my own breakfast. How hard is it to pour cereal?" Still, he remained standing at her side.

She patted the bed next to her and moved toward the center. "What's wrong?"

"Nothing," he said, sitting carefully on the edge, "and everything."

Reaching for the other pillow she pushed it behind her shoulders and slipped her hand into his. "I know this is hard on you. I've had a month to think about it and it doesn't get easier to understand."

He nodded.

"Know what I'd like?"

"What?" he said. "God, Lil, I'd do anything to make this easier for you—to make this go away."

"I know, but we can't do that. Guess you didn't sleep much last night."

"Not much."

"Funny. I slept better than I have in weeks. Must be the relief of finally telling you."

"What do you want?"

"I'd like us to keep things as normal as possible for as long as we can."

George sighed, "I don't know how we're going to get the kids to come home in April."

He squeezed her fingers, felt her thin bones move with the pressure and immediately released her hand. Why hadn't he seen this coming? Why hadn't he noticed her losing weight?

She smiled. He said *we*; last night it was *you*. "I've written to each of them. Maybe we'll hear soon and if not I'll call them. I don't want to tell them yet. If they come here just because they pity me—or you—it won't be the same."

He turned slightly so that he could see her face better. "Know what I thought about all last night?"

"No. What?"

"I thought about how much I'd failed you over the years. I wasn't a good husband or father."

"Stop that. You were always good to me, a good father to our children."

"You know that's not so."

"We can't redo the past, dear, but we do have now." Her voice broke slightly. "It's all we have and suddenly 'now' isn't much. Doctor Bob says there might not be a lot of pain, just some weakness, shortness of breath." She watched him wince. "We can deal with that. The one thing I really want, besides keeping things as normal as possible, is to have the kids home one more time."

"You're going to have to tell them. Then they'll surely come home for the visit."

"No. I don't want pity."

"It won't be pity, Lil. They love you. Besides, they should know the truth."

"They will know when the time is right. Please, promise me you won't tell them until I'm ready. It's more than *us* being reunited with *them*. I want the kids to realize how important family is. I want them to be interested in each other. I want them to be friends." She looked into his eyes and saw the frustration. "It'll be okay, honey. They will come home. Somehow it'll work out."

Their fingers lay twined on the wrinkled sheets. He gave her hand a soft squeeze. "Okay, I promise. How can I argue with faith like that?" He bent down and kissed her gently. "We'll wait to hear from them."

For several minutes neither spoke. The morning light, filtering through the closed blinds, brightened the room. When their eyes met, they smiled.

"You're a gem, Lil. I always knew that but I didn't say it or show it often enough."

"Have I ever complained?"

"No."

"Well then. Move and let me get up. In thirty-five years there haven't been many days I didn't watch you walk down that back path to the garage. Now," she said looking at the clock, "you won't be getting any breakfast and you'll be late for work. Get going."

George didn't move for a moment and then stood, holding out his hands to help her from the bed. "I'll get coffee and a Danish at the cafeteria before I punch in." They stood in an awkward embrace, his work-roughened hands snagging the soft material of her nightgown.

For a fleeting moment she felt like a bride, excited at the warmth and strength of his arms as he held her, aware once again of the maleness of the vibrant young man she had married. Where had that gone? *Nowhere,* she counseled herself. *It's here and it's been here all along. We never really forgot it. How sad we let it just slip into an emotional never-never-land.*

Halfway down the stairs she turned, looking up at him expectantly. "Do you want to talk to Bob? I could call and make an appointment."

He hesitated then shrugged. Would it make it easier to bear if he knew all the details? "Might be a good idea. I have some questions and I guess that's the best place to go for answers. If there are any answers," he murmured.

At the back door he kissed her goodbye and she clung briefly to his arm.

Lily watched him walk to the garage and disappear around the corner. She stayed bent over looking through the window until she saw the roof of the car behind the fence. She'd watched it so many times she knew the routine. He'd lift the heavy doors, move the car to the alley, get out and close the doors, then drive off to work. Routines like that were part of life and now she knew how precious simple things like that were. Her eyes filled with tears and she angrily wiped them away.

"Don't go getting sentimental about every little movement," she muttered to the empty house.

In spite of the brief emotional moment, she felt happier and more at ease than she had in a month. *Kate was right.* She turned on the radio and put water on for her tea. She looked at the clock, and decided it was too early to call Kate.

#

"You feel better?" Kate stood in her kitchen, the telephone cord stretched tight as she put the last of the breakfast dishes in the cupboard.

"Yes. You were right. You love to hear that, don't you?"

"I'm not gloating, just happy that you've finally told him. It had to be done. How was he this morning?"

Lily hesitated. She'd shared most of her adult life with Kate, the ups and downs, good and bad, sad and funny times. They'd never crossed the border of intimacy, though, and this morning's conversation in the bedroom was intimate. She smiled, remembering.

"He's doing okay. I'm going to make an appointment for us to see Doctor Bob. It might make it easier for George if he can ask some questions or find out more about what lies ahead for both of us. Now that I've told him, there are questions I have, too."

"It'll be okay. You have each other."

"And you, Kate. You've always been there for us—for me. Don't for a minute think I've forgotten any of that." She struggled to keep the emotion from her voice.

"You're my best friend."

Lily heard the poignancy that softened Kate's words. For one of the very few times in her life, Kate sounded lonely.

"I'll need your help." Lily's voice brought them back to the present.

"You've got it."

For several moments no sound traveled along the telephone line that connected them. Lily realized something much stronger than the wire disappearing into the wall joined them.

"I'll see you later. Okay if I stop by?" Kate asked.

"Of course. Come for lunch."

"No. You don't need extra work. I know—I'll bring lunch over and we can have an indoor picnic in your kitchen. Maybe I can think of something to tempt your appetite."

They laughed. Some things never changed.

CHAPTER SEVEN

The aggravation started with his telephone call to Simone at five-thirty. Michael guessed from the tone of her voice that he'd probably caught her in the bathroom where she was beginning her elaborate preparations for their night at the theater.

"Hi, honey. Sorry but I've got bad news. I'm going to be delayed."

"Delayed? How late will you be?" Already her pique was apparent; Simone didn't like her plans changed.

"Mister Harris—Max Harris—just called. He wants to see me this evening."

"No. Don't tell me you are not coming home in time to go to the theater with me. I will not…"

"Simone," he interrupted. "It's business—it's important."

"So important it cannot wait one other day?" The more disturbed Simone became the stronger her

French accent became. Born in New York City of French parents who had immigrated to this country after World War II, she clung possessively to the accent, wearing it as a badge of distinction.

"His brother is flying in to New York early this evening to meet me. They have joint business interests and want me to represent their corporation on a stock option program. They're flying to Tokyo tomorrow morning. The Harris account is my biggest, Simone, I can't…"

"You can," she shouted. "Have someone else gather the information. You can work on it another time."

Michael didn't respond immediately, drumming his fingers on the desk. He forced himself to stay calm, reluctant to give in to the anger he felt pushing into his throat. Simone loved the townhouse, clothes, and nights at the theater his salary provided. Well, this was the price. Surely she could understand. "I can't go with you tonight. You can still go with Michelle and Andre."

"I hate being the *extra*," she whined.

" Please, Simone, they're friends, you won't be an 'extra.' You know you'll have a good time." He hated begging and yet he seemed to be doing it often lately.

"I'll also go to supper with them," she challenged.

"Fine. I want you to. I'll be there when you get home."

"You'll miss seeing my new gown." By the petulant sound of her voice, Michael knew she was pouting, pushing her full lips out and frowning slightly.

"I'll see it when you get home."

"It's not the same."

"I know."

Awkwardly, they ran out of things to say and hung up.

Michael had dinner with Mister Davis and his brother, Herb. Together they covered the stock option program for several of the companies acquired in a large merger operation. Michael made notes and took a folder of documents with him when he left them at ten o'clock, promising to have their portfolio ready for them when they returned the following week. It was a large account and he was pleased at their confidence in him yet he was anxious to get home even though he knew Simone probably wouldn't return until eleven at the earliest.

When he entered the vestibule of his home on 37th Street, he was greeted with the haunting scent of Simon's distinctive perfume. The house was cool and quiet. Entering the den to the right of the main hallway, he threw his jacket on the back of the sofa facing the fireplace, and poured himself a brandy. Before sitting, he lit the gas logs in the fireplace and watched the flickering tongues of the flames for a few minutes before he went to his desk.

The letter from his mother was at the bottom of the stack of mail. Simone hadn't mentioned it to him earlier and she never opened anything from his parents even though it was always addressed to Mr. and Mrs. Michael Hoffmann.

He was rereading the letter when he heard Simone's key in the front door. Carrying it with him he met her in the hall.

Strikingly beautiful, her jet-black hair pulled back in a severe style emphasized her classic features. Prominent cheekbones covered with flawless pale ivory skin made her dark eyes appear huge. The brilliant red gown she wore clung seductively to her body. She dropped her jacket on a chair.

"You are home." Her voice was clipped and tense.

"Yes. Did you have a nice time? How was the play? Did you…?

"I'm tired Michael. It has been an exhausting day." She moved toward the flight of stairs leading to the second floor.

"Wait, please." He reached for her.

"I'm tired."

"Come have a brandy or sherry with me. I'm sorry I had to cancel tonight but surely you understand. Tell me about the evening. Did you have a nice time with Michelle and Andre?" He held her arm, guiding her into the room. "I need to talk to you."

"Michael, I am tired. This cannot wait for another day?" She shrugged her arm away from his and stood at the end of the cream leather love seat that flanked the fireplace.

He pointed to his brandy on the end table. "I'm having a drink. Join me. Sherry?"

"Oh, very well." She sat on the edge of the cushion, her shoulders squared.

"Tell me about the play."

"It was a bit boring. The cast did the best they could with the script. It will never last long."

"That's too bad. I thought the first reviews were good." He handed her a small wine glass. "What did the others think of it?"

"They were pleased but," Simone shrugged, an expression she used often, "you know how gullible Michelle is and Andre is a fool when it comes to her. We ran into Malcolm at the intermission."

"Was Kay with him?"

"No. She is still away. He says she is visiting friends but we all know where she is." Malcolm, older than Michael and Simone, was active in the Thespians Alliance charity, as they were. It was well known that Malcolm's wife had a severe drinking problem and periodically went away to a rehabilitation hospital in upper New York State.

Michael sat next to Simone. "You didn't mention the letter from my parents. You know you can open any mail that comes to us from them. I've told you that before."

"It is not proper. Besides, the message would be for you anyhow. What did dear MaMa have to say?"

"It's a strange letter. Here let me read it to you." He started to rise.

She put a restraining hand on his arm. "Don't bother. Just tell me what she wrote."

"She wants us to come to Eagleton for a weekend in April."

"April?"

"That's what she said."

"And her reason?"

"None, really. Only that it's important for us to all be together."

"And who is 'all'?"

"She's contacted Debbie and Patty, too."

Again Simone shrugged. Michael knew her shrugs could mean many things, confusion, disinterest, or questions.

"Apparently it's important, but the strange thing is the letter doesn't even sound like Mom. It sounds as if someone had dictated it. I'm puzzled."

"Well," said Simone putting the almost empty glass on the table, "you will have to telephone her and find out what she really wants. I don't think a trip to Eagleton in April sounds appealing at all. If *you* want to go…"

"No, please. Don't suggest I go alone. Mom specifically invited you, too. She wants all of us to be together."

Simone walked across the room, stopped in the doorway and turned to face him. "Really, Michael. Why would *I* want to go to see *your* parents in *April*? Either plan to go alone, or reason with her. Suggest a more suitable season. Late summer perhaps." She turned and disappeared. "I'm tired; I'm going to bed." She hesitated a moment, then added, "Please don't disturb me."

He watched her move up the stairs.

She paused, glancing over her shoulder, dramatically poised halfway up the gleaming oak staircase. "You didn't even mention my new gown." Her petulance was sharp.

"You look lovely, Simone. Really lovely."

She smiled, turned and continued upward.

With increasingly regularity over the past year, Simone had made it clear that when she said she didn't want to be *disturbed*, it meant that Michael would sleep in the guests' suite on the third floor. Michael leaned against the wall and closed his eyes.

Damn. What the hell is wrong at home? Why would Mom want us all there in April? Simone's right. It's a foolish time to plan a reunion. Is it Dad? Are there money problems? He drained his glass. In the den he picked up Simon's glass and went down the long hall to the kitchen. *And, what the hell is wrong here?* He'd asked himself that before, never out loud and never coming up with any answer.

The sparkling chrome and white of the room made him squint. He put the glasses on the drain board. Hester would be in tomorrow. Standing in the kitchen, he thought again of his mother and pictured her in the kitchen in Pennsylvania. Not that there was any similarity between the two rooms. A scent of chocolate chip cookies came to him and he shivered and left the room where such a smell would be totally foreign. When he reached the landing on the second floor, he saw a light beneath the bedroom door and heard faint sounds of classical music. Simone was in another of her strange moods.

Punishing me for disappointing her, he muttered as he climbed the stairs to the next floor. He didn't have to be concerned about clothing on the third floor. Months ago his wife had shifted half his wardrobe to the guests' suite closet.

"It will be less crowded in our closet, darling," she'd reasoned.

Michael wished he'd brought another drink along with him. Somehow he knew he wasn't going to get much sleep tonight. He had carried his mother's letter with him and now put it on the bureau, thoughtfully stroking the plain white envelope. Whatever was wrong, he didn't want to delve into it right now, and yet questions kept running through his mind. *Dad? Mom? Money? Troubles?* When he did go to sleep, his dreams were muddled. His sisters' faces drifted through his thoughts, but they were silent. Mister Davis appeared to be angry. Simone was there, too, only she just smiled and shrugged.

When he woke he felt more tired than he had been when he finally went to sleep last night.

Standing in front of the mirror the next morning his thoughts were as tumultuous as his dreams had been. "I never could deal with emotions," he muttered to the face that watched him draw a razor through the thick foam.

Michael stepped out of the elevator at the thirty-second floor. At seven thirty in the morning the building was almost empty. His steps rang hollowly as he strode along the corridor to the double glass doors with the gold lettering that read Matson and Dolby, Investment Brokers. Balancing his briefcase and a cardboard container of coffee, he used his key to open the door. The office was his haven—a place where he felt safe and confident. Ten years earlier, he hadn't had a key or an office of his own. Originally one of the anonymous clerks who occupied the floor below these offices, six months ago his most recent promotion changed all that.

He flipped on the lights illuminating the plush reception area. To the left were the luxurious offices of the senior brokerage officers. They had heavy oak doors protecting them from the common area, and windows offering a spectacular view of the city.

He moved to the right, past the empty receptionist's desk and went through the gate in the highly polished brass railing that separated the reception area from the offices occupied by the junior officers. His office had a large window facing the waiting room. In a few years, with any luck, he would be assigned an office with a real window that looked out across the city. The blinds, that afforded privacy when dealing with clients, were now pulled to one side. The unlocked door to his office was closed and he pushed it open and entered.

He turned on the light and his computer. As he settled into his chair, he watched the stream of numbers and stock symbols as they ran across the screen, recapping yesterday's market activity. He shuffled through a pile of order confirmations, then sipped the lukewarm coffee, feeling himself slide into the challenging atmosphere of his business world.

Reaching into the inside pocket of his jacket, he took out his mother's letter. *It's as if a stranger wrote it. These words aren't Mom's; they're stilted and rehearsed.* Tapping the envelope on the desktop, he was startled by a loud rapping on his door.

"Whoa. You're here early. You looking for an office with a solid door and a view?" Kevin MacBrien filled the doorway with his huge frame. Looking more like an NFL player than a stockbroker, a broad smile covered his ruddy Scotsman's face. He ran one hand through unruly red hair waiting for Michael's answer.

Michael returned his grin. The two men had started with the firm the same year and had progressed at a similar pace. More than office friends, Kevin and Michael found they really enjoyed each other's company.

"Hell no. This office suits me fine. Had some portfolios to go over and it's a lot quieter now than after the market opens." He gestured toward a stack of manila expanding files.

"How was the meeting with the Davis boys?"

"It went well. I've got a lot of work to do but they won't be back in the country until the end of next week."

"You had coffee?"

"Yeah. I picked up a cup in the lobby," he said, shaking the empty container.

"I'm going to the deli. Want me to get you something?"

"No thanks. I've got to get to work."

"See you for lunch?"

"Sure. We can go to Luccio's if you like."

Kevin waved at him through the window and loped across the reception area.

Michael watched him disappear through the glass doors before turning back to his desk. But, instead of picking up one of the bulging files, he opened the envelope and read the letter from his mother again.

CHAPTER EIGHT

"Michael, I do not wish to discuss this further. I am *not* going to your parents' home in April and that is final." Simone balanced her cup on the saucer she held.

He turned his back to her and knelt to light the gas logs in the fireplace. It was the same routine every night when they had their after-dinner coffee in the den. Tonight, however, tension filled the room.

"You're being stubborn. Mom specifically asked us to come that weekend."

"Have you called her? Have you asked what is so important about that date? No. Like a sheep called by the shepherd you are ready to turn and follow."

He gritted his teeth and closed his eyes, hating the confrontation. Angrily, he threw himself into the wing-backed chair to Simone's left. In the office he welcomed challenges; that was where competition belonged, not here. He realized part of this was his fault, always giving in to Simone. He'd left their social life up to her; proud of the way she entertained friends and clients. Many envied her beauty and grace and he chose to overlook her periodic moodiness. Long ago he'd convinced himself she wasn't as cold as she sometimes appeared.

Dammit, why was his mother's letter such a puzzle, and why was Simone being so adamant? The two women were never close. Close? That was a joke. From their first meeting he felt the charge of mutual animosity. His mother, however, was too polite to put what she felt into words.

Simone, on the other hand, was not so reluctant to voice her opinion. Shortly after their wedding he remembered her saying, *"Your mother is disappointed in your choice, Michael. She would rather you'd married a more domesticated woman. I could never please her."* She'd dusted her hands in front of her as if brushing away some troublesome lint.

Her voice brought him back to the present. "Maybe if she chooses another time, sometime in the late summer or early fall, I would consider it but what in the world would I—would we do there in April…"

"That's the date she chose… "

"It will probably rain the whole time. We will be shut up in that cramped house…"

"You don't know it'll rain at all."

"No, I will not do it. Besides, the end of April is always the busiest time for Thespian Alliance." She stared into the fire, reluctant to meet his eyes.

Restlessly, Michael stood and paced behind the love seat where Simone was seated.

"Maybe I'll call Debbie. She must have received her letter. I'd feel better talking to Mom if I really knew what the story was. What do you think?"

"Call her." Simone shrugged and rose, moving across the room toward the hallway. "But please do not commit me to a visit in April. I won't go."

She smiled to herself as she walked to the kitchen. *Why would he think I'd want to visit that hateful old woman? We are worlds apart. A good wife bakes cookies and mops floors.* Simone put the cups into the dishwasher and snapped the light off. She certainly wasn't going to spend any more time thinking about the mother-in-law she had dismissed a long time ago.

"I'm going upstairs, Michael," she called from the foot of the stairs.

"I'll be up shortly."

"Don't hurry. I'll probably be asleep before you come up. I know you have a very busy day planned tomorrow, and I'll be gone most of the day with Michelle. The art show for the benefit of Thespians, remember?"

She didn't wait for a reply. Her nightly ritual with bath and skin care would take an hour. She hoped Michael would choose not to come to bed with her again tonight but hesitated to suggest the third floor again so soon.

Simone sprinkled perfumed bath salts on the hot water gushing into the deep tub. Her face warmed but it wasn't from the steam. Turning on the jets in the tub sent the fragrant water swirling into whirlpools of motion—she thought of tomorrow afternoon. She wouldn't be attending the art show. Of course, Michelle would *say* she'd been there, should it become necessary. *French girls protect each other. They understand*, she thought, letting the scarlet robe slide down her naked body and fall in a shimmering heap on the black and white tiles.

#

George cradled Lily's arm in his as they walked down the concrete steps from the doctor's office. She wanted to tell him to stop handling her as if she were made of china but the words would have sounded too harsh. She regretted her critical thoughts when she saw his hand tremble as he opened the car door for her.

He was acting as if she were an invalid. *Well, if I'm not one now, I'll probably be one before long.* She sighed and waited for him to settle himself behind the wheel.

The chill March air penetrated the car's interior. He started the motor, fiddled with the heater settings, then said, "I should have come out first, started the car and the heater so it would be warmed up for you. Sorry. Sometimes I don't think."

"It's okay."

"No, it's not okay. I should have… " He turned to look at her. "There are so many things I should have done."

She put a gloved hand on his arm. "Stop. You promised, remember? No recriminations, no 'we shoulds' and 'what ifs.' We have today and all our tomorrows. Who knows how many? No absolute schedule. You heard Bob. He's pleased with the way I'm doing."

"Said you should eat more."

"I'll try. Kate is always trying to fix something to tempt me." She remembered last week's kitchen picnic. Funny how she could recall every minute now where a few months ago she forgot what she'd had for dinner the previous day. She watched him stare ahead through the windshield. He'd been so quiet in Bob's office it was Lily who asked most of the questions, feeling calmer than she had during her earlier visits.

"Are you okay?" she asked.

"Sure." He slid his hands around the wheel, still not attempting to put the car in gear.

"I think Bob answered all our questions pretty clearly, didn't he?" She watched him tighten his jaw and purse his lips.

"I don't know if I can do what you're doing, Lil. I don't know if I can…"

"You can."

He grasped her hand, making her flinch with the pressure. "Do you want to see another doctor, get another opinion?"

"No, I don't, but I will if you want me to, if it will ease your mind."

"No. If you feel sure that Bob's got this thing right…"

His voice caught and Lily recognized his difficulty at putting his acceptance of the truth into words.

"I do."

"I was glad there weren't any other patients in the waiting room when we got there tonight."

"Bob's thoughtful. He didn't have any patients the day he told me either."

He put the car in gear and moved forward. They held hands. *Like we did when we were courting,* she thought. For several blocks neither spoke, then Lily startled him by saying, "Know what I'd like to do?"

"Uh…"

"Of course you don't. George, I want to do something fun. Something crazy. I want to be silly and laugh."

"What—uh now?" George said, slowing the car and turning into the alley.

"I don't know. We'll think of something."

He pulled up to the garage doors, put the car in neutral and turned to look at her, his hands still clutching the wheel.

"When…?" he repeated.

"Don't worry about it tonight, dear. It's a silly whim. We'll think about it."

"Whatever you want. Whatever…"

"I know. Let me out here, it's easier than tripping over that junk in the garage. Another place we should clean out," she said, opening the door. "I'll put the kettle on."

He watched her go through the gate in the tall fence. "What the hell is there to be silly and laugh about?" he muttered. His words rang hollowly in the cold garage. He knew, though, if anyone could find something to laugh about it would be Lily. His heart felt an ounce or so lighter than it had in Bob's office as he shut the door behind him and stood in the chill night air. The light was on in the kitchen and he could see his wife moving around behind the closed door. As normal as possible, she'd said.

"Okay," he murmured. "As normal as possible.

CHAPTER NINE

Debbie heard the telephone ringing and fumbled with her keys in her hurry to open the door. She dashed across the short hall to the living room and snatched the receiver from the telephone.

"Hello," she snapped.

"Hello yourself. I was about to give up."

"Mike? I just got in. You forgot the time difference."

"No, I didn't. It's after eight there. I thought you'd be home by now."

"I often work late. Let me catch my breath," she said, stretching the cord as she plopped down in the soft white leather chair facing the wall of windows. The drapes were still open and the windows looked cold and blank, like sightless eyes. "What's up? Haven't heard from you since—was it New Year's Day?"

"I guess. Did you get a letter from Mom?" he asked softly.

"Yes. Why are you whispering?"

"I'm not whispering."

Debbie stretched her legs and pushed off her shoes. "Oh? I thought maybe Madam Simone was monitoring your calls."

"Cut it out, Deb."

"Sorry. That was bitchy. And speaking of bitchy, how is Simone?"

"She's fine. She went upstairs to get ready for bed. Can we get back to the subject?"

Debbie read his defensiveness. "What subject?"

Michael sighed audibly. "The letter from Mom. Did you get one?"

"Yeah, yesterday, what's that all about?"

"Mine said we were all getting a similar letter. I don't know what's behind this, do you? Have you figured it out?"

Debbie looked across the room to the desk where her copy of the letter rested. It was hidden from sight but she looked anyhow. "I don't know. Are you going? I haven't a clue about what she's hinting at. A family reunion? Reestablishing connections? We're grown up and doing our own things. Maybe she's getting sentimental in her old age."

Michael recognized the glib offhandedness. Juggling immediate emotions with the obligations you felt to family members wasn't easy, he knew. Yet, ever since her divorce, Debbie had been distancing herself more than ever.

"I don't know what to do. I miss seeing Mom sometimes but..." He hesitated. "I hate the thought of clashing with the old man again. I never know what subjects to bring up, what's safe to talk about."

"He's mellowing a bit."

"I haven't seen it."

"When was the last time you were there for any length of time?"

Michael ignored her question. "This meeting seems important to Mom. Do you think there's something wrong there? I've thought about it a lot over the past two days. It can't be financial. Dad's worked at the foundry for over thirty years. He's got a good retirement plan. In choosing my career, it was one of the sterling features he thought I overlooked, don't you remember?"

"You always think of finances don't you? Well, I don't think it's that. Maybe Dad's not well and she's worried? Until now they've both been pretty lucky health-wise." Debbie thought briefly about the cancer scare years ago but rationalized, *no, that was all over long ago.*

Michael shifted his position and slid onto a stool. He'd been leaning across the breakfast bar in the kitchen.

"My life work *is* finances, Deb. Thinking of that was natural. I considered one of them being sick but Mom would have told us if it were that, wouldn't she?"

"I suppose so."

"And what about Patty? She'll never come. She wasn't even part of the family when we were a family. Do you even know where she is?"

"In Florida I think, seems to me in a letter a couple of months ago, Mom mentioned she was in Florida working as a waitress somewhere. Who knows? She probably couldn't afford to come home anyway."

Neither brother nor sister spoke for several moments.

"Well, are you going?" Michael fiddled with the telephone cord.

"I don't know. Are you? It's not exactly the most convenient time. The summer would be better for me. I always go home for a week then anyhow."

"We hadn't made any vacation plans this year yet. Simone's so involved in her charity work and since I received a promotion my workload has increased. How were they last summer when you were there?"

"I didn't notice anything different but then I guess I'm not very observant."

Michael didn't say anything but he thought, *you don't observe because you don't let yourself get involved.* The sour taste of guilt flooded his throat as he applied those same thoughts to his own behavior.

"When I go home I spend the days with Mom and most of the evenings visiting friends. Dad doesn't pick on much anymore. In fact, he's very quiet when I'm there. Not like when we were home. What's so important about April twenty-sixth? I can't think of anything."

"Me either. It's not a birthday or anniversary. Well, I don't know what to do. It would only be a long car trip for me. You'd have to fly from Chicago and you say Patty's in Florida? I think I'll call Mom and see what's up. Unless you want to."

Debbie noticed that he said 'a long car trip for *'me'* and not '*us*'. It was pretty obvious the ice queen wouldn't be with him.

"No, you call. You're the oldest." She didn't add 'and the favorite' as she'd always felt. First children, especially sons, always seemed favored by mothers. At least sisters thought so. "Call me after you've spoken to her. I don't want to start worrying prematurely and it's probably just a whim. Maybe we can change the date to something more convenient. I'm assuming that it's not terribly convenient for you either. Will Simone go?"

"Who knows? As I said, a weekend isn't too difficult for me to arrange. We're only 140 miles away."

After she'd put the receiver back in the cradle, Debbie walked across the plush carpet to the windows and stared at her reflection mirrored in the glass. She looked through the image and across the section of Chicago framed between the drapes. Echoes of her childhood reverberated in her head. Nothing she ever did pleased her father. Her good grades never received praise. According to her father, she'd be better off excelling in home *economics*. She heard his voice echo in the silence of the room.

Dreams of becoming an architect are foolish. You'll get married and have children like every other woman. What is there away from Eagleton that's so wonderful anyhow?

She couldn't answer his questions then and she couldn't now. She sighed and drew her shoulders together, arms defensively across her chest and stared out the cold windows.

Across the city, millions of lights sparkled in the cool night air. Darkness obscured the view of Lake Michigan, one of the reasons she paid the exorbitant rental for the apartment, one of four perched on top of a tall building. Elegant and luxurious, it was her personal reward after the divorce. She was content with the new life she'd established for herself. But then, maybe *content* wasn't exactly the word she should apply to her guarded existence.

Michael's concern and confusion echoed her own. Getting in touch with her wasn't unusual for her mother. She'd written religiously over the years, keeping her informed as to family matters and up-to-date on local back-home news. Debbie had laughed once, telling her mother she was the eyes and ears of Eagleton. Her mother's open invitations were always unspoken, but setting up a family reunion? She, too, struggled with the strange, elusive message in her mother's request.

Well, the letter had caused one immediate change. Debbie had thought about her brother and sister more over the past two days than she had in the last five years. Is this what her mother meant when she mentioned reuniting the family? That was absurd; they were never the *Brady Bunch.*

She pulled the heavy drapes across the expanse of glass, shutting out the rest of the world, ending the reminiscing before she got to the more painful details.

Still, as she went into her bedroom she continued to think about her brother and sister. It sounded like Michael had problems with the difficult and moody Simone. Patty was always a wanderlust, independent and uninvolved in family matters, but then she'd always been the oddball. As for herself, she wasn't a problem. She hadn't told them the sordid details that led to the divorce, but that was best kept to herself; they didn't need to know.

After she'd changed from her business suit to a silk caftan, she went to the kitchen. A small casserole and salad from the local gourmet delicatessen would be dinner, as usual, unless she was spending the evening with Charles. Not tonight though. She purposefully limited their engagements to three a week at the most, and they had tickets for a concert tomorrow.

She slid the casserole into the eye-level oven, carefully lined up the salad and silverware on the place mat on the breakfast table, and poured a glass of white wine. Her book lay on the coffee table in the living room. Another perfect evening waited for her. Perfect except for the nagging discontent her mother's letter had kindled. Without realizing it she'd already made up her mind. Her vacation was scheduled for August. She *wasn't* going home in April.

CHAPTER TEN

The house was quiet. Tonight the quiet, however, took on a new depth. Was it because he felt there was an ominous overtone in his mother's letter? He thought he'd feel better, less confused, after talking to his sister, but the opposite was true. His stomach tightened and a slight dull thud began behind his temples. Maybe he shouldn't have had the drink he'd just finished.

Restlessly, he wandered from the den to the hall and stared up the stairs. Should he try to talk to Simone again?

The telephone rang and Michael jumped in surprise. Was it Deb calling back? His mother? He hurried back to the den and picked up the telephone.

A thin line of perspiration covered his upper lip and his hand trembled when he gently replaced the receiver. The caller was only a co-worker calling to confirm a meeting set for the following day. Why had he thought it would be his mother?

He glanced at the clock on the mantel over the fireplace. It was twenty-five minutes to ten. His parents wouldn't have gone to bed yet. If he remembered correctly, his father always watched the ten o'clock news before retiring. Why not call tonight? Why wait and agonize another twenty-four hours?

He dialed the familiar number and waited. It rang four times and his frown deepened with each ring.

Finally his mother's voice, breathless as if she'd run from outside to answer the telephone, broke the string of electronic signals.

"Hello?"

"Mom, it's me. You sound as if you've been running. Did I call at a bad time?"

"Heavens no, Michael. Your father and I were looking through some things in the cedar closet. I'm so glad you called; it's good to hear your voice. How are you? How is Simone?"

"We're fine. We're fine," he repeated. "How are you and Dad?"

He waited through a slight hesitation before his mother replied, "We're fine, dear. Wait, I'll call your father so you can talk to him, too."

"No. Wait. Mom? I wanted to talk to you first. I got your letter." The choppy sentences emphasized his nervousness and his cheeks warmed. "I mean, I wanted to see how everything was and why it was so important for us all to be in Pennsylvania on the twenty-sixth of April. Is it a special occasion?"

"No, dear. No special occasion. I've been worried and concerned for some time about our family and I decided to do something about it. Honey, we're never together anymore. You children aren't close. No one makes any effort to keep in touch, to…I don't know." She sighed. "You all have your own lives to live but, still, there should be some connection."

"It's the times, Mom. We're busy with our careers, or at least Deb and I are. That doesn't mean we've forgotten our family. I feel guilty that you think we have."

"I don't want you to feel guilty. That's not what this is about. I knew you'd think I was crazy." She stalled. This wasn't the way she thought it was going to be but then if she hadn't known what she expected, she shouldn't be surprised should she? Talk about communication.

"I don't think you're crazy. You worried me by your reference to family problems. I didn't know any existed. I spoke to Debbie tonight and she was confused, too. We're scattered but I guess since I'm closest I should be more attentive."

"It's not *attention* I want. I'm not blaming you or anyone and I certainly didn't mean for you to feel guilty. It's just…"

"Are you all right? Is Dad okay? Deb thought maybe Dad wasn't well."

"Oh, he's fine. Strong as an ox and looking forward to retiring in three years." She sighed with relief. The truth was so much more comfortable.

"I'm glad to hear that. Well, I don't know what plans I can make for the trip. I haven't checked my calendar or spoken to Simone," he lied. "What about Patty? Deb thinks she's in Florida. How in the world would she get up here for a weekend? Deb could afford air fare and I'll drive, but what about Patty?"

Lily hesitated before answering, not that she was ashamed of offering to pay for Patty's travel expenses. "We've offered to pay for her trip. We're able to do it and it's important to me—to us, for you all to be together for this one weekend."

"I guess that's what we don't understand, Mom. What's so important about this one weekend?"

"It's something I want to happen, that's all. Maybe it's selfish but I want you and Simone, Debbie and Patty all here under the same roof, in the same house so we can talk and be a family again. So you can be friends again. I know you all have busy lives away from us but can't you indulge your old mother this one wish?"

Mom putting pressure on us? This was so unlike his mother Michael felt his heart quicken. He brushed the hair from his forehead, licked his lips and switched the telephone to the other ear. "It's not a question of indulging you, Mom. We want you to be happy. We don't see the problem, but I'll contact the girls and see what we can arrange. Does it *have* to be that weekend?"

"That's the weekend I'd like it to be, dear." His mother's voice was soft.

"Well, I'll see what I can do. Do you have a telephone number for Patty?"

"No. I have the name of the place where she's working as a waitress. Would that help? Maybe you'll have to write to her."

"Give me the name of the restaurant. I can probably get the telephone number and leave a message for her there if I can't find a home number."

Later, as he went down the hall to the kitchen, he tucked the paper with the name of Patty's place of employment into his shirt pocket. He took a beer from the oversized refrigerator, popped the top and tilted the can to his lips. Simone would have a fit if she saw him drinking from the can. Maybe that was why this beer tasted so good tonight. He leaned against the sink and stared into the darkness. When he finished his beer, he crushed the can in his fist and tossed it into the recycle bin at the head of the cellar stairs.

I might as well shower and read in bed. He began to climb the carpeted stairs. *What's the real reason behind Mom's request and why are Debbie and I both feeling guilty?* He stopped midway up the stairs. *Both?* He leaned into the wall for a moment realizing the guilt he had heard in Debbie's voice echoed his own.

When he reached the second floor, he hesitated, staring up the dark stairs that lead to the upper floors. On the third floor, two small, completely furnished bedrooms, and a bathroom lay hidden in the darkness. Five years ago, when they purchased the five-story brownstone home, helped by money his grandfather had left him, he'd hoped those rooms would be for their children, but there were no children. And, in his heart he knew there would never be any children if Simone had her way, and when didn't Simone have her way?

CHAPTER ELEVEN

Carlos Espinosa watched the pretty young girl cross the parking lot behind the restaurant. The breeze caught her light brown hair and swirled it across her face as she turned and ducked through the narrow opening in the fence behind El Diabolo. Heat intensified the pungent aroma from the dumpster and he closed the door to the kitchen.

Patty Hoffmann was different today, not her usual bouncy self when she stopped by to pick up her paycheck. Reliable though. She'd be back at seven o'clock tonight for the late shift. A good employee, he decided, patting himself on the back for recognizing something in her a little more special than the usual parade of girls who drifted through the restaurant trade. A touch of class, he thought. Efficient and quiet, she worked hard and was a favorite with several of his best customers. Of course, most of them were men but that wasn't difficult to understand. Patty was pretty.

Patty didn't think of herself as pretty. She didn't see herself as any classier than the other girls she worked with either, but she knew she occasionally got special treatment from Carlos. Not that he asked for anything in return. She'd kicked around enough to know it was best not to get involved personally with owners or other waitresses. It usually led to conflicts, or worse. No, Carlos had been good to her without any strings. When she started, she was hired for the lunch shift, which meant lower tips and cheaper, crabbier tourists with noisy children. She was lucky to get evenings so quickly and didn't mind the hours. Working late, sleeping late and having the days to herself was a good routine.

She waited on the corner for a bus. In a little over seven hours, she'd return to the restaurant and begin another six-hour shift. She checked her watch, enough time to go to the bank, cash her check, sit on the beach for a while and take a nap before going to work. Tidewaters, the rooming house she called home, had window air conditioners; they were noisy but she could at least sleep in comfort.

Patty left the bank and walked to a beach not far from Tidewaters. It wasn't much of a beach, just a strip of sand stretching along the coast near some commercial fishing docks. The fancier beaches were north of here where the tourist hotels and condos were. When she reached the sand, she shed the oversized tee shirt and white shorts she wore over her bathing suit. The battered bench she'd come to think of as hers was vacant. Two tall coconut palms offered some shade but she chose to sit in the sun. She closed her eyes and listened to the sea gulls' cries as they circled overhead. The breeze was brisk and when it gusted, sand stung her bare skin. Still, it was March and warm.

She rolled her shoulders trying to release the taut muscles. *That damn letter from Mom. What did she mean family connections?* Well, she couldn't possibly go home for a weekend. What a crazy idea. She couldn't afford that, even if they paid the airfare; she couldn't risk losing her job. It was the best money she'd made in five years and now she *had* to work as long as possible. Patty didn't usually look too far into the future. Not until six weeks ago anyhow. Now there was another reason to make plans, save money, and keep working. When she first started at El Diabolo it was with the same sense of chance she'd employed for all her ventures. If it didn't work out, there was something else down the street or in the next town – or state. Life was different now.

Always a loner, strangely she wished she had someone to talk to. For two days she'd thought about her mother's letter, her parents, and her brother and sister. Odd how she rarely thought of any of them. They were family; they just weren't all in the same place. Mom was right when she said they were different. Michael was the brainy one. Her earliest memories of her brother were vague. Eight years older than she, he was well established in school and studies by the time she entered kindergarten. He'd always been tolerant but busy when it came to his youngest sister. As children, he and Deb fought a lot over stupid things, but she hadn't been included in the conflicts. She'd always been envious of her sister who she thought of as much prettier and smarter. Deb had an air of purpose and confidence about her, finishing projects and completing plans. Patty wondered what could have gone wrong with the marriage everyone thought was perfect. *Couldn't have been so perfect*, she thought.

She looked down the body that had never pleased her. Her legs and arms were a golden brown and she wondered how long it would be before her waist got even thicker and how Carlos would take the news when she announced her pregnancy.

Later, after a fitful nap, she ironed her shirt on the bed. Learning to iron on floors, beds, and unpadded tables had been part of her nomadic education. She was quite expert at it. The shirt was a wild print of tropical flowers and birds, so small wrinkles didn't show anyhow. The black slacks didn't need ironing because they stretched tightly across her hips and thighs.

Dressed, she sat on the side of the single bed. The letter from her mother lay on the nightstand. She unfolded the single sheet of paper and read the message again. How could she go to Pennsylvania for a weekend, even if they sent her money for a ticket? Her hands trembled and she was overcome with a longing to see her mother and father, an alien emotion that brought rare tears to her eyes. What would they think? Her mother always talked about grandchildren but not to her. Once long ago, she'd heard her mother drop a grandmother hint to Debbie, but that was a lost dream now she supposed. *I guess she thinks Mike is their only hope for a grandchild.* Would her mother be excited, shocked, or both? Patty dropped the letter on the bed, rose and wiped the salty tears from her eyes.

"Damn fool," she muttered as she closed the door behind her and ran down the stairs.

At six-thirty Patty checked her workstation. She liked to have everything in order before she began her shift. The restaurant was filled to capacity and she looked at the reservation list before going to the back room to sign in. They'd be busy until after ten with regular diners and then the late crowd would come in. It amazed her how people could eat fried seafood dinners at eleven o'clock at night, but she was glad they did. The later the customer, the more they drank and the more they tipped. Her hand automatically ran under her apron across her abdomen. Still fairly flat. She was folding cloth napkins when she felt a tap on her shoulder and spun around. Never easy at being touched unexpectedly, she scowled at the offender. It was Carlos.

"You got a call earlier today. I left the message on my desk."

"I got a call?"

"Yep. You got a brother in New York?"

Michael had called? How had he found her? Why…? Then she remembered the letter. She smiled at Carlos. "Thanks. I'll get the message and call him tomorrow."

"Hope it's not bad news. Long distance calls from relatives usually mean trouble." Carlos knew that from experience; his family was scattered along the east coast of this country with the rest of his relatives still in Cuba.

"Probably trying to track me down. I'm the rebel in the family."

The paper on Carlos' desk was grease-stained and wrinkled but the numbers and message were clear. "Patty—call Michael at his office tomorrow. 1-212-555-7500." She tucked the note into the pocket of her slacks and went to work.

Making a telephone call when you had no telephone wasn't easy. The next morning Patty checked with the old lady who ran the rooming house and was firmly told that no long distance calls could be made from her telephone, no matter what. "Unless," Mrs. Jankowski added piously, "it's a matter of life or death." She folded her lips over her badly fitted teeth and glared at Patty from her doorway. She'd dealt with drifters before.

Patty could have paid her but she was so angered by the old bag's attitude she slammed the front door and walked away from the scruffy building. As she walked along the gritty sidewalk, her mind churned through her possibilities. She'd have to find a public phone booth and make a collect call. A collect call was her only option anyhow, but phone booths were hard to find. It was lucky to find a whole telephone stuck to an outside wall at a convenience store.

The rooming house was in a rundown urban part of town, several miles from the center of the city. She turned the corner and walked along a street she hadn't explored yet. As she walked, the houses became a bit nicer; the yards actually had grass and flowers. Most of them had two sandy ruts leading from the sidewalk to an empty carport. The adults were probably at work, the kids at school.

After several blocks she noticed a stucco building surrounded by Spanish Bayonets and Queen Palms. A sign at the side of the double doors read, Branch Library, Hillsborough County. She crossed the street and tried the door. It opened and a blast of cool air engulfed her. The room she stepped into was quiet, and she hesitated just inside the doors.

"Can I help you?" asked a stout woman behind the counter. She wore a colorful shift and huge rose tinted glasses. The smile she offered lit her brown, lined face surrounded by gray, frizzy hair.

"Do you have a public telephone?" Patty asked.

"We do, it's down that hall outside the research office." The woman pointed, her large fleshy arm quivering with the gesture. "Can't make long distance calls unless they are collect," she warned.

Feeling obligated to walk quietly, Patty tiptoed along the hall. Halfway down the corridor she found a shelf set into an alcove. There was a telephone, some scrap paper, stubby pencils and a chair pushed under the shelf. She pulled Carlos' message from the pocket in her shorts, sat on the chair, and stared at the telephone.

Finding such ideal conditions was more than she had anticipated but now that she faced the instrument she was unsure of what to do next. What did Mike want? It had to be about her mother's letter and that stupid weekend she was planning. What did it have to do with her? She wouldn't be going north. Not now.

She sighed, picked up the telephone and gave the long distance operator the numbers for the collect call. Someone came out of the room behind her and she glanced up to see a woman carrying several heavy books walk quietly toward the front of the building. The connection was made and she heard a voice say, "Matson and Dolby."

The formality of the voice and the firm's name surprised Patty. She listened as the operator asked for Mister Michael Hoffmann, stating it was a collect call.

The answering operator accepted the collect call without question, which surprised Patty, and she stuttered as she asked to speak to her brother.

"Mister Hoffmann is in a meeting. May I have him call you later or do you wish to speak with another investment counselor?"

Damn. She wasn't used to dealing with such propriety. If he wanted her to call, why the hell hadn't he stayed by his telephone? She was annoyed. "This is his sister in Florida. I'm returning his call. I'm not going to be at a number he can call back so tell him I called."

She was ready to hang up when she heard, "Oh, wait. Mister Hoffmann said if his sister called he was to be interrupted. Please hold."

Patty listened to classical music and drummed her fingers on the shelf. She watched the unknown woman, who smiled at her, return to her office. After what seemed like an eternity, she heard her brother's voice.

"Patty. I'm so glad you called. I wasn't sure my message would even get to you. The fellow who took it didn't seem to speak much English but he said he knew you."

"That was Carlos. He speaks English, he just doesn't let strangers know it." Patty tried to picture her brother. Had it been three or four years since she'd seen him? The last time she'd been home he hadn't been there. "Why'd you want me to call?"

Michael stretched across his desk and pushed the door shut. The blinds at the window that looked out on the reception area, were open. Unless he had a client in his office who demanded privacy, his blinds were usually open. His secretary turned to look at him when he closed the door. He nodded and she smiled.

"I got the name of the restaurant from Mom. I spoke to her last night—and to Debbie in Chicago." He paused, waiting for a response from Patty. Nothing interrupted the silence. "Did you get a letter from Mom?"

"Yeah, something about a weekend in Pennsylvania. Is she crazy? I can't take a trip. I just got this job and it's a good one. Waitresses don't get vacations, the only time off we get is when we're unemployed."

"Well this one weekend seems to be important to them, or at least to Mom. I haven't talked to Dad yet." He frowned as he suddenly remembered he hadn't spoken to his Dad last night and that, too, was strange. Anytime he called home, his mother always made sure she put his Dad on the line before hanging up. "I understand Mom's promised to send you air fare so you can come."

"What the heck is this about? All of a sudden we have to be joined at the hip?"

"Don't be flip. I don't really know what it's about. But it's important." He wasn't at all sure that was the truth either.

Again there was a difficult silence. Patty couldn't think of anything to say and Michael knew so little about his younger sister's life he, too, was at a loss.

"How's your wife?" Patty finally said, breaking the uncomfortable quiet.

"Fine." He wondered if Patty even remembered his wife's name. "Simone's fine and

I'm fine. Busy. And you? I haven't been able to keep up with you, you move around so much."

"Yeah. Well, I think I might be pretty well set for a while. I like it here. The weather's great and the job's good. Lots of tourists, although the girls, the other waitresses, tell me it slows down a little after May but there's still enough tourists to make a living. The restaurant is kind of plush. Tips are good." She ran out of things to say.

"Well, that's good to hear. How long have you been in Florida? Simone and I thought we might take a winter vacation this past year, but it didn't work out. Too many things going on. Maybe next year."

"I came here in December, three months ago." Patty counted the months with three fingers walking across the shelf. "I can't come north now though."

"Can't you consider it Patty? It seems important to Mom and it's only one weekend."

"God, what's so damn special about this one weekend? It's not like we do this regularly or if we even care if we get together. I haven't seen you or Deb in four or five years. I saw Mom and Dad the summer before last." Patty's fingers tapped nervously and she glanced over her shoulder to see if the woman in the research office could hear her or was paying any attention. She couldn't see anyone.

"I don't know what the reason is. I'm going to call Mom tonight and tell her I spoke with you. What should I tell her?"

"Tell her…" A sudden sadness engulfed her and she was shocked to realize her eyes were filled with tears and her hand holding the telephone quivered. What was the matter with her? It must be the pregnancy causing these weird feelings. And maybe that was what she wanted to tell her mother. Not Michael—her mother. She wanted to tell her that a grandchild was on the way. She wanted to feel her mother's arms around her and see the astonishment on her father's face. "Tell her I don't think I can come to Eagleton," she whispered.

"Even if she sends you the money? Patty, I'll send you the money if you don't want to ask them. No questions asked; no one else needs to know."

Patty rested her head on her hand. The urging from her brother to make a decision right now turned to resentment and then anger. "Dammit, I don't care what you say. Tell them anything you want. I can't come home. Not now."

She was tempted to hang up.

"Don't fly off the handle! Think about it okay? You can call me here or at home, collect, any time. Think about it, please?"

"I'll think about it but I can't see me running up there in April. It's just not possible."

"Do you have a pencil and paper? Take my home number too, in case you want to call me. Are you sure you're okay?"

"I'm okay," she shouted into the phone, reaching for a scrap of paper and one of the stubby pencils. "Give me your number."

She scribbled his home telephone number on the paper. The pencil was blunt and the numbers were thick and uneven.

"Read the number back."

He was checking to see if she really wrote them down and she knew it. She recited the numbers and said, "There. You thought I didn't write it down, didn't you?"

"No. I wanted to make sure you had the numbers right. Patty…" He hesitated.

"I'm okay, Mike. Really. Better off than I've been for a while."

He stared across the busy office, recognizing a client waiting for him in the reception area. Michael smiled and waved. His secretary looked at him anxiously. "I have to go, Patty. But keep in touch, okay? Call me here—or at home, anytime. And promise me you'll think about coming home in April. Okay?" Strange how he felt more protective of his sibling than ever before and he hadn't seen her in years. With shame he realized he rarely thought of her.

"I promise—and thanks. Sorry I was bitchy. I don't like this kind of pressure and I don't understand it. I'll call you." She didn't say when and they both knew it was an empty promise.

After she hung up, she left the library quickly. Suddenly the cool, calm confines of the building closed in on her and she needed to be out in the air. Unaware of where she was walking, she was surprised to find herself several blocks away from her rooming house. She walked home more slowly than usual.

In her room she picked up the letter again, slowly rereading it. Why did she sense urgency in her mother's words? Taken word for word there was no crisis outlined. It wasn't a special occasion that she could think of and Michael said he didn't know of anything.

She lay across the bed listening to the churning window air conditioner. If anyone had an emergency to plan for, it was she. The flu she thought she had at the end of January turned out to be a child in her womb. Ten weeks pregnant the doctor told her. No real home. No insurance. No father for the baby. Now that's a crisis.

A single tear slipped from each eye and ran across her temples and into her hair. She wasn't crying because she felt sorry for herself. What was it then? If she were honest with herself, and she usually was, she'd have admitted she was lonely and scared. For the first time in her life she was faced with an issue she couldn't ignore or run away from. The doctor had offered to refer her to an abortion clinic, the easy answer, and probably the most sensible one. Why had she instantly turned it down? What did she need a kid for? Even *she* couldn't invent an answer to those questions.

CHAPTER TWELVE

Kate allowed the kitchen door to swing shut with a bang as she tossed her purse on the counter top. “Tell me,” she demanded.

Lily grinned at her. “I told you on the telephone. Michael called last night.”

“Well, I know that, but I want to know all the details.” She slid into the chair opposite Lily and thumped her folded arms on the table.

“There’s not much more to tell. He said he’d have to talk to Simone, check his calendar, and he’d get in touch with the girls. He’d already called Debbie.”

“And?”

“Well, I don’t know exactly what they talked about. You know Michael, he doesn’t gossip.”

“Lil, this isn’t gossip. This is important.”

“I know, Kate. Remember? It was my idea.”

"You know what I mean. What did Debbie say to him? Is she coming? Is she going to call you?"

Lily motioned toward the stove. "There's tea, get yourself a cup."

Kate reached for the pot and poured tea in the mug already sitting on her side of the table. "I should think she would have called you as soon she got the letter."

"That's because you know the reason behind the plan. I guess I surprised them." Lily's shoulders slumped with the weight of this thought. She heaved a sigh then continued, "George is being very cautious. He doesn't want me to get too excited and then be disappointed if they don't come."

"If they don't come, I'll personally wring their bratty little necks." Kate glowered. "I still think if they even hesitate, you should tell them the reason for the get-together."

"No," Lily shook her head. "I don't want that. Think about it. It would be maudlin and I couldn't stand that."

"But George might be right. If they don't know how important it is to you, they may think they can come another time."

"The uncertainty of time seems to find it's way into every conversation lately," Lily muttered. "See what I mean? You know, and you can't help but hint at the questionable amount of time I have. At least you're not being sappy."

"Thanks." Kate studied her friend. Ever since Lily had told George there was a definite improvement in her attitude. "Mike didn't even hint at Debbie's reaction to your invitation?"

"He said she was confused about the timing and the reason." Lily absently stirred her tea and then, looking at Kate, said, "I gave him the name of the place where Patty's working. He's going to try and call her, too. I hope he gets to speak to her and then calls me."

"What if he can't reach her? Do you think she'll call—or at least write?"

Lily shrugged. She knew Kate's concern was genuine. "It'll be okay. Deep down inside I know they'll come. And who knows, I may have more time than we think. Bob said no two cases are alike and there are no absolutes—except the final one."

Kate scowled at the reference to Doctor Bob and reached across the table taking Lily's hand. "You are a wonder. I don't know how I'd handle this but if it does ever happen to me, I'll have had a great role model."

Lily stood and took her mug to the sink. "Well let's pray it never happens to you. You're a good friend. You put some laughter into my days now and what more could I ask?"

"Speaking of laughter," Kate said, grateful for the change of subject, "How about going to the little theater production that opens next week. I hear it's a comedy."

"That might be fun. I told George the other night I wanted to do something silly. He thinks I'm crazy but he's being such a dear. I think if I asked for the world, he'd have it gift wrapped."

"Think George will want to come, too?"

"He might. He's acting like he did when we were first married. Even brought home a funny card yesterday. I was shocked. Imagine him stopping on his way home from work and going to a card shop."

"Imagine," Kate said, hoping she hid her reproach. "I'll call and order three tickets."

Lily stooped and peered out the window in the back door. "It looks like a nice day. Why don't we go downtown, look around and have lunch?"

"It's Wednesday."

"I know. Is it cut in stone that we only go to town and splurge on lunch on Friday?"

Kate chuckled, "You're right. Get your coat and purse. I'll bring my car around to the front." She was already pushing her arms into the sleeves of her coat.

"I need to stop at the pharmacy, too. Another prescription to fill."

Kate stopped halfway out the door. "Another prescription?"

"Same one. I need a refill, and stop panicking every time I mention doctors or medicine. It's going to be my way of life and I'm resigned to it so you better be too if you're going to hang around. Get going. I'll see you on the sidewalk in a minute."

#

Michael tapped his pencil on the pad centered on his desk. It was five-thirty and the office was quiet. He knew Kevin was still in his office because the lights were on.

He looked at the papers he'd been working on when Simone called. Something gnawed at him. It wasn't the first time she'd called at the last minute to tell him she wouldn't be home for dinner. Still, her voice seemed different, low and flirty, as if she'd been drinking. She hadn't mentioned where she was but he'd assumed she was still at the gallery sponsoring the benefit art show. Now that he tried to remember everything, he was sure there were no background noises, no voices. Strange. Still, she might have slipped into someone's office to make the call.

He rolled his shoulders and returned to his work. No sense leaving now. He'd stop and get something to eat on his way home later.

"Burning the candle at both ends, Mike?"

Startled, Michael looked up to see Jack Matson, Jr. standing in his doorway. "No sir," he said, smiling and pushing his chair back from the desk. "Come on in, Jack. I have some free time tonight and thought it would be a good time to go over these figures while everything is quiet." He motioned for the youngest of the senior partners to sit.

"Can't stay, just noticed you were still here. Every time I come in early, you're already here. We appreciate your dedication, Mike, but don't burn yourself out."

"No fear of that. My wife is involved in a charity thing today and she called to say she's running late, so I'm batching it this evening. Good time to clean up some loose ends."

"Well, don't work too late. See you tomorrow." Michael watched him cross the room and disappear through the huge glass doors. The security lights were on and the reception area had an air of muted solemnity.

Half an hour later Kevin knocked on the window as he walked by. Poking his head through the doorway, he said, "Still working? I thought I was the last of the Mohicans."

"I'm closing up shop, too." Michael switched off the computer and pushed his drawer shut, pressing the lock firmly. He stood. "You going right home?"

"Yeah, Kathy's waiting for me. She just called. What about you?"

"Simone is tied up with that charity art show. I'm going to stop for a bite to eat before going home. I'll walk you to the garage."

He snapped the light off and pulled his door closed.

"Hey," Kevin said, punching a huge finger into the elevator button. "If you're alone why don't you come home with me? I'm sure whatever Kathy is holding in the oven will feed the three of us. She's used to my erratic hours and plans casseroles that keep indefinitely."

"No, thanks, Kev. Nice of you to offer, but I've got to phone my mother later and I don't want to make that call too late."

"Everything okay?"

"Yeah, I guess. She's planning some kind of family get-together and I'm the liaison between her and my sisters."

The doors opened, they stepped in and traveled downward in silence. In the garage they bid each other goodbye, separated and walked to their assigned parking spaces. Kevin's steps echoed a jaunty rhythm while Michael's were at a more solemn pace.

Trying to recall Simone's words, he still felt anxious or uncomfortable and couldn't decide which. *What's the problem? This isn't the first time she's been late. Must be this business about Mom*, he thought.

CHAPTER THIRTEEN

Lily sat at the kitchen table twisting a damp paper towel in her hands. When Michael called half an hour ago, she'd been folding clean towels, still hot from the drier. It was Thursday, George was bowling and she was alone. Dinner had been a can of *Campbell's* tomato soup and some crackers.

At the sound of Michael's voice her heart jumped. "Hi, honey. Oh I'm glad you called. Does this mean you spoke to Patty?"

"Yes, I did, Mom. In fact, it was a lot easier contacting her than I thought it would be."

"Is she all right? I wish she'd get in touch with us more often. I worry about her being so far away."

"She seemed fine. She called me collect this morning and we had a nice chat."

"Well, did she get my letter?"

"Yes."

"And…?"

"We talked about it. She isn't sure what the real reason for the get-together is either. She did say she was doing well at her job. Seems happy there."

Lily sensed the tension in her son's voice, pushed the towels aside and sat at the table. "Is she coming home?"

Michael hesitated. "Gosh, Mom, why is it so darned important for us to be there in April?"

"What did she say?"

After a brief tense silence, he said, "She's doing really well with this job, Mom. She'd lose it if she left. At least that's what she said."

"She's not coming?" Her voice broke; her best efforts couldn't hide the choked-back tears.

"I don't think so."

Lily's left hand gripped the telephone and her right one curled into a tight fist. She would not cry! She struggled with her composure. "I'm disappointed. I thought she'd try to come home just this once. I thought…" Tears slipped from her eyes and her lips trembled.

"Mom, are you crying?"

Silence.

"Mom, for God's sake answer me. Are you crying?"

"No, dear," she lied, reaching for a paper towel to stem the tears that suddenly poured down her cheeks.

"You are. What's this all about? Damn! I can't stand it when you cry. You never cry. Is Dad there?"

"It's Thursday."

"He's bowling. You're crying aren't you? Mom, what the hell is going on?"

"Michael I wanted you all to be together. I'd counted on it." She gave up trying to conceal her emotion. Her breathing was strained, her lungs ached, and her words were muffled. What was the use?

"Mom, I'll be there. Whatever it is, Simone and I will come home in April. Maybe Deb will, too. Are you still crying?"

"Yes, but I'll be all right, dear. I'm being silly. It's not—it's not that important."

"Maybe if we made it later in the summer…"

"No. It's okay. Maybe Debbie will come, too."

"I wish you weren't alone. Are you okay? Is something wrong?"

She felt physically sick; her stomach churned sending bile to the back of her throat. She fought to regain control of herself. She couldn't give her secret away; it would defeat the purpose of her plans. "I'm fine, honey. Aunt Kate is coming over in a few minutes and we'll have a laugh and a cup of tea."

"Oh, that's good. You sure you're okay?"

"Yes. For heavens sake I don't know what happened to me. I'm getting silly in my old age. I miss Patty—and you and Debbie." She was losing her battle for control and bit her lower lip until it hurt. "We'll have a good visit. Don't worry about me."

When she hung up, she missed twice before getting the receiver in the cradle. She'd been so sure. So sure the kids would come home. With her head resting on her crossed arms, she sobbed uncontrollably. When she finally forced herself to become calm, she glanced at the clock. Nine o'clock. George wouldn't be home for at least another hour and she didn't want him to see the ravage the crying spree had caused.

She'd lied when she said Kate was coming over. Should she call her? No. What good would that do? Suddenly tired beyond belief, she gathered the folded towels, threw the tear-soaked paper towel in the garbage, snapped off the light, and started up the stairs. *A hot bath and bed*, she thought, hiccups from crying still shuddering her chest. She stopped at the top of the stairs, clutching the handrail. Lord, she was tired.

In the bathroom she put the towels in the linen closet, automatically aligning them so that the folded edges were forward. Her hands trembled as she did this familiar chore and tears threatened again. *I can't believe Patty is not coming home. I was always there for her. She could at least...*

Lily leaned her head against the closed door and fought for control *Stop it*, she ordered herself. *It's not the first time you've been disappointed. Maybe there's still hope Patty will come home. I could write another letter.*

While the tub filled, she shook two tranquilizers from the bottle and swallowed them with a paper cup of water. Normally she only took one before bed. Tonight she wanted to be sound asleep before George came home. Tomorrow would be soon enough to tell him of Michael's telephone call.

The woman who watched her from the mirror looked old and haggard.

#

Michael's hand lingered on the telephone as if by holding it he could hold on to the connection with his mother. He rose from his chair behind the desk, his mouth dry and his hands trembling as he refilled his glass. Automatically, he swirled the brandy in the snifter and then brought it to his lips. He felt as if he were coming to after an anesthetic, groggy, numb, and helpless.

What was behind his mother's request? Why was it so important for them all to be there? And why had she cried? He had no answers and a nauseous feeling of fear settled upon him. His mother never cried over simple disappointments. She'd always been the strong one in the family, his father distanced himself from problems whenever possible, unless he was the instigator. He tried to chronicle the times he'd witnessed his mother's tears; his grandmother's funeral was the only thing he could think of. When they were all home he recalled brief tears of pride at something one of them had done, or a special gift she received, but the grief he'd heard in her voice meant something was wrong. He threw himself into the chair and stared at the unlit fireplace.

The hall clock chimed the half hour and he looked toward the hallway. *Where the hell is Simone? How long did that damn thing last?* Restless, he rose and wandered through the darkened living room and down the hallway to the kitchen. The house had an eerie emptiness about it.

With the drink still in his hand, Michael climbed the stairs and wandered through their bedroom. Several pairs of Simone's shoes were tossed on the floor between the bed and the closet door. Frowning, he stooped and put them back on the racks on the closet floor. It wasn't like her to leave her things scattered about. *She must have left here in a hurry. Probably primped too long.* He glanced at his watch and muttered, "Where the hell is she?"

Returning to the den, he stood next to the desk, staring at the telephone. Should he call Debbie? No, his mind was in too much of a muddle to call her and yet he wanted to talk to someone.

He heard a key in the front door and hurried to the hall. "I'm glad you're home. I was beginning to get worried. What kept you so long?"

Simone shook her arms free from the leather coat she wore, opened the closet door and carefully placed the garment on a hanger. "Why would you worry? You knew where I was."

"You're later than I thought you'd be. How was the show?"

"Successful, but tiring."

"Come and have a drink with me, I need to talk." He turned and went into the den.

"Michael, I'm tired. I really don't want a drink. Can't it wait until tomorrow?"

He spun around. "Dammit, Simone, you have time for everyone else. I need to talk to you. I called my mother a little while ago and I'm worried."

His sudden and uncharacteristic demand startled her; his face was twisted with anger. "Perhaps a small sherry," she said, entering the den. She perched cautiously on the edge of the sofa.

Michael handed her a glass and put the bottle back in the cabinet. "I'm sorry I shouted. Today hasn't been easy. Nothing to do with business," he said, holding up a cautioning hand. "I spoke to my sister, Patty, this morning and I don't think she's going to come home in April. Then tonight I called my mother. She…" He paced away from her facing the front windows behind the desk.

"It is a foolish request. Did you tell her…?"

He turned to face her. "She cried!"

Simone studied her husband's face. Michael rarely lost his temper or became overly emotional yet his eyes were filled with unshed tears and the brandy snifter in his hand was shaking.

"That is unlike her."

"I know. I'm worried. She was upset and trying to make light of it. I promised her we would be there in April. She…"

"Michael I asked you not to commit me to the trip. It's such a busy time for Thespians. You knew that."

"Yes, I know but you can make an exception, can't you?" He was pleading again.

She lowered her head and swirled the amber liquid in her glass, realizing now was not a good time to add to his anguish. "I will have to see what can be arranged."

Michael sat next to her, taking her hand in his. "I knew you'd understand. Whatever her reason is, this weekend is very important. I'll call Debbie tomorrow and see what arrangements she's made. At least the three of us will be with them." He pulled her into his arms, burying his face in her hair that hung loose around the pale ivory of her face. Her warmth comforted him; her perfume filled his nostrils yet he stiffened slightly. He detected another scent. Pushing away slightly, he looked down into her face. "Your hair smells of smoke."

"I told you, Michelle, Andre, and I had supper together. The restaurant was very crowded."

"Where did you go?"

Simone hesitated. Usually they went to Marcello's but she and Michael were well known there. "A little place in the Village. I don't remember the name. Andre chose it."

"I thought the show was from ten until four this afternoon."

"It was but there is so much work before and after."

"Maybe you do too much for them."

"No. Not nearly enough. There is such need."

Michael pulled her closer and felt her stiffen. "I'm tired, dear," she whispered. "Let me go and get ready for bed."

He stood, pulling her up with him, keeping her in his arms. "I'm tired, too. I'll put our glasses in the kitchen."

She started toward the stairs and then turned and said, "Give me forty-five minutes. You know I can't rush my bath." Her smile was brief; she hurried up the stairs.

"I'll read the rest of the paper. I didn't get to finish it this morning. Don't rush, darling." At least she hadn't said she didn't want to be disturbed tonight. He grinned as he took the sticky glasses to the kitchen. Passion had a way of soothing anxiety. Tomorrow night he'd call Debbie and together they would plan for the weekend that seemed to dominate his mother's wishes.

Upstairs in their room Simone closed the door behind her and leaned against it. She was tired but not from any work done for the benefit of the charity she supported. Across the room she saw her reflection in the mirrored closet doors. Still dressed in her pale blue silk suit, she looked tired. Not at all as she appeared when she left the house this morning, elated at the thought of the daylong rendezvous she and Malcolm had planned. Not at all like the beautiful woman who had spent the day in a luxurious hotel room with a passionate and sensuous partner. Her cheeks flushed as she recalled their mutual desire. Malcolm. Even his name brought a heated bloom to her pale body.

She hurried to the bathroom, stripping the clothes from her body as she went. She would need a hot bath to revive her. Michael, too, had hinted at his desire and she couldn't afford to invite questions.

#

Lily hadn't been able to hide her disappointment or distress from George in the morning. He sat on the side of the bed holding her hand while she wept. This time the sobbing was subdued.

"Dammit, I was afraid of this. I'm going to call them. They'll change their minds when they know the reason. We've never asked them to drop everything and come home before. The kids need a reason, Lil, especially so early in the year. Maybe if we could have waited for summer…"

"We can't."

"I know." He patted her hand gently, desperately trying not to show how angry he really was. "Stay in bed. Do you want me to call Kate?"

"No," she shook her head. "I'll be all right. She's coming over anyhow. It's Friday. We're going to the library."

"Oh, yeah."

"Don't worry about me." She sat up and kissed his cheek, smelling the shaving cream he'd used for years. "It was foolish of me to think everything would fall into place. Sometimes these things take some effort. We'll think of something."

He stood, unwilling to move from her side.

"Go on. You'll be late. They'll think you don't have a wife anymore with you eating breakfast in the cafeteria so often." The joke fell flat as they stared at each other. She forced a smile. "Go on. I'll see you after work."

She leaned back on her pillows.

"Go back to sleep for a while."

"I will," she lied.

When she was sure he had left, she crept out of bed. Still tired, and a bit groggy from the extra pill, her body ached. She avoided as much eye contact as possible when she stood in front of the mirror brushing her teeth and combing her hair. Maybe she could convince Kate that puffy eyes were a result of taking two pills instead of one, but she doubted it. She wasn't looking forward to telling Kate about Michael's call. She shuddered and slowly descended the stairs.

She poured *Corn Flakes* into a bowl and took the milk from the refrigerator. *I'm not givin up. There has to be a way to convince them without telling the truth.*

CHAPTER FOURTEEN

"You've got to tell them."

"No. I won't. Think about it Kate. Do you want them to arrive with long faces and hearts torn apart with anticipated grief? What kind of a visit would that be with everyone tiptoeing around the inevitable truth. I don't want them here out of duty."

"For God's holy sake, you've got to tell them sometime. Look at how George has changed since you told him about your illness."

"Right. But George and I have a different kind of relationship, a different kind of love. A long time ago we made promises—sickness and health, good times and bad. It's not the same with children and parents."

"They aren't children, they're adults, responsible adults."

"I know, but they're my children and they always will be. They've made good lives for themselves."

"They deserve to know."

"And they will when the time is right."

For several minutes they drove in silence, then Lily said, "Let's not go to the library today. How about going back to Wilburn's. Remember that dress I saw the other day?"

"Sure. Do you think you'd like to try it on?"

"Yes, I'll need something for their visit. Most of what I have is too big now. "

"I told you you were getting too skinny. But what the heck, a new dress is a new dress." Kate kidded.

When they reached the parking garage at the back of Wilburn's Department Store, Kate pulled into a slot, turned the engine off and remained staring through the windshield. She sighed. "I want this to work out just as much as you do, Lil, but it doesn't seem possible."

"You want to make things easy for me and I appreciate it. But telling them I'm dying to force them home isn't going to work—not for me—not yet, anyhow. We'd all be walking on hot coals. The purpose of the weekend is to reunite the family."

"Knowing about you would reunite them."

"I guess you're right, but it wouldn't be a happy reunion. Remember when I first thought of this idea? I said I wanted them to be friends. Friends, Kate, not joined by mutual tragedy; that will come later, hopefully by then they'll realize there's more binding them to each other than grief."

Kate looked at her. "You've come a long way since the first time you told me this."

"Thanks to you, and George," Lily admitted reluctantly. "I haven't given up yet. God's performed greater miracles than convincing three stubborn kids that they belong to a pretty nice family. They'll come. Now, let's go shopping. "

Kate took the key from the ignition and opened her door. "We're going to have lunch at that fancy restaurant on the top floor of Wilburn's today. Soup to nuts—and dessert. My treat."

"It's expensive."

"Who cares?"

The children and the weekend weren't mentioned again until they sat in the elegant atmosphere of the rooftop restaurant. Lily was obviously tired. She'd been quiet as they shopped and now she fiddled nervously with the silver.

"I've been thinking about the kids. You know, Kate, maybe I'm all wrong about this weekend reunion."

"Wrong?"

"Well, it's purely selfish of me. Michael, Debbie and Patty are all where they want to be, doing what they want to do. Why should they change their lives?"

"Oh, come on. You said this was the only thing you wanted before…"

"Before I died. Yes, I did. But what real purpose will it serve? It won't change them."

"You don't know that and it might make them realize how thoughtless they've been over the years. Look at George," she reminded Lily.

"They aren't thoughtless, just…"

"Yeah, just what?"

"They're good kids."

Kate looked away, staring at the scene framed by the huge window next to their table. Soft music and muted conversation surrounded them. "You're right, Lil. They are good kids. They're good kids because they have a great mother. Their father…"

"Please, don't."

"Let me finish. You know I've never offered an opinion on your family matters or interfered. There were times when I had to bite my tongue over some of the petty things that George and the kids got upset about. You were always the mediator."

"That's what mothers do."

"Yes, to a point. But you always sacrificed yourself to make everything smooth for the rest of them. I watched, Lil, so don't tell me I'm wrong."

Lily chewed her upper lip and folded her hands in her lap. "You may be right in some instances. But George was a good father, he provided well, he loves the children—and me."

"And now you are going to give up the one thing that really matters to you? It must be important, Lil, because it was the first thing you decided you wanted to happen in the time you've got left.

"I know."

"Well, why would you abandon the idea? Michael said he was coming."

"I haven't heard from Debbie, and Michael feels Patty won't be here."

Kate saw her swallow and noticed a nerve tic rhythmically at the side of her mouth.

"It isn't fair for you to give up on this."

"I haven't given up. I'm trying to be realistic. If they can't, or won't come, why should I spend the little time I have left dwelling on something that's not going to happen? George and I have things we can do together."

The waiter came to the table and placed their salads in front of them. Lily looked at the elaborate combination of greens, tomatoes and lobster and felt her throat close.

"Don't forget our desserts," Kate said to him and motioned that their teapot needed to be refilled. When he left, she looked at Lily. "You don't have to eat all of that to get your dessert today," she smiled. "It's not like you have to clean your plate."

"Thank goodness. It's a lot of food. You shouldn't have ordered dessert, too. Everything is so expensive here."

"We're splurging and we're worth it. You can take the salad home and share it with George tonight for dinner."

Lily couldn't imagine George enjoying leftover salad but didn't say anything. She picked up her fork and started to rearrange the food on her plate. "I'll do my best. Now, let's enjoy this elegant place and pretend we're rich enough to afford it."

#

After dropping Lily at her house, Kate drove home; her hands gripped the wheel as if they were around the necks of three ungrateful children. She was still furious over the news Lily had shared with her earlier. They had come close to an argument over the news that Patty wasn't even going to consider coming home. How dare Patty dismiss her mother's invitation so casually? The thought of Lily giving up the whole idea because of their blind selfishness made Kate shudder.

Maybe Lily's right; maybe it is a waste of time. George changed because he's feeling guilty for all the time he lost being thoughtless and a damn fool. The kids don't have that kind of guilt although they should have kept in closer contact with their mother. But they've ***got*** *to come. Deep down in her heart she still wants to see them together. I know it, and if they won't come home, she'll pretend it's okay but it won't be. Dammit she's going to get what she wants if I have to go there and drag each one of them home by the ears.*

She grinned as she pictured herself descending on Lily's kids like an avenging angel. Still her mind churned through possibilities.

If I could talk to Patty...but I don't even know where she is. Somewhere in Florida, Lily said. That's a big help. I can't question her about where the kid is; she'd want to know why. And even if I could, what would I say? I could call Michael and tell him he had to convince Patty to change her mind but then what reason would I give him? Maybe I should call Debbie.

Kate went around and around, looking for a solution to something that didn't seem to have any. Before she went to bed that night she repeated her prayers as always. This time, though, she included a fervent plea for some guidance to help her friend. It seemed like a futile expectation, nevertheless she prayed for the miracle.

CHAPTER FIFTEEN

Michael's telephone call disturbed Debbie. *Mom cried because Patty wasn't coming home? That's not like her. Surely he's over-exaggerating her reaction to the news. Why would she think Patty would suddenly change? She'd never marched to the same drummer as the rest of us.*

The doorbell broke into her thoughts and she hurried to answer it.

Charles Wellmont, six foot two inches tall, with a muscular body that spoke of hours in the gym and on the racquetball court, was boldly handsome. No one ever called him Charlie.

Debbie's heart jumped and she struggled to keep the cool calm distance she affected every time she saw him. He was so different from her ex-husband, Jim, and yet she couldn't bring herself to trust him, even though he'd been a persistent caller for the past four months and she was well aware of his intense feelings for her. She was thankful he was not as aggressive as he appeared.

"Hi. You're early."

"Couldn't wait to see you, Honeypot." He crushed her to his chest and kissed the top of her head. "Can a man get a drink here?" he said, stepping into the living room.

"A man could if he helped himself. You know where it is. I'll be out in a minute. I just got off the telephone with my brother, so I'm not quite ready."

"Michael, isn't it? How's he doing? I'd like to meet him someday."

"You probably will—someday."

Charles, the only son of wealthy parents, didn't need to work but intelligence and a healthy restlessness kept him involved in various business interests. A major investor in the firm where Debbie was employed, he also traded heavily on the market. He and Michael had much in common but Debbie was reluctant to begin exposing him to her family. *Too early*, she thought as she turned and went toward her bedroom.

"What are you drinking?" he called after her.

"Nothing right now. I'll wait for the party." They'd been invited to a cocktail party at the home of one of the senior architects.

"Everything okay at home?"

She hesitated. No, everything wasn't okay at home. Had it ever been 'okay'? Still, she didn't want to open that can of worms. "Sure," she said and closed the door.

When she returned he was sitting in one of the chairs that faced the wide expanse of windows. "I never get tired of this view," he said, gesturing with his glass.

"Me either. I wasn't a city girl and Chicago scared me to death when I first moved here, but now I love it. I love my work and this apartment."

"You love anything, or anyone, else?" he teased.

"Charles, we've only been seeing each other four months."

"I've been watching you for a year."

"Sneak. I remember you hanging around the office while I slaved over a drawing board."

"You're special, Deb."

"Thank you." Ashamed of her bland remark to his compliment, she thought, *Damn, I want to lighten up but I'm scared. And, he's never given me any reason to be scared. It's a miracle he's still interested.* She sighed and sat on the arm of the chair.

He took her hand in his, gave it a squeeze. "I know who hurt you, Deb, and I'd like to be alone with him for five minutes," he shuddered, then seeing her pained expression at the reference to her ex-husband, said. "You look tired tonight. We won't stay long."

"I'm okay. Michael had some upsetting news about my mother. I'll have to write to her."

When they returned three hours later Debbie had a pounding headache. She threw her coat over one of the dining room chairs and asked, "Want a nightcap?"

"No thanks. I've imbibed my limit. You look pale. Anything wrong?"

She shook her head. "Just a slight headache. I'll be fine in the morning. Sorry if I was a wet blanket tonight."

He reached for her and drew her to him. She loved the musky scent of his cologne. His arms circled her and one hand rubbed the back of her neck. "You are never a wet blanket."

"Ummm. That feels good."

"Want me to stay?" He felt her stiffen. "Just to rub your neck? The muscles are tight." He steered her toward the couch.

"I'll be all right," she said but she moved with him.

He sat next to her, his fingers stroking and kneading the back of her neck and shoulders. She felt herself relax and was aware of his body close to hers.

"This isn't fair to you."

"What's not fair?"

"You know," she felt her face warm.

"Honey, I told you, you're special. I can wait."

Not forever, she thought. She turned, offered her lips to him and he responded with passion. She felt his hands drop from her neck and circle her body, pulling her even closer. Debbie melted into his embrace, feeling him press her into the back of the couch.

"No. Oh, God, Charles, I'm sorry," she said, pushing him away.

He sat up and looked at her, puzzled. "I know this has something to do with your divorce. He must have been a real bastard. Have you tried counseling?"

She nodded. "I went through twelve months of therapy after my divorce. I'm a lot better than I was, if you can believe that."

He stroked her face, "You can trust me. Don't you know that?"

"I do. At least I feel I do. Give me a little more time."

"I'm beginning to love you."

"I know."

He waited. She knew he wanted her to say she loved him, and while the words were in her head and heart, she couldn't bring herself to say them. *Will I ever be able to say 'I love you' to another man?*

"I really like you, Charles. You're..." Again he waited and still she couldn't continue. "If..." She touched his face with trembling fingers.

"If what?"

"If you can wait just a little while longer..."

He saw tears in her eyes; her lower lip trembled, and he bent to gently kiss each eyelid. "I'll see you Saturday. We're going riding, remember?"

"I've never ridden before."

"I'll teach you." He rose and pulled her up with him. "I'll let myself out. You go get some rest."

"No. I'll come to the door with you."

They walked hand in hand across the luxurious room. At the door she kissed him with more feeling than usual. Again, she wanted to say 'I love you,' but couldn't.

After he left she remained in the dim living room, looking out the window at the twinkling city lights. *He's a very special man and I'll lose him if I don't get over my fears. Unfounded fears where he's concerned.*

She crossed the room, snapped the light on and sat at her desk. Tired but not sleepy, her pounding headache was almost gone. Drawing a piece of notepaper to her she picked up her pen and began to write to her mother. *She'll understand that I can't come to Pennsylvania in April. I'll go home in August as I always do.* Earlier that day the firm had made reservations for her to attend an important conference in San Francisco in April. It was the first time she'd been asked to be a part of this event and it was an important move in her career. Nevertheless, she felt a strange sense of guilt as she scribbled her excuses.

CHAPTER SIXTEEN

There was no comfort in the stiff breeze that blew Patty's hair across her face and she angrily brushed it back, tucking it behind her ears. Usually the sun, the sea air, and the peace of the open expanse of sand and water calmed her fears, repaired her tired muscles, and gave her a lift. Monday was her day off and she enjoyed sleeping late, doing her laundry and spending time on the little beach, but today she couldn't separate herself from her troubles. *Too damn much thinking time, that's the problem. When you're up to your ears in fried grouper platters, you don't have time to think about troubles.*

She pushed her toes deeper into the sand and stared out at the soft waves that lapped the shoreline. Unless there was a storm brewing, the waters of the Gulf of Mexico were usually calm.

Absently watching a little cabin cruiser as it sped across the horizon, she tried to understand what was really bothering her. Her pregnancy? Of course. But also crowding her mind was the worry caused by her mother's letter and the telephone conversation with her brother. And weren't they all tied together? If she weren't pregnant, she'd be able to truthfully tell them why she wasn't about to take a trip to Pennsylvania in April. She couldn't afford to lose the best job she'd ever had to satisfy a whim. Then again, if her mother hadn't written, she wouldn't have talked to Michael. And if she hadn't talked to Michael would she even be thinking about a trip home? *Am I thinking about a trip home?* She kicked the sand with both feet, sending it flying into the breeze and felt it sting her legs in retaliation. *I am,* she admitted to herself.

She stood quickly, felt the world tilt, and had to steady herself by touching the back of the bench. The sand and the breeze that brushed her cheeks were hot as she talked to the water's edge. Shocked by the realization that she was actually considering going home, seeing her parents and brother and sister, Patty was suddenly covered with goose bumps. Walking across the sand, she felt more frightened than she had at any time in her life. The warm water washed over her feet as she turned and followed the shoreline, each step making deep impressions in the soft, wet sand, impressions that disappeared with the next wave.

And how would she keep her job? Why worry about it when she knew she'd have to quit to have the baby. Who knew how long she'd be able to work? *A baby. Jesus, how am I going to have a baby here? Who would help? Where would I go? Imagine bringing a baby home to Tidewaters and that old hag?* Tears stung her eyes and she turned and retraced her invisible footprints.

Since she'd talked to Michael, she'd thought more about her family than she had in the past five years. It wasn't as if she didn't care for her brother and sister, they were just different. Michael, the financial wizard, married to a strange woman who was cold and condescending; Debbie apparently had a wonderful career, drawing plans for skyscrapers and shopping centers, but then she always seemed to do everything perfectly. Everything except her marriage, and that was still a mystery, at least to Patty. Even as children they didn't have much in common, now they seemed worlds apart.

Patty walked to the sidewalk that led home. Home. That was a laugh, although it was a cut above some of the places she'd stayed in. Head bowed, she moved slowly along the gritty sidewalk. *I want to go home, really home. I want to see Mom...and Dad. Funny when I think of them I always think of Mom first. Dad's kind of an afterthought because he's there. I always thought of him as such a jerk. Now...*

She crossed the street, took out her key and opened the door.

Mrs. Jankowski looked up from her sitting room where she watched endless daytime soaps. "Been to the beach, dearie?"

"For a walk."

"No work today?"

"It's Monday."

"Oh, that's right."

Patty climbed the steps, her feet thumping on every riser. "Damned old bat. She knows perfectly well I don't work on Monday. Nosey old hag," she muttered as she opened the door to her room. She wanted to slam the door but she felt guilty at the nasty remarks she'd made and closed the door softly. Looking around the room she assessed her belongings and thought of moving them home. The die had been cast; she'd already made her decision.

She threw herself on the hard bed. *At least now I know what I want to do. How I'm going to do it is another matter. Another worry.* She closed her eyes, feeling older than her twenty-five years.

During a restless night she decided to call Michael rather than her mother. She doubted she would be able to talk to her without crying, or at least hinting at a problem. It would be easier to talk to Michael and he was less likely to ask questions.

The following day she called Michael's office. He was unavailable but she left a message. "Tell him I'll be home in April. They can send the airfare to me at The Tidewaters." She gave the anonymous voice on the other end of the line the address.

She was glad he wasn't available. *I'd love to be a fly on the wall when he gets the message,* she thought feeling a strange sense of relief.

#

Lily sorted the mail, putting the circulars and junk in one pile and the bills in another as she always did. She'd set aside the smaller envelope carrying the return address of her older daughter. Now she picked it up, holding it gently as if it were something fragile. Shrugging her shoulders, which were suddenly, unaccountably taut, she slid her thumbnail under the flap and removed the single, folded sheet of paper. Debbie always used pale gray stationery with her first initial in Gothic scroll in the upper left-hand corner. She also always used green ink. After scanning the message quickly, she reread the letter, then slid it back into the envelope and put it on the top of the pile of bills for George. For several moments she sat quietly at the kitchen table, then stood and took the receiver from the wall telephone. She dialed Kate's number and listened. On the fourth ring, Kate's cheerful 'hello' ended the mechanical buzzes.

"Hi. I have good news, bad news and surprising news, which do you want first?"

"Whoa. Wouldn't you know the one day I don't check in with you, you go on an information binge? What's all this news? Tell me."

"Well, I guess the bad news first. We got a note from Debbie and she's not going to be able to come home next month. She…"

"Oh, no. Dammit, she can't do that. What's her excuse?"

"She has to attend some kind of conference in San Francisco. It's connected with her job and it's important—so much for that. I'm not upset."

"The hell you aren't. I know you."

"No, really. I made up my mind if any of them couldn't come, I wasn't going to get upset."

"Still, I thought she'd be the one you could count on. I'm furious."

"Well, don't be. Don't you want to know the other news?"

"Yes. Tell me."

"Michael called a few minutes ago. He heard from Patty and she **is** coming home. He gave me an address where I can send her money for the airfare."

"Oh, Lily, that's great news. If anyone wasn't going to show up, I would have bet it would be Patty. Damn! We've got to get Debbie here now. Then it will be exactly what you wanted."

"I don't want you to be upset about her. I told you..."

"I'm not giving up yet. But, you said good, bad, and surprising news. What's the surprising news?"

"Remember I had an appointment at the doctor's office early this morning? Last visit they'd done more blood work and taken more x-rays. Today he had the results and he told me he was surprised at what they showed. Seems there hasn't been any 'appreciable deterioration or intensifying of the cancer cells in either lung since last time.' Those were his exact words."

"You mean you aren't getting worse?"

"That's what I thought at first but he said because my lungs aren't getting worse right now, doesn't mean I'm getting better. He told me that if I were willing, I would be eligible for some new experimental drugs and treatments."

"Are you going to do it?"

"I have to think it over. He gave me a lot of information and talked for a long time about how this isn't a cure and might have no effect at all. In fact, it's so new that they're not sure what the results might be."

"Wait a minute. You'd be a guinea pig?"

"I don't think it's primitive but he stressed it's experimental and there are no guarantees."

Kate was silent for a moment, then said, "Have you made up your mind?"

"I think I'll do it. I'll talk to George about it tonight. But what have I got to lose? We all know there's no cure, it's inoperable, and the end result will be the same. We might get a bit more time. In fact, I asked him if that was a possibility."

"What did he say?"

"He didn't give me any hope of more time but he didn't say it was impossible either."

Lily heard Kate exhale.

"Well, you were right. Good, bad and surprising news, and all in one day. How do you feel?"

"The same. I'm excited about Patty coming home, that's good news and a surprise. I'm disappointed with Debbie's response but I understand her reasoning. She doesn't know—and don't jump in and tell me I should tell her. That subject is closed. The medical news is surprising but since it's so iffy I'm not getting excited about it, yet. I think I'll do it though."

"Do we have time for a celebratory cup of tea?"

"Not today, Kate. I'm tired. I want to take a nap before I think about dinner, although George said something about going to the diner for a bite tonight. He's trying to make things as easy as he can for me now."

"Okay. I'll see you tomorrow anyhow. I got the tickets for the show. Want me to come by and pick you both up at about seven-fifteen? Curtain goes up at eight. If you're not too tired afterwards, we can go for an ice cream sundae."

"Sounds great. I'll take a nap tomorrow afternoon."

"I'll call you tomorrow morning anyhow."

"I know. You're so predictable."

"I like reliable better," Kate quipped.

"That, too."

"Get some rest. If you need me, call."

CHAPTER SEVENTEEN

Kate watched George guide an obviously exhausted Lily up the seven concrete steps to their front porch. They'd enjoyed the comedy and Kate and George exchanged knowing glances over Lily's head when she laughed out loud at some of the banter on the stage.

During the evening at the theater, and later at *TCBY* while they ate their sundaes, no mention was made of the experimental treatments Doctor Bob had offered. Kate wondered if Lily had made a decision yet. *She'll tell me when she's ready.* She pulled away from the curb and drove home.

Kate was used to living alone and considered the fact that she could have long conversations with herself one of the advantages. As she got ready for bed, she thought about Lily's news. Patty was coming home. "Strange isn't it that the one you think won't, does, and the one you think surely will, doesn't," she reasoned. She couldn't help wonder at the cause behind Patty's sudden change of heart. Was it that she'd lost her job, needed money, or was in some kind of trouble down there? Whatever it was she was thankful there was no need of outside urging to get her here. "The reunion is only four weeks away. Now I have only Debbie to persuade, and how do I do that?"

Kate was convinced the planned get-together was absolutely necessary for the Hoffmann family and especially Lily. A restless night provided no answers and the next morning after she'd spoken to Lily, still no solution was evident. Lily's decision to talk to Bob further about the new medical treatment also left her uncertain, but Kate knew she couldn't interfere with that. "It's one thing to meddle in personal matters, but medical areas are another thing," she rationalized. By evening, Kate had a plan. She was uncomfortable with it but it was the only answer she could think of. There wasn't time to be cautious.

At eight o'clock, knowing it was seven in Chicago, and with no confidence at all, she dialed Debbie's number and waited for a response. When she heard the familiar voice, her heart fluttered in her chest. *No turning back now.*

"Hello."

"Hi, it's Kate. Hope I haven't called at an inconvenient time."

"Aunt Kate! What a surprise. No, I was sitting here thinking about dinner."

"Wow, you eat fashionably late out there."

"Actually it's earlier than I usually eat but I left the office on time tonight. So, what's up?"

"Not much—just wanted to touch base with you."

"Well, I'm fine. Busy at work and enjoying my new apartment, but I love it. You should see it, Aunt Kate. You'd love it, too."

Debbie stood in front of the windows looking across the city. The sun's last rays glinted on the tops of the building to the west, giving the scene a golden glaze. "Why don't you come out to visit me sometime? You've never been to Chicago. We girls could do the town."

"We girls? Any young men circling the camp site?" Kate struggled to keep the conversation light, delaying her real mission.

"Well, I've been seeing someone but it's not serious. I know Mom would love me to find someone but that's not in the cards. Not soon anyhow."

Kate heard the hurt and uncertainty.

"Why did you call? Is everything okay in Eagleton? I mean, I'm always glad to hear from you but you don't usually call me." Actually, Debbie couldn't recall a single time when she'd heard directly from her mother's best friend.

Swallowing the lump in her throat, Kate said, "Well, there is something, honey. You know I don't usually interfere but I'm calling to try and persuade you to come home next month and be with your family."

"I can't. There's a really important convention in San Francisco that same weekend and the firm has asked me to attend. It's kind of a feather in my cap at work and my career is important to me."

"I realize that but this is important, too."

"I'm coming home in August like I always do. Mom and I'll have a good time together then. I spoke to Michael on the telephone a couple of times recently. I know we should keep in closer touch and I'm going to do just that. Of course, with Patty…"

"It's important that you come now, Deb," Kate interrupted.

Debbie heard an ominous tone in Kate's voice and a chill ran through her. "Why?"

"Your mother really wants you all to be together."

"I know, that's what her letter said. Really, Kate, it sounds like a good idea but it's not practical."

"Your mother…" Kate hesitated.

"What's the rush? Why can't I see them in August?"

Gripping the telephone as if it were a lifeline, Kate cleared her throat. "There's a problem. I've been sworn not to tell you or anyone. Deb, you know I don't break promises, especially to your mother. I don't lie and I don't meddle but there's something…" Her throat closed around the words and she felt as if she were drowning.

"What problem?" Debbie's voice grew stronger, "Dammit, tell me, what problem."

"Your mother's very sick. She needs you to come home."

"Sick? Why didn't she tell me?" The chill turned to ice as she lowered herself into the chair. "How sick?"

"Isn't it important enough to grant her wish? What difference does it make—she's sick and she wants you home."

"How sick?" she repeated.

"I swore not to tell any of you kids. Do you know how hard it is for me to break a promise?" Kate's voice broke as the combination of fear and regret gripped her. "Your mother is very ill and the one thing she wants is to have you kids together at one time. The date she's chosen is four weeks away. This is important."

Debbie rested her elbow on the desk cradling her head in her free hand. "How sick? What's wrong?" she whispered again, fear tearing at her empty stomach.

"Dammit, I told you it's serious. Do you have to know the details?" Before she'd said the words, she knew the answer. Of course, Debbie would have to know the details. "I'm sorry I yelled. This isn't easy for me and I know it won't be easy for you. Your mother has cancer. It's terminal."

"No. Oh, no."

Debbie didn't realize she'd screamed the words and Kate listened to sobs wracking the child she loved as a niece for thirty years. She wished with all her heart she was in the same room with her. She wanted to put her arms around her and comfort her as she had so many times before—only then it had been for skinned knees.

"I'm so sorry. So sorry," she repeated not knowing if Debbie still had the telephone to her ear. "Deb? Deb, crying doesn't do any good. I know."

Still the sobbing continued, until Kate heard, "Oh no, no, no. Not Mom."

"Honey, listen to me. All the tears in the world won't change a thing. The one thing your mother wants right now is for you all to be together. Patty and Mike have told her they're coming home. You have to come, too."

She listened intently for a response.

"Debbie are you there? Can you hear me?"

"I hear you," she whispered. "I'm sorry. I can't believe it, I don't want to believe it."

"I know, but it's true. I couldn't believe it at first either."

"I thought the cancer had been cured when she had surgery years ago," she whispered.

"It metastasized. Reappeared in another area."

"Where?"

"Her lungs. Both lungs. It's inoperable, but Doctor Bob is pleased with how she's doing, given the circumstances. In fact he's suggested some new kind of medicine and treatments. That might help, who knows?"

"How long does he say…"

"Medicine isn't an exact science," Kate said, quoting Lily's quote from Bob's report. "They can't say for sure."

"A year?"

Kate hesitated. She hated this subject. "Probably not that long. Maybe six months."

"Oh, God. When did she fine out?"

"In February."

Neither spoke for several moments.

Debbie finally broke the silence. "What about Dad?"

"He knows. He's handling it okay. In fact, he's changed."

"Changed?"

"He's very attentive and kind." Kate didn't know how else to tactfully say he realized too late that he'd been a jackass for much too long. "Can you make arrangements to be here?"

"Of course. I'll have to. They'll understand at work," Debbie said the words automatically. "Oh, Kate, this can't be happening. Not to Mom."

"Now listen to me and listen carefully. Your mother is *not* to know that I told you this. Do you understand?"

When Debbie didn't reply quickly, Kate continued, "You do whatever you have to do, but it had better be an Oscar-winning performance to keep this secret a secret. It's important to her that you kids come home because you want to, not out of pity. She's said that repeatedly."

"I understand."

"Do you? Think about it. You can't arrive all teary-eyed. You can't even notice she's lost weight and is tired all the time. It's not going to be easy."

"I know."

Kate knew the answers were too automatic. The reality of what Debbie was facing hadn't penetrated yet. "I know this has been a shock, it's understandable. Do you have my phone number?"

"I think so."

"Write it down," she ordered. "Ready?" She recited her telephone number then said, "I want you to call me. Anytime of the day or night, you understand? We can talk about whatever you want but don't let anyone know that you're aware of the trouble, or that I called you. Can I count on you?"

"Uh huh."

"I'm so sorry I had to give you this news. I told your mother you'd find out eventually but it's so damned important to her that no one knows until she's ready to tell."

"Do Michael and Patty know?"

"No, and don't you tell them either. If your mother finds out I've broken my promise you can't imagine the wrath that will come down on you. My wrath. I might not be able to trust all of you to put on an act that will fool her. I trust you to do it. Can you? Will you?"

"I will, Aunt Kate."

The sobbing had abated but Kate knew she was still weeping. "I wish I could be there with you."

"So do I." Debbie looked around the room. The luxury was cold comfort.

"Do you have someone you can call? I don't like the idea of you being alone right now."

"I'll be okay."

"Can't you call anyone? A girlfriend? Someone you work with?"

"Yes, don't worry about me."

"I'll worry about you all I want." Kate said, trying to insert a sliver of humor in a situation that begged for it.

"Thank you, Aunt Kate. Thanks for telling me."

"It wasn't easy but it was the only thing I could think of to get you here. I don't break promises easily."

"I know. I've trusted you with a few."

Kate was relieved. At least Debbie was talking about something.

"Remember, if you want to talk, call me. I don't care when it is."

"Okay."

"You going to be okay now? I don't want to hang up until I'm sure."

"I'll be okay. I'm numb. If I need you, I'll call later."

"I'll be here."

Neither wanted to break the connection.

"Make yourself a cup of tea."

“Mom’s cure for everything,” Debbie said and started to cry again.

“Mine, too.” Kate wept quietly.

They hung up reluctantly, the child unwilling to cast herself free of the familiar comfort, the adult hating to release the suffering child.

CHAPTER EIGHTEEN

She was used to being alone, used to facing adversity, yet never in her life had she felt more isolated, more terrified. Debbie rose and walked to the windows, snatching the drapes across, shutting out the glittering world outside. She went back to her desk and sat in the chair she'd just left. Her fingers rolled a pencil across the pad; her mind searched for something that made sense; her body ached with sadness. She loved Kate for calling her but hated her for the news.

Kate, always there for the Hoffmanns as long as Debbie could remember, through happy and sad times, showing up when an extra pair of hands was needed or a celebration was planned. How like her to be the one to know and share her mother's secret. Debbie and Michael always referred to Kate as Aunt Kate in public but secretly, to each other, they had called her Sister Kate because of her calm, caring presence and her no-nonsense discipline when she was in charge.

Thinking of Michael she reached for the telephone but drew back as she remembered. She couldn't call Mike, she'd promised. Call someone, Kate had said. Her body still quaked with remnant weeping and she wiped her eyes as she wandered through the darkening apartment.

In the kitchen she snapped on the light over the sink and saw the frozen dinner she'd planned to zap for her evening meal thawing on the drain board. She wiped the puddle with a paper towel, slid the moist, limp box back in the freezer, and looked at the telephone on the wall. *Call someone, Kate had ordered.*

Her hand shook as she dialed. When he answered, she was slow to find her voice.

"Hello?"

Silence.

"Hello?" he repeated. "Anyone there or is this a very quiet heavy breather?"

"Charles," her voice cracked.

"Deb? Is that you? What's the matter?"

"I need to…"

"Debbie, are you all right?" He heard her whimper. "What happened?"

"I need you—I need to talk," she whispered.

"I'll be right over. It'll take me twenty minutes. Are you okay? Are you hurt? Sick?"

"No. I just heard from my mother's friend, the one I call Aunt Kate. She told me…" The tears streamed down her cheeks and she forced her words through lips that felt stiff and swollen. "She told me my mother's dying."

Charles listened to her sob. "Deb, go unlock your door and then lie down. I'll be there as soon as I can. Will you do that?"

She nodded her head.

"Will you do that? Can you hear me?"

"Yes." She didn't remember hanging the telephone up, or saying goodbye—she didn't even notice he'd already disconnected the call at his end.

Eighteen minutes later he opened her front door and hurried through the apartment. The door to her bedroom was open and a small bedside lamp lit the room. He stopped for a moment in the doorway, then hurried to her bedside. She was leaning back against several pillows, a box of tissues at her side, her eyes swollen and red, her breath coming in stuttering gasps.

He sat next to her, taking her hand in his. "Tell me," he said gently.

She lay in his arms, her head against his chest. He stroked her hair. For half an hour he listened as she told of her conversation with Kate, ranting at the unfairness, questioning the consequences. She asked him questions, yet didn't wait for answers. At first he sat next to her, wiping her eyes and throwing the tissues on the floor as they became soaked, letting her cry until her immediate grief spent itself. Then he pulled her into his arms, her body across his as he sat on the side of the bed. She calmed and then became quiet. For a few moments he thought perhaps she was asleep. Moving slightly so that he could see her face, he saw her eyes were open.

He wanted to kiss her, to soothe her hurt and promise nothing and no one would ever hurt her again. Instead he increased the pressure of his arms around her, pulling her closer to his body. She didn't resist.

A small clock, somewhere in the room, chimed softly with a tinkling sound. He searched for it with his eyes, unsure of the time.

"It's nine o'clock," she whispered, pulling away from him.

"Shall I fix you a drink? Have you had anything to eat tonight?"

"No."

"Want something?"

"No." She remained in his arms.

"Are you comfortable?"

"Not really, and your arms are probably numb, holding me like this." She pushed herself away, teetering on the side of the bed. He reached to steady her and stood, watching her tuck her blouse into the waistband of her slacks.

Their eyes met and she looked away, embarrassed. "I'm sorry."

"Sorry?"

"Sorry I called you. No, I'm not, but I'm sorry to have fallen apart like this with you. You've been…"

"Helpful?" he finished for her.

"More than that." She stood facing him.

He brushed her hair away from her face. "Why don't you go wash your face and comb your hair? You'll feel better. I'll wait for you in the living room."

She tried to smile. "Okay. Make yourself a drink. I'll be right out."

In the bathroom mirror she looked at her ravaged face and barely recognized the haggard woman who returned her gaze.

When she went into the living room, he had lit several lamps and was sitting on the couch.

Patting the cushion next to him, he said, "Sit here. I've poured you a glass of sherry."

He slid his arm across her shoulder and pulled her close. "It's rotten news, darling, but you'll get through it. I'll help."

"You have more faith in me than I have."

He put his glass on the coffee table in front of them and turned toward her. "You can be as strong as you need to be. This is too fresh in your mind to think clearly about what you've got to do in the next month."

She shivered at the mention of the limited time she had to prepare for her visit, and then sat forward, twisting her hands. "Oh, God, I'm worried about how I'm going to manage the next month and my mother is facing…"

He took one of her hands in his. "And your mother is facing death."

She nodded.

"Deb, you're not going to accomplish anything tonight. Do you have a sleeping pill?"

"No."

"I didn't bring anything with me. I didn't realize…"

"Of course you didn't. You've been wonderful. Really, I don't know what I'd have done without you."

"Listen. Do you think you could go to sleep if I stayed here on the couch?"

"You don't have to do that."

"I know I don't."

Debbie studied him. The little line between his eyes had deepened. She leaned forward and kissed his cheek.

CHAPTER NINETEEN

"You've done enough for one night. I'll be fine. When you leave I'll take a shower and get ready for bed. I may not sleep much but I'll rest."

"I'll call you in the morning, but if you need me or want to talk during the night, call me, okay?"

"Okay."

"Don't plan on going in to work tomorrow. I'll come over when you're ready and we'll go to breakfast. Maybe a ride along the lake will help. We can talk."

She smiled weakly, realizing that never before could she recall anyone having such concern for her. *Except my mother*, she thought, fighting her tears back.

"Thanks, but I think it will be best if I go into work. Keeping busy will help."

"We'll go to dinner then."

She nodded.

They rose together and he put his arm around her as they walked to the door. "I don't like leaving you." At the door, he smoothed her hair back from her face again and kissed her.

Her response surprised them both as she clung to him, her lips parted slightly, her body pressed against his. When they separated, their eyes locked, exchanging emotion they hadn't openly acknowledged before.

"I'm so glad you called me,."

"I'm glad I did, too."

Charles gave her a quick kiss, opened the door and left without another word. For several moments after he left she leaned against the door, her forehead pressing against the cool wood, then turned and went to her room. She cried in the shower, her salty tears mixing with the pulsing water. Washing away the grief was impossible, but hot water eased the tension.

From the bathroom door she looked at her bed, the spread twisted and crumpled, a reminder of the time she'd spent there earlier, pouring her heart out to Charles. She didn't want to go to bed.

In the living room she turned out all the lamps and opened the drapes; the glow of the city lights illuminated the quiet room. It was cool. Curling up into one of the soft leather chairs facing the windows, she hugged herself.

Her thoughts ran rampant, racing from her phone conversation with Kate to her time with Charles. She rose quickly and walked to the window. Her time with Charles. The warmth of his arms continued to encircle her. With startling reality she realized how deep her feelings were for him. *I love him. Oh, God. What now?* Turning, she threw herself into the chair again. *Marriage? Love? How can I even think of those things? My mother is dying.* She shivered but didn't cry. She hadn't shed many tears in her life, not even following the breakup of her marriage. After she stopped going to therapy, she'd adamantly refused to even think about her marriage. Now with her every emotion scraped raw by the heart-rending situation she was in, it was impossible to dam the surge of remembrance. Jim…

Jim…in the quiet, cool room Debbie reminisced.

#

They met at college and dated occasionally. Jim Branson, not a large man, appeared deceivingly rugged. His handsome features were dominated by startling blue eyes set below well-defined brows. They were friends.

Their dates slipped into a familiar pattern, dinners, theater, concerts, and quiet Sunday walks. The relationship drifted toward something neither seemed to recognize until they were making plans to be married. Debbie once laughed and told Jim, "You never asked me to marry you. You just said 'after we're married', as if it was a foregone conclusion."

The wedding was quiet because they wanted it that way.

"Shall we invite your parents?" Jim swung her hand as they walked through the park they spent so many Sunday afternoons in.

"I don't think so. Why have them travel all this way for a civil ceremony they won't approve of? They're Catholic, remember?"

"Are you disappointed it won't be a big, fancy church wedding."

"No. All I want is you."

"How about Michael and Patty? You know I'm not going to ask Doug."

Debbie knew that Jim and his brother Doug, ten years older, had a friendly but distant relationship because Doug was a regular Army man and usually stationed overseas.

"No. Michael is in New York and who knows where Patty is. No, let's just have a quiet ceremony and a wonderful honeymoon in Hawaii." She squeezed his arm.

Debbie called her parents after the honeymoon, sent them a personal note, extolling her happiness and inviting them to visit 'sometime.'

Jim continued his work as a research physician and she returned to her job with the architectural firm.

They established their home in an old, well-kept house in the suburbs. Jim's father had left him a considerable inheritance so they started off married life with what most young people had to wait years for. To their friends and acquaintances, they appeared to be the epitome of a modern, career-oriented couple. Neither mentioned a family of their own in the future. They were part of the upwardly mobile, though not so mobile, young crowd.

There was, however, none of the closeness or passion Debbie had dreamed of. She credited Jim's intense work schedule at the lab for their infrequent and casual lovemaking. The trouble didn't boil over until one evening three years after they were married.

It started with a simple question. "Jim, don't you think its time we gave some serious thought to starting our family?"

He stopped eating and stared at her. "It's too soon, Deb."

"Soon? We've been married over three years. How long do we have to wait? You know all about biological clocks and things like that." She smiled weakly and leaned against the back of her chair.

"Let's say I'm not ready yet."

"But," she insisted, "When will you be ready? We both have good jobs and are financially secure. I'm willing to put my career on hold for a couple of years."

"It's not about money." He didn't look up.

There was a cold finality in his voice. Debbie was stumped for a minute. They had never talked about this subject before. Her best friend and old college roommate, Sally, had recently given birth to a darling little boy. Holding little Danny in her arms, Debbie began to think about children of her own.

"Jim, seeing little Danny makes me think about babies. I want to have children. Why do we have to wait? Can't we even discuss it?"

Her husband pushed his unfinished dinner away, arms straight and stiff. His fists were clenched, and he looked at her with steely eyes. "I said I'm not ready for children. I'm not ready to be a father." His voice was harsh and strange.

"But..."

"No. I'm not ready."

He rose and paced across the kitchen, stopping at the counter near the door that led to the garage. He stood silently for a minute, arms braced against the counter top as if by doing that he could push the problem away. Suddenly, he turned to her. She couldn't remember ever seeing him so agitated.

His eyes blazed and his face was contorted with anguish.

"I don't want to talk about it; I'm not ready to be a father; I thought you were content with our marriage the way it is."

"My wanting a baby doesn't mean I'm not content with our marriage..."

"Stop!" Jim's voice ricocheted off the walls. "I don't want to be a father. I don't think I'll ever want to be a father. Debra, please!"

He shook with emotion. Suddenly he looked small and vulnerable.

"Jim, I just..." She was close to tears, her voice rose defensively. "You're not being fair. You can't mean this. Why didn't you say anything about this before?"

"No, dammit, no," he whispered, then turned and fled to the garage.

A strange silence in the kitchen formed a backdrop for the words they had hurtled at each other. She listened as the garage door opened and closed. He was gone.

Alone, numbed by the heated exchange, she mechanically cleared the table, slid the dishes into the dishwasher, sorted the silverware, and wiped the counters. In the living room she waited for him to return. At eleven o'clock she went upstairs to bed, leaving a light on in the hallway. At one o'clock she heard his car pull into the garage and knew he was home. He didn't come upstairs.

In the morning, she saw he had slept on the couch in the study. Following a silent breakfast, they parted without sharing a word. That evening they resumed a distant, polite reserve that continued for the next two weeks, discussing only the most ordinary topics. The atmosphere was as if they were unfriendly boarders rather than husband and wife.

Debbie spent the time during this two-week period immersed in thought, reflecting on their true relationship. She realized she had been blind to many of the abnormalities of their marriage. Why did Jim have so many late nights? Was there someone else? Had there always been? Was that the reason behind the limited sex, the distant lovemaking?

One evening as they shared another strained dinner in the kitchen, Jim broke the silence. "We've got to talk. This can't go on this way."

"What can't go on? Our marriage? The way we are living?" Debbie's voice was testy.

"Let's talk in the living room." Jim took his wine glass and moved through the archway. She followed, sitting on the couch. He took one of the chairs facing her and placed his glass on the table next to him; she cradled hers in both hands, staring down into the red depth of the wine as if to find solace there.

He leaned forward, his arms folded, elbows resting on his knees. He stared down at the carpet and without raising his eyes, began, "I haven't been honest with you from the beginning. I don't know how to make it up to you. I don't know how to fix it."

Her stomach contracted; her breathing became difficult, as if her lungs were suddenly filled with cotton.

"I know we can't go on like this," he continued. "I don't want to hurt you any more than I'm going to."

When he looked at her, she was shocked to see tears flood his eyes. Not like him, yet over the past few weeks she'd seen a side of him she hadn't known existed. She started to speak but he shook his head, freezing her with his intense stare. "Please—don't say anything. Let me finish. I've agonized over these words for days. I have to say them."

The room shrank, squeezing them into a tiny space, the quiet remaining unbroken for several moments.

"I thought I loved you. Even thought I could overcome feelings of the past. I tried, really, really tried. I hoped marriage would be the answer but it wasn't. Our marriage has been unfair to you and I don't know how to correct it without hurting you more."

"I don't..."

He raised his hand to stop her. "Time isn't the answer, things aren't going to change. I hope when you hear what I have to say you can somehow forgive me and go on with your life. You deserve so much more." His voice broke and she saw him fold his lips into a cruel straight line. He paused, then said quietly "I'm gay."

She stared at him. The words he had spoken reverberated from a great distance. Her eyes sought his; she was unable to speak.

He buried his face into his cupped hands. Again, his words muffled, he said, "I thought I could change, but I can't. At first I really wanted to. You must know it wasn't anything you did or didn't do." He paused, she couldn't respond, numbed by the revelation.

Silence thickened the air in the room. "Is this because I wanted a baby?"

"No, of course not," he stood and paced away. "You must see the marriage was wrong from the start. Your wanting a child just made me realize…" He hesitated and turned back to her. "I've contacted an attorney and gone over the facts with him."

Her face stung with the finality of his words and she shuddered.

"You can get a quiet divorce. I've already made arrangements to transfer assets to you in a separate account. I owe you much more than mere money but…"

Debbie looked at her hands, twisted together in her lap, her knuckles gleamed white in the dim light. When had she put the wine glass on the table?

"We can sell this house and you'll get half the proceeds. My life insurance policies will still name you as beneficiary." He stood facing her, arms hanging limply at his side. "It's a small payment for the guilt I feel, the hurt I've caused.

Defeat permeated the aura around him and if she hadn't been so numb maybe she would have felt pity—pity for him or for them, she wasn't sure. "I'm moving to San Francisco in a couple of months—to a research facility there." His words were muffled with grief.

There was nothing more to say and he knew it. She knew it, also. Answers to questions she hadn't had the courage to ask were suddenly clear.

She didn't remember the rest of that night, or even the intensity of the pain she felt at first. There were periods of time she couldn't remember at all.

Jim moved out sometime during the following week. The house was put on the market and sold quickly. Debbie thought of taking time off from work but realized that keeping busy was the best medicine for the hurt she was experiencing. A few of their friends appeared to be surprised but some of them had little to say, suggesting the breakup of their marriage wasn't something they found extraordinary.

She didn't confide the painful truth to her family. After a couple of lonely, agony filled weeks, she called Sally.

"Hi," she croaked, her throat dry, her voice brittle.

"Are you okay? Are you crying?" Sally gripped the phone with one hand and cradled her son in the other arm. "What are you doing? Where are you?"

"I'm home. Doing nothing. Oh, Sally…"

"Get over here. I can't come out now I have Danny affixed to my hip. He's fussy."

"I don't want to go out —or talk to anyone."

"Nuts, you called me. I can hear you're crying. I'll look for you in twenty minutes."

Debbie was sure that sharing the sorrow and hurt wouldn't help anything but Doctor Maria Phillipi had convinced her during this afternoon's session that she had to talk to someone other than her.

Two hours after she'd arrived at Sally and Dan's home she returned to the lonely house she had shared with Jim for three years. The "For Sale" sign welcomed her but the house was cold and silent.

Her visit to Sally hadn't really solved anything; perhaps her pain wasn't quite as intense, perhaps she had been absolved of some of the guilt she carried along with her.

"You didn't know, Deb. He was the one who entered the marriage with lies and deceit not you."

"I should have seen the problem. Maybe if I'd seen it we could have worked it out."

"Debbie, there is nothing you or anyone else could have done to make that go away."

"'That' meaning his being gay?"

"I hate talking about it, Deb. It's a sad, sad thing and I hate him for doing this to you. But you have to go on and you won't until you unload that baggage. Take a vacation. Get out of that damn house. Come here if it will help you but I think you should get away. Go home. See your parents."

"No!" Debbie thrust herself from the chair and picked up her purse. "No, I can't tell my Mom. I told you because I trust you but if you ever tell another soul, even Dan, I'll hate you forever. I'll never forgive you."

They hugged in Sally's driveway. "Promise?" begged Debbie.

"Promise." Sally said, following her friend to her car.

The divorce was quick and quiet, but not as painless, as her lawyer had intimated, nor as swift. Irreconcilable differences covered a multitude of sins, none of which had to be enumerated on the divorce decree. Her agony was not quick or painless. Counseling helped, but nothing seemed to fill the void in her life. Her emotions raged from self-pity to fury as she realized the betrayal her marriage represented.

Questions were always present. Should she have recognized Jim's problem? Was it a problem or an illness? Should she pity him or detest him? What could she have done? The last question always received the same answer, *nothing*. The depth of her naiveté haunted her. She was ashamed, but knew the shame wasn't really hers. Her friends didn't fully understand her moods because they didn't know the reason for her anguish. Her counselor told her she was experiencing a period of grief. Mourning for the death of a marriage was as real as mourning for the death of a loved one, she told her.

When the house was sold, Debbie bought a luxury apartment on the top floor of a building with a prestigious address. The sadness and isolation she had inflicted on herself moved in with her. Strangely, it was the intensive work during this period of her life that saved her sanity.

She thought she'd buried the painful reason behind the failed marriage. She thought she'd conquered her loneliness with her work. Her mother's letter and Charles' comfort had brought those memories to life again.

#

The first rays of the sun striking the buildings between hers and the lake brought her back to the present. She rose, stretched and groaned at the stiffness she felt from being curled up in the chair all night. Her mind reverted to the previous night; Kate's voice, the devastating news, and then Charles. She hugged herself in front of the wide expanse of windows and felt his arms around her, his lips on hers, and she remembered his kiss when he left. A remnant of last night's headache tugged at her temples and she shivered in the early morning sunlight as it crept over the quiet city.

I can't think of anything else right now. I have to deal with my mother's illness—and death. I have to—and I will.

CHAPTER TWENTY

In the living room, Lily sat on the couch next to George. Kate, perched on the edge of a chair, leaned forward and nervously massaged her hands. It was Friday evening and Lily had called Kate as soon as they returned from the doctor's office.

Kate twisted her hands and urged, "Tell me exactly what Doctor Bob said."

"He said she's not to climb stairs. This new medicine isn't working worth a damn," George blurted out.

"Now, George." Lily patted his hand and smiled at Kate. "He really said it's too soon to say if the medicine is working or not."

"You've been on it two weeks and look at you. You can hardly walk the length of the house. You're thinner than ever. Damn him. Why'd you let him experiment on you?" George looked away, grinding his teeth.

"I've noticed it's harder for you to breathe lately," Kate said softly.

Lily nodded. She knew they were worried. "What we have to do is figure out a way so I don't have to climb the stairs much."

"You won't have to. I'm putting a bed in the sunroom. It'll be warm enough. You can use the bathroom off the kitchen. I'll get you some help, too."

"What help? You've already got Mrs. Getz coming in once a week to do the cleaning, and her daughter Ellie doing the washing and ironing." Lily turned to Kate. "That Ellie does a great job on the ironing. She even presses the pockets in George's pants."

"What the hell do I need with pressed pockets?"

"They lay flatter if they're pressed. Anyhow, what other help do I need?"

"Me," Kate said. "I'm coming in every day. You know I love to cook. I'll fix the meals. And don't start arguing, I've made up my mind."

"Kate, you can't give up all that time to be here."

"I can and I am, so that's the end of that subject. Whether you like it or not, I'm here every day for a while." Biting her bottom lip, she finished, "You know I want to help you."

"I know, Kate. You've always been here for us. I really think the medicine will work. Bob said it might take a few weeks to see any improvement. That means he's looking for improvement and I'm willing to go along with his hopes." She leaned back against the cushions, trying to fill lungs that seemed to shrink every time she said a few words.

She felt a thin line of cold perspiration form on her upper lip and patted it with a tissue.

George and Kate both noticed the gesture and their eyes met, held for a moment, then looked away.

"Tomorrow is Saturday. I'll start turning the sunroom into a bedroom." George stood and went toward the kitchen. "Anyone want a cup of coffee or tea?" He snapped the light on and began to fill the kettle.

"Tea would be nice," Lily called. She looked at Kate and whispered. "I'm worried."

"So are we, dear," Kate said, moving to sit next to her.

"No, I mean, I'm worried about the kids. What will they think when they come home and find a bedroom in the sunroom? What will they think when they see me?"

"Dammit," Kate whispered, "what the hell do you care what they think. They're going to know, Lily. Face it. For God's sake stop playing this game. You've got more to worry about than the kids."

They listened to George putting cups and spoons on the table. The kettle whistled and Kate called, "Do you need help?"

"No. It'll be ready in five minutes. Lil, where's the cookies?"

"In the cabinet next to the refrigerator." She smiled and whispered to Kate, "Right where I've kept the cookies for the past twenty years."

"So, the kids are all coming home?" Kate asked.

"Like an answered prayer, Kate. Michael called last week, and I got a note from Debbie, someone else is covering her conference. I hope she won't have any trouble at work because she changed her plans."

"Shoot. Why do you always dream up problems?" Kate felt a twinge of guilt when Debbie's response was referred to.

"I don't dream them up."

"You do so. Patty is the surprise. When's she coming?"

Before Lily could answer, George called them to come and drink their tea. In the bright light of the kitchen, Lily's pallor seemed accentuated

Later, when Kate got ready to leave she said, "See you tomorrow. I'll be by around nine, is that okay?"

"Fine, but you don't have to come that early."

"I know," she said, closing the door gently.

George and Lily were alone. She started to rise but George put a restraining hand on her arm.

"Sit. I'll put this stuff away and then get you upstairs."

"What are we going to do about getting a bed downstairs? I still don't like the idea but I guess we're stuck with it until this medicine starts to work."

She didn't see George's grimace at her mention of the new miracle drugs. "I'll take our bed down and put it up in there."

"Our bed?"

"You don't think I'm going to let you sleep down here alone, do you? We've shared that old bed for too many years. I'd never be able to sleep up there alone." He feigned gruffness but Lily read his tenderness.

Later, he held her elbow gently, slowly taking one step at a time, as they worked their way to the upper floor. Lily liked the feel of his hand on her arm. At the top of the steps they paused while she took some deep breaths. She leaned against him, the soft flannel of his shirt caressing her cheek. "I love you, George."

"I love you, too."

As they walked down the hall to their bedroom Lily dragged her hand along the wall, feeling the flocked paper. *I'd have scolded the kids for doing this,* she thought. At the door they paused as if waiting for a signal to enter the room that held their most intimate secrets. Still holding her arm, George guided her to their bed.

She sat on the side of the bed while he brought her a nightgown. When he handed it to her their hands touched and they didn't move for a moment. Looking into his eyes, she said, "I feel like a bride. Silly, isn't it?"

George bent down and kissed her lips gently. "You'll always be my bride, Lil. Nothing you do or say is silly." He left and she heard the bathroom door close softly.

I'll never stop loving him. Damn, I can't be as sick as they say. The new drugs have to work. I have to be better by the time the kids get here.

#

Patty looked at the check in her hands. Drawn on the First National Bank of Eagleton, signed by her father, the amount was more than enough to cover her round trip airfare. She felt guilty as she thought of explaining everything to her parents and not using the return trip ticket. They might be angry when they heard the real reason for here return to Eagleton. Would they welcome her?

What did the future hold for her and her baby? She didn't have any answers to these questions she'd asked herself over and over again during the past two weeks.

She slid her hand under her tee shirt. So far she'd been able to hide her pregnancy from everyone at Diabolo's but it wouldn't be possible much longer. She sighed and threw herself across the coverlet, staring at the ceiling. *You expecting some miraculous answers to appear up there?*

She pushed herself upright knowing she'd made up her mind; she wanted to go home. Now. She wanted to see her mother; to be truthful and honest with herself and her family. Slowly she peeled the shirt over her head, pulled her soft shorts down, shed her socks and went to the closet. She pulled her bra off and tossed the clothes she'd worn onto the laundry pile on the floor of the closet. Slipping a soft cotton nightgown over her head, she got into bed, pulled the covers down, punched her pillow into a comfortable shape and turned out the lamp.

Slipping between the rough sheets, she thought, *Okay, Smartie. If that's what you want to do that's what you'll do. Tomorrow you'll make reservations, give your notice and get the hell out of here. If they're shocked so what, you've faced rejection before.* She had no alternative plan if her parents weren't supportive, but again, she'd faced that kind of thing, too. Her mind was more at ease than it had been for weeks.

Sleep came to Patty quickly that night.

CHAPTER TWENTY-ONE

The regular Monday morning think-tank meeting at Matson and Dolby was postponed due to the unavailability of two of the three managing partners. At three-fifteen in the afternoon the receptionist buzzed Michael and told him the meeting was going to start in fifteen minutes.

He met Kevin coming out of his office and together they walked to the boardroom. The other junior partners were already there, stacking their folders in front of them on the shiny, long conference table. Bob, the newest to join their ranks was holding court with the junior partners, as well as the secretary and several clerks who had been invited.

"You should have seen old Matson at lunch at The Tavern today. We were there with clients and he gave one of his monologue's on moral behavior."

"What the hell were you doing at The Tavern for lunch?" Kevin asked as he plopped his folders on the table. "They must be paying juniors more than when I began."

"Hell no. You guys got all the perks when you were promoted. Now the system is crappy as far as perks go. I was pitching a big time account this morning, and Matson suggested lunch. Could I refuse?"

"Anyway," said another, "what was he spouting off about."

"Seems he knew this guy who was in the restaurant and you should have seen him and the babe he was with. They sat in one of those cozy alcoves, but you could see everything. The old guy was all over the girl, a lot younger girl, I might add."

"And?"

"And Matson said this Malcolm somebody was a big contributor to lots of charities he's involved in. Said the guy had an alcoholic wife stored away someplace and he must have picked up a floozy to replace her."

Michael stopped in the doorway, ice suddenly replacing the blood in his veins. Malcolm? He listened.

Bob, enjoying his audience, went on. "The 'lady,' and I use the term loosely, was well lit already and it was only one o'clock. It was pretty dim in the alcove but you could see enough to know what was going on." Feeding on his audience's interest, he continued, "Dressed like a model and really pretty. French. When they were leaving," he cupped his mouth with his hand and added, "to go to *their* the room, I heard her say something and she had an accent. Probably an aspiring actress or model, or something."

Kevin's face turned redder than ever. He looked at Michael, who was frozen in the doorway. Their eyes met and Mike looked away quickly, then took the seat next to Kevin and began to shuffle his papers, keeping his eyes on the worksheets and ledgers.

The door closed softly behind them as the senior partners entered the room and took their places at the head of the table. For the next two hours, sales strategies and market reports claimed their attention. Michael felt nauseous and cold as he stumbled through his presentation. As soon as the meeting ended, he gathered his papers and left the room. Kevin caught up to him in the hallway.

"Mike, maybe that was a mistake."

Michael turned to him, seeing compassion in his friend's eyes. "I think you're right. It was a mistake." He hurried into his office, closed the door and drew the blinds.

Sitting at his desk, he felt drained. Bob's words echoed in his ears, replacing everything that had been said during the meeting. It had to be Malcolm and Simone. Bile flooded his throat and for a moment he thought he was going to be sick. He checked his wristwatch, ten minutes to six. Standing, he took his topcoat from the hanger on the back of the door. There wasn't any use in trying to remember what he had to do with those case files. Not tonight anyhow.

In the garage he noted Kevin's parking space was empty. As he walked across the concrete, his heels made a hollow lonely sound with each step. At his car, he pressed the access button on his key ring and heard the locks pop up but he didn't open the door. *I need a drink.* Turning quickly, he returned to the elevator and thumbed the button to the lobby.

The lobby was still brightly lit, he could see the doorman through the wide glass doors, and the night security man was already seated at the reception counter. "'Night Mister Hoffmann," he called as he looked up to check the elevator's passenger. "Not working late tonight, huh?"

"Not tonight Casey. I think I'm drinking early tonight."

Casey laughed and went back to the monitors he'd just turned on. On the sidewalk, late shoppers and office workers hurrying to bus stops filled the pavement, sweeping around either side of him as he stood uncertainly in the middle of the walkway.

At the end of the block neon lights danced around a sign which read, *The Brokerage*, a grand name for a small gin mill often frequented by other brokers in the building. Michael turned away and walked in the opposite direction. He wasn't in the mood to socialize with anyone he knew. He needed time; he needed to think.

Several blocks later, he stepped into an anonymous bar. The room was crowded and smoke-filled. Every stool was taken and patrons stood two and three deep behind those seated. He scanned the tables and seeing none empty, joined the crowd at the bar. It was noisy and Michael thought, *this is a mistake. How can I think in here with this racket?* Nevertheless, when he caught the bartender's eye he ordered a Scotch and water and thrust the bills across the shoulders of those in front of him. Taking his drink, he moved to the wall across from the bar and behind the tables. He leaned there, needing the support. His head reeled. Malcolm and Simone? Could it be a mistake? They often met to discuss the financial needs of the Thespians. Is that what they really met for? He tried to remember mentions of Malcolm lately. Several occasions came to mind. Tossing the drink down the back of his throat he turned to leave and bumped into a man he recognized but he couldn't put a name with the face.

"Hey, Mike. Don't move so fast in a crowded place like this. You'll do someone harm." The familiar face was crossed with a big grin and Michael felt strong fingers grip his arm.

"Sorry. I was on my way out."

"You'll have to leave that," the unknown man said, glancing meaningfully at the glass still gripped in Michael's left hand.

"Oh, right." Michael looked at the friendly face, "Forgive me, but I can't recall your name or where I've met you."

"Don Stevens," the stranger said, putting out his hand. "You don't really know me. We've met several times at fundraisers. I know your wife through the Thespians. I do stage settings for some of the plays. It was chaotic then, too," he said, his arm gesturing at the noisy crowd around them.

"Sorry. I should have recognized you. Just stopped in for a quick one."

"Have to get home to the Missus huh?"

"Yeah." Michael didn't move to leave. Something in the friendly voice and face made him want to stay. "You had dinner yet?" he asked with uncharacteristic impulsiveness.

"Me? No."

"Plans?"

"No."

"Let's get a bite. I need a break and Simone isn't expecting me," he lied convincingly.

"Where?"

"How about that little Greek restaurant around the corner. Is it still there?"

"Yeah, in fact it's one of my favorites."

They pushed through the door into much cooler night air and walked around the corner to the restaurant. It was crowded but they were able to get a table for two in the back corner near the service door.

"You're in stocks, aren't you?" Don said, unfolding the big red cloth napkin.

"Yes. It was kind of a rough day today." Michael ran one hand through his hair, his brow creased. He was tired.

"You have them. Not many people think stage settings are very critical, but we have pretty frantic schedules, too. Especially right before opening night." Again, Don smiled, and Michael felt the strain in his shoulders relax a bit.

"We all have tough times, I guess."

They ordered wine and their meals and sat watching the other diners for a few minutes.

"You see Simone much?" Michael asked.

"Rarely, mostly at fundraisers. I never run into her at the offices because I'm hardly ever there and she doesn't come to the theater until the show is ready to go on. Or, at least, I've never seen her there. Why?"

"Just wondered. She's very involved in that charity."

"She's got a great name as a fundraiser."

I'll bet she's got a great name as a 'fun raiser', too. Michael's hand shook as he picked up his wine glass. His rage started to fester and he forced it to the back of his mind as he chatted with Don. He consumed the food automatically, not really thinking about what he was eating.

When they left the restaurant, they stood on the nearly empty sidewalk for a few minutes. Their conversation during the evening had been easy, touching on local politics, the theater, and charities in general. Now that they were parting, it was awkward.

"Well, have to get home. I didn't ask. You married?" Michael reached to shake his hand.

"No. I was but it didn't work out. I have a girl but we aren't on the same playing field most of the time. She's in accounting. Very practical, I'm more Bohemian." He smiled. "Well, it was fun running into you this way. Or, more accurately, you running into me. See you around. Maybe another fundraiser?"

"Maybe," Michael said. They turned away from each other simultaneously. Don's steps became faint as Michael turned the corner and walked back to the parking garage. At the gate he showed his identification to the security guard.

Traffic had thinned out and the ride home took far less time than it would have at six o'clock. Michael's thoughts were of confronting Simone, the nagging doubts that had surfaced and the role he might have played in this. How blind had he been? What signs had he missed? Was it really true or was he panicking prematurely? He sighed. *On top of worrying about going to Pennsylvania and the mysterious reunion, now this*, he thought, pulling into the five-story garage complex where he rented a monthly space. He walked down Thirty-Seventh and cut across Park Avenue. As he lifted the latch of the wrought iron gate, he noticed lights from the hallway glowing in the kitchen windows. His eyes traveled up the back of the house. Simone was home; there were lights on in her bedroom. *Her bedroom? I guess that says a lot when I automatically refer to our bedroom as hers now.*

He squared his shoulders as he entered the kitchen and walked down the hall to the foot of the stairs. She'd left a light on in the den. From the doorway he noted the fire hadn't been lit and the mail was on the corner of his desk. He hesitated. Did he really want to go through the mail or did he want to talk to her right away?

He hung his coat in the hall closet. Grabbing the rail, he began to climb the stairs. He felt beaten down and lonely. *Why the hell should I feel this way? She's the bitch. How much of what he had heard and then surmised was true?* "Well, I'll find out," he muttered to himself as he reached the landing.

CHAPTER TWENTY-TWO

Michael stood in the doorway, seeing their bedroom as it really appeared. *I was right—it is hers not ours.* Simone was propped up in bed with several pillows behind her shoulders. The soft light from the frilly lamps on either side of the bed cast a seductive glow across the silky sheets and comforter that covered the lower half of her body. She wore a red silk gown and her hair hung loose around her face. Everything was tinged with pink, the lights picking up the soft rose of the walls and carpet. *Didn't I see all that damned lace before? It looks like a mistress' salon, not the average American couple's bedroom.*

She glanced up from the book she was reading. His face was emotionless yet it broadcast an icy message. Her smile was anemic. One thin strap slipped off her shoulder, pulling the silk away from her breast, exposing the soft, full swelling.

Placing the book on the table next to her, she said, "Michael, you're late. I didn't know of an evening appointment."

"I didn't have one," he said stepping into the room, remaining several feet from the foot of the bed.

"Oh? Have you eaten?"

"If I said no would you get up and cook me something?"

A faint frown flickered across her forehead but didn't linger. Simone didn't allow frowning, it caused wrinkles.

"Is something wrong? Problems at the office?"

"No. I think my problems are not associated with the office."

Again her eyebrows raised and lowered and she watched his face with feline interest. "You look tired," she said patting the bed next to her. "Rest and tell me what is troubling you."

Michael paced to the windows. He couldn't look out; the blinds had been drawn behind the sheer curtains. The heavy magenta brocade drapes suffocated him and he turned back to her.

"Did you see Malcolm today?"

"Malcolm? Of course not, why would I see him today?" She swallowed with difficulty and stiffened against the soft pillows.

"Tell me, Simone, what do you think of Malcolm?" Michael's tone was cool and controlled.

"Think of him?"

"That's what I asked."

"Well, he is a kind man, generous to the Thespians."

"Besides being kind?"

Simone pushed the covers back and swung her legs over the side of the bed. She appeared smaller than usual as she sat there, back ramrod straight, dark hair spilling seductively over her bare shoulders.

Her voice betrayed her fears. "I don't know what you're talking about, Michael. Have you been drinking?" She stared at the closed bathroom door, avoiding his eyes.

"Come off it. You were seen with Malcolm at The Tavern today at lunchtime. Ring a bell?"

She stood, not moving away from the bedside. "We needed to discuss the new contribution program."

"You said you didn't see him today."

"I forgot."

"Forgot? From what I heard, you weren't doing much talking."

Simone rushed to the bathroom door but Michael darted forward, putting his hand on the door to prevent her fully opening it. "Oh, no you don't. Sit down, we're going to talk." He grabbed her arm and pulled her across the room, pushing her down into one of the heavily padded chairs beside the windows. She glared at him and rubbed the place on her arm where his fingers had left marks.

He towered over her. "Malcolm is more than just a contributor, isn't he?"

She made no answer, pushing back into the cushions as far as possible, but keeping her head erect.

"Tell me," he shouted, his hand cupped her chin and forced her to face him. "Tell me about all the fund-raising meetings. Tell me about the secret luncheons and God knows what else."

"There's nothing to tell. We had lunch. We talked about the Thespians."

"The Thespians!" He spit the words out of his mouth as if ridding himself of some ill-tasting spoils. "A convenient excuse. Everything was convenient for you, wasn't it? Kay upstate in that funny farm drying out again? The pretense of charitable involvement?" His voice rose with every exclamation. "How long, Simone? How long?"

Her chin trembled and her eyes smarted as they filled with tears.

"How long has this been going on? How naive have I been?" he whispered.

She pounced on the hinted defeat in his voice. "Really Michael, can't you be more cosmopolitan?"

"Cosmopolitan? That's a word you use with a magazine, museums and art shows, not something you apply to behavior. At least not in my world. What the hell do you think you're doing? Are the rules different for 'French girls?'" he sneered.

"I don't know what you're talking about." She tried to stand and he put one hand on her shoulder and forced her backward.

"You do, I can see it in your face, Bitch. "

Her eyes blazed. "You will not touch me again in such a rough manner." Her words dripped with resentment and her accent coated each syllable with indignation.

He leaned down so that his nose was inches from hers. "I can smell your guilt. You thought you'd have it all didn't you—me paying the bills at home, Malcolm providing the fun and games. Is that it?"

"No. He is a cultivated experienced gentleman. I enjoy his company. We have a deep friendship."

"Friendship? I think it's gone beyond that." His voice croaked in anger and pain. "What have you done besides hold furtive meetings, drink in the afternoon, and destroy two marriages?"

"Two marriages? Really Michael, you are blind. Kay is not a wife. She hasn't been one for years."

"Oh, and that's your excuse? You can take her place in Malcolm's life because she is unable to perform? Do you mean…?" The full meaning of what she had intimated thundered into his head.

Their eyes locked. Michael realized how far the affair had progressed and Simone's confession without words.

"You whore," he snarled.

"Stop it! You have no right. Your interpretation of that word is far different from mine."

"Oh really? There's only one definition for a whore, and it fits you perfectly." He turned his back, unable to look at her, afraid to admit to the emotions boiling inside of him. He stepped away a few feet; he wanted to pound her with his fists. The longtime pacifist was being crowded out by the outraged and defiled man he'd become in just a few hours. His fists were clenched so tightly his hands hurt and he held them out, glaring at them as if they belonged to someone else. Distracted for a moment, he took a deep breath. "You're disgusting. How can you have the nerve to justify this behavior?"

"It is not so strange in today's times," she said flatly.

"Oh," he thundered, turning back to face her. "You think that because others sin it's perfectly all right for you to join in on the fun? What kind of morals do you have? I thought you were different. Different? Ha! I had that right."

"You are being superior. What I did was not so strange, given the times and the circumstances."

"Circumstances? Maybe that's what I don't understand. What circumstances, Simone? That everything was clear for you and Malcolm? No stumbling blocks like an inconvenient husband or wife?"

She slid forward and he moved back to confront her, daring her to leave the chair, yet afraid to touch her.

"Stop shouting at me. The neighbors will hear us," she spat into his face.

"Is that what you're really worried about? The neighbors? I'm sure something as mundane as letting the neighbors, who don't even know us, in on our little secrets won't bother you."

"Michael!"

"I want to know what went on, Simone. All of it." Again he pushed her shoulders back, forcing her into the cushions.

She stared at him, her dark eyes flashing with contempt. "How dare you shove me like that? Have you forgotten who I am?"

"No, Simone, you've forgotten who *I* am. In fact you seem to have forgotten you even have a husband." He moved a small step backward, "Stay where you are. I'm trying very hard not to become as violent as I feel."

The acid look in her eyes did not change, "What do you mean you want to know what happened?"

"How long has it been going on? Where? When?"

"You are a fool. Isn't it enough that I have confessed to being—indiscrete?"

"Indiscrete is putting it mildly, but yes, Simone, I want to know it all."

She hesitated, her sensuous mouth drawn into an unaccustomed hard line. A nerve at her jaw line ticked rhythmically. "You want to know it all, Michael? You may be sorry."

The room deepened with the intensity of the moment, then in a small voice she repeated. "You'll be sorry."

"I'm already sorry." He waited.

"Malcolm is different, mature, lonely yet able to cast aside his problems and find happiness. We are much alike. I have been seeing him for almost a year."

He drew in a quick breath and held it, his mind wanted to fly back in time but he forced himself to the moment again. He croaked, "And? In this year?"

"At first it was luncheons and sometimes dinners when you were too busy to be with me." She pouted.

Too busy to be with you? I was building a career. I was providing for our future. He didn't speak and she continued.

"We found we had many of the same interests."

Like an unconscious desire to say 'the hell with others.'

"We enjoyed each other."

I'll bet you did.

"When we discovered we held the same fascination and passion for each other, we were unable to stop. He is an ardent lover. We didn't mean to hurt anyone. It wasn't done with malice."

"Not with malice?" Michael backed away and sat on the corner of the bed, the words 'ardent lover' carved into his heart. "How can you apply any sense of reason to what you've done."?

"We love each other." This time she shouted the words.

Michael shook his head. "You don't know what love is. Love is trusting, caring, feeling each other's pain. It's honest and gentle, never cruel or uncaring."

"That is in fairytales."

Michael thought of his parents. He thought of Kevin and his wife and other married couples who lived up to their commitments through good times and bad. "I feel sorry for you Simone, but even my pity can't repair the harm that's been done. I never realized how cold and unfeeling you really are. But I will get even." He stared coldly, his hands lying calmly in his lap.

She twitched in the chair, pulling at the soft material on the arms.

"You have made your bed." He stopped at the absurdity of that statement, then corrected himself "You have made your choice. You can't have both and obviously you don't want me or you wouldn't have done what you did."

Still she didn't speak.

He stood, towering over her. "I'm going to Pennsylvania in two weeks. I'll be gone a week. When I come home you will be out of this house. Do you understand? Out, completely. Get whatever lawyer you want. Take whatever action…"

"Lawyer? Out of this house? It is my home. You…"

"No, Simone, it's not your home any longer. You leave. You destroyed our marriage. Now, go to Malcolm."

"I will not leave my home."

"Oh, yes you will. You had better be out of here when I return. I won't live with a whore." His lips curled harshly around the word. "Not any longer."

Her face froze, her pale cheeks became paler, her dark eyes deepened in color. "You will regret this."

"Possibly, but I doubt it. I already regret a great deal. You may think you can break me financially; I can recover from that. What you have destroyed can't be recovered but you won't destroy me. There is life beyond you, Simone. Hard as it is for you to believe, I will go on without you. I don't need you."

He rose and left the room, shutting the door quietly behind him. Downstairs he picked up his mail and turned off the lights. His steps were slow but steady as he climbed to the third floor. In the room he had occupied for so many nights over the past year he stopped and reflected. His room. Yes, this was his room.

He put the mail on the corner of the dresser and removed his suit and shirt. In his underwear he sat on the side of the bed and flipped through the envelopes and junk mail, returning them unopened to the dresser. He lay back across the spread, his hands behind his neck, staring at the ceiling.

He was uncommonly calm. Had he known before and been unable to admit that his marriage was a failure? Was the failure the devastating blow it should be? To his ego maybe but not to his soul, he decided. Maybe he had steeled himself for the ultimate hurt with the repeated small doses of withdrawal Simone had fed him over the past year. He pulled himself upright and went into the bathroom, turning on the shower.

Standing beneath the pulsing water he lathered his body, watching the foam slide down his flat stomach and muscled legs, results of twice-weekly squash matches. It swirled clockwise as it disappeared into the drain. Without realizing it, he was watching some of the tension and anxiety he'd felt earlier this evening leave his body along with the grime of the day.

Later, lying between the cool sheets with the lights out, he reflected on his life. He was proud of what he'd accomplished thus far. His mother's face floated before him and he felt as if he could reach out and touch her. Why did she want him and his sisters to be there with them in April? And what about his Dad? Maybe he'd been too hard on the old man. He wasn't a bad guy. Sighing, he thought about the trip in two weeks and the ultimatum he'd given Simone. The thought of her not being with him wasn't that hard to accept and he felt guilty. Had he ever really loved her, or was it her aura of beauty and mystery that had captivated him? No, that was wrong. He had nothing to be guilty about as far as she was concerned.

As for his guilt about not being the son his parents wanted, that was another thing. But he'd be with them soon and deal with that then.

A small smile flickered across his lips in the dark room and he surrendered to sleep he wouldn't have thought possible a few hours ago.

CHAPTER TWENTY-THREE

Every time Patty looked up she found the same pair of eyes on her. The waiting room was beginning to fill and she moved to a chair farther away from the check-in desk. She was already cleared for boarding and had her seat assignment. She glanced at the man who had been watching her. Tall, in his fifties she'd guess, medium brown hair, thick glasses, and nice looking but not handsome, she tried to recall if she'd seen him before coming to Tampa International Airport this morning. *Maybe I waited on him at Diabolo's.* If she had, he didn't look familiar so he wasn't a regular.

She tried to rekindle her interest in the magazine she'd bought at the shop along the concourse but her mind wandered. Giving Missus Jankowski notice of her leaving Tidewaters had been easy. Leaving Diabolo's had been difficult. Without realizing it, she'd established a quiet friendship with several girls and with Carlos. They'd given her a small travel bag as a going away present and Carlos provided coffee and cake at the end of her last shift.

She'd bumped her duffle bag, filled with all her worldly possessions, down the stairs at five-thirty this morning. Her hope of escaping Missus Jankowski proved futile. When she reached the foyer, the landlady's door popped open and she crept out of the room as if not wanting to awaken anyone. Not that there was anyone in her apartment but an ancient, annoying parrot, but who knows, maybe she had an admirer. Patty smiled at that thought.

Clutching her threadbare bathrobe around her, the old hag had given her a pat on the shoulder and told her she'd be missed. *Yeah, like a case of flu,* thought Patty as she exited the rundown building for the last time.

The PA system announced boarding for US Air flight 763 to Philadelphia and Patty rose and moved to the gate that now stood open. Checking her duffle bag, all she carried was her purse, the small travel bag the girls and Carlos had given her, and a magazine. As she walked down the aisle looking for Row 17, Seat C, she was shocked to see the man who had stared at her already seated in the window seat of Row 17. She smiled and seated herself, pulling the seat belt across her lap. Oh, well. What harm could he be on a crowded plane, and hopefully someone would take seat B between them.

When the thrust of the takeoff pushed her back against the seat, there was no one in seat B. Mister Mysterious was occupied with his newspaper and Patty opened her magazine again. When the flight attendant offered them a breakfast tray, she ordered milk and he chose decaf coffee.

"Nice flight so far," he volunteered.

"Yeah, so far."

"Traveling to Philadelphia?"

Since that was the destination of this nonstop flight, she thought the question was a bit foolish. "Yep."

"Me, too. I'm attending a seminar at the University of Pennsylvania School of Medicine. Should be interesting. New procedures on neonatal care." He crumpled the plastic wrap that covered the tray and pushed it into the pocket in front of him. Reaching across the empty seat between them, he extended his hand. "Philip Branigan," he said.

"Hi. I'm Patty Hoffmann." She felt awkward shaking hands with him.

They ate their breakfast in silence and after the trays were removed, Patty went to the restroom at the back of the plane. When she returned, she hoped he would be reading his paper but he was staring out the window.

"Would you prefer to sit next to the window? I was looking at those clouds; I wouldn't mind changing with you."

"Oh, heavens no, but thank you."

"I think Florida has such interesting skies. The sunsets are some of the most beautiful in the world."

She smiled. "Yeah. I only lived there for five months and I worked the late shift so I didn't get to see a lot of sunsets though"

Patty wondered why she was so free in sharing information about herself. She didn't confide in strangers as a rule. I *must think he's harmless*, she thought with a smile. Buckling her seat belt again, she reached for the magazine and then decided she didn't really care about the latest in makeup and fashions. She leaned her head back and closed her eyes. The flight would take two hours and twenty-five minutes. At Philadelphia she had booked a commuter flight to Wilkes-Barre where Kate would meet her. She was lost in thoughts of Eagleton and her parents when he spoke again.

"Are you okay?"

"Sure."

"I couldn't help notice you're pregnant."

Patty was stunned. She didn't think it showed that much. Panic engulfed her. If a total stranger noticed it right away how was she going to get past Kate and her mother until she found the right time to tell them?

Staring at him, she said, "How did you know? I thought I didn't show very much."

He smiled. "You don't really. I'm a doctor. For twelve years I was a GYN but three years ago I switched to neonatal care, specializing in care for infants born with life-threatening problems," he added.

Patty didn't answer.

"Say, I hope I didn't upset you by noticing. I wondered if the flight was bothering you."

"That's okay. You surprised me though. I managed to keep it from everyone where I worked and I'm going home to tell my family."

He waited a moment before speaking. "I noticed because I'm trained to notice, I guess. Sorry."

Patty shook her head. "It surprised me."

They rode in silence for several minutes then Patty asked, "Do you have children?"

"No. Not that we wouldn't love them. My wife had surgery years ago and we aren't able to have children. She fills her life with other people's children. She's a kindergarten teacher."

"That's why you changed to neonatal?"

"Maybe. I had a couple of patients who had terribly fragile babies. One made it and the other didn't. I felt as if *I'd* lost a child. Made up my mind to learn how to help." He turned to look out the window.

Patty couldn't think of anything to say. She'd seen the pain in his eyes as he spoke of the baby who died.

When he turned back he was smiling again. "Your first?"

"Oh, yes. And probably my last."

"Why do you say that?"

She hesitated. "I'm not married."

"You're to be praised, Patty. At least you haven't decided to destroy this life. So many young girls do these days. Don't they realize there are people who ache to hold a child of their own? I get so angry..."

She hadn't felt especially noble when she decided to keep her baby, but she heard the passion in his voice.

"Did you and your wife think about adoption? Oh, God, that's a thoughtless question. Please. Don't answer." Her face glowed with embarrassment.

"No. Don't be upset. It's a very normal thought." He patted her hand resting on the empty seat. "Yes, we did think about it. But, it took Elaine so long to recover from her surgery. She had her teaching career and I had my practice, so we decided to help other children in our small way."

"I'm not ashamed of my decision to have the baby. To be honest, I don't know why I didn't choose to have an abortion. The doctor in Tampa suggested one."

"He did?"

"Yes. And, it would have been easier for me. Now I've lost my job, and I have eighteen or nineteen years of raising a child by myself ahead of me."

"You won't always be alone, I'm sure. You're a pretty girl, Patty. And, you'll have your family to help. Are they excited?"

"They don't know yet."

"Oh yes, you mentioned that. Sorry."

For God's sake, we haven't known each other for more than forty minutes and we're apologizing to each other like old friends. Still, Patty felt comfortable talking to Doctor Branigan. *Must be his nice bedside manners*, she thought.

The flight attendant's voice came over the PA, interrupting any further thought or conversation for the moment. "Ladies and gentlemen the Captain has asked that you keep your seat belt fastened and remain in your seats as there is some turbulence ahead of us. It shouldn't last very long and he's going to try and move up over the storms. We will advise when it's safe to move about the cabin again." The metallic voice and crackling background noises were silenced with a click.

Patty and Doctor Branigan looked at each other, checking to see if the seat belts were fastened. For the next half hour they were jolted and jostled as if they were on a *Tilt-a-Whirl.* Patty wondered for a while if her breakfast was going to remain in her stomach and had to swallow carefully several times. When the flight attendant came down the aisle, Doctor Branigan leaned over and caught her attention.

"Miss? Could you bring the young lady a ginger ale? She's not feeling well."

"Thanks," Patty smiled. "I didn't think of that."

"The doctor knows best. You okay?"

She nodded, thankful for the cool glass of bubbling soda the attendant handed her. She tucked the half-filled can in the pocket, then turned to him, "Want the rest?"

"You keep it. You may need it."

"Thanks," she said again, closing her eyes.

In Philadelphia he held her arm as they walked through the tunnel to the main concourse. When they reached the escalator, he stopped. "You'll be okay here now? I could wait until you get your next flight."

"I'm fine. You go on. You don't have to bother about me."

"It's no bother."

Patty studied him carefully. There was no ulterior message behind his words. "Why are you doing this?"

"Because you're young and alone and pregnant, I guess."

"Thanks." Impulsively she hugged him. "You'd have made a wonderful dad."

He grinned. "You'll be a great mother, too. Just remember, Patty, it's a gift. A baby is the most precious gift you'll ever receive." He patted her shoulder and stepped onto the moving stairs. She watched him disappear and then leaned over the wall to watch him stride along the lower level toward the baggage area.

She had an hour's wait for her next flight so when he was out of sight, she turned and checked the monitor on the wall. Walking toward another concourse, she felt happier than she had in months. She patted her stomach underneath the oversized shirt she wore over her jeans. *It's gonna be okay, Squirt. We're gonna be okay.*

CHAPTER TWENTY-FOUR

Kate was too nervous to sit in one of the hard plastic chairs. Instead she stood in front of the grimy window overlooking the runways, watching the constant flow of small airplanes as they took off and landed. Occasionally a larger commercial plane would taxi past the window and Kate would remind herself that Patty was arriving on a small commuter plane. She glanced at her watch and then at the large clock over the arrival gate. Patty's plane should have been here ten minutes ago.

Last night she'd spoken to Lily confirming Patty's flight numbers and time of arrival. Lily and George had agreed it was more sensible for her to meet Patty. The drive to Wilkes-Barre would have been out of the question for Lily, and George wouldn't have to take another day off from work.

Lily's anxiety was obvious. "I can't wait to see her. I'm so glad she's coming early. We'll be able to visit longer." She hesitated. "Are you going to tell her?"

Kate sighed. "We've discussed this. You know how I feel. I can't see letting her arrive and be confronted with you being so obviously ill. How are you going to hide the oxygen?

"I don't have to wear it all the time."

"You should."

"Well for a few minutes, when she first comes in."

"You're crazy."

Lily didn't respond. She hated the fact that she needed the oxygen. It had been one of the deciding factors in the change in sleeping arrangements. The home unit, as the visiting nurse referred to the big machine, was hidden in the corner of the sunroom next to her bed. The long clear vinyl tubing allowed her to move around the first floor. She wore a portable unit when she left the house.

"If you insist on holding me to my original promise," Kate said guiltily, "I'll do it, but I think it's wrong,"

"You're right," Lily admitted reluctantly. "I wanted to keep it from them but I guess that was foolish. Maybe you could drop a hint and not come right out… oh, damn. That's foolish, too. I don't know, Kate. Do whatever…"

"Let me feel my way after she gets here, okay?"

"Okay. I know you'll do what's best. Have a safe trip."

Kate became aware of some movements behind her and turned to see the attendants busy at the arrival gate. *The plane must be coming in*, she thought and watched as a small commuter plane appeared from nowhere. It taxied cautiously toward the terminal as if feeling it's way through the clutter of baggage vehicles and people. The ground crew hustled through their routines and rolled the steps to the side of the plane; the silver door slid back and passengers began to descend. Kate remained at the window watching. Most of those arriving were obviously businessmen and women, dressed in suits and carrying briefcases. When Patty stood for a moment in the doorway, Kate recognized her immediately. Long light brown hair swirled around her face as she came down the steps.

Kate hurried across the waiting area and watched for her to come through the door leading to the terminal. She waived when she saw her.

Patty stepped into her waiting arms. Kate was surprised at the intensity of Patty's embrace. Stepping back, she said, "You look great. Florida must have been good for you, you're tanned and not as skinny as the last time I saw you."

"Yeah, well—God, it's cold here." Patty shivered, hoping to take the conversation away from her additional weight, at least for now.

"Well, we think it's lovely but I guess compared to Florida it's chilly."

"Chilly. It was seventy-nine degrees when I left and it wasn't eight o'clock yet."

"Wow. You'll have to tell me all about it. Now, what about luggage?"

"My duffel, that's all." Patty looked up to check the directory overhead. Pointing to the left, she said, "Baggage area this way."

Chatting about the trip and the weather, they walked down the concourse to the baggage pick-up area.

They left the airport and instead of taking the interstate, Kate took the old highway toward Eagleton. Patty thought it strange but didn't comment. In the car Kate questioned Patty about her travels and jobs over the past two years.

New spring growth was softening the mountainsides and natural springs were gushing from rock formations along the road. They had been traveling for thirty minutes when Kate slowed the car and pulled between rough stone posts leading to a recreation area on a lake.

Patty was familiar with the area and looked surprised. "Where are we going?"

"For a picnic. I thought you wouldn't have had much to eat on your trip since you left so early. What have you eaten today?"

Patty laughed. "I had a rubber omelet and a sticky bun the size of a quarter for breakfast on US Air, and a bag of peanuts and a diet coke on the commuter."

"Thought so. There's a small cooler on the back seat." She pulled into a deserted parking area and stopped the car. "Can you reach the cooler? I'll take a blanket from the trunk to put on the bench. They haven't officially opened the park yet so everything is probably covered with winter grime." Kate got out and went to the back of the car.

Carrying the cooler, Patty followed her. She was still puzzled but decided it was Aunt Kate's practical way of making sure she ate sensible food. Her stomach growled and she grinned as she followed Kate down the sun-dappled path to the water's edge where several picnic tables were scattered across the rocky shore area.

The lake was as deserted as the park. No boats bobbed or streaked across the water as they would when the season began. The quiet was deep and comforting.

Choosing a table in the sunshine protected from the breeze by a huge bank of rhododendrons, they spread the blanket on the bench and put the cooler on the table. For several moments they sat quietly.

"Nice here, isn't it?"

"Yeah. I remember coming here with some kids the last summer before I left. One guy had one of those inflatable boats and we took turns paddling around in it. There's a beach not far along there," she pointed to the right.

"I remember. When you were little, your family and I would come here a couple of times each summer. Do you remember?"

"A little. I remember Dad always wanting Michael to go fishing with him and Mike didn't want to."

Kate nodded. She reached for the cooler and began unpacking. "I brought your favorite sandwich. Pimento cheese spread on rye." She smiled at Patty as she handed her a sandwich wrapped in clear plastic wrap. "Still like it?"

"Oh, gosh, yes. I can't remember the last time I had this. Thanks Aunt Kate." This unexpected thoughtfulness almost brought tears to her eyes. "Mike and Debbie used to say it was the worst choice in the world," she said, masking her emotion.

"There's lemonade and fresh grapes, too."

Patty hadn't realized how hungry she was until she began eating. She was picking grapes from the plastic bag when she felt, rather than saw, Kate staring at her.

"What?"

"Nothing. Just glad to see you, I guess. It's been so long."

"I know. It seemed to work out that way. I'm glad I came home though."

"That's good. It means a lot to your mother."

Patty turned to face Kate. "You know, when I spoke to Mike he wasn't sure what the reason for this trip was and at first I was kind of annoyed about the whole thing. Now I'm glad they got in touch with me."

"I am, too."

"What *is* the reason?"

Kate looked across the wide expanse of water. This was the opening she was hoping for and now that it was here she was scared to death. She hesitated. "Sometime things don't always work out the way you want them to. And sometimes things that you think will never happen, do."

They looked at each other, Patty's face puzzled, Kate's softened by the sympathy she felt for Lily's baby daughter.

"That sounds like a riddle," Patty said, popping the last grape into her mouth. "But, I know what you mean. I've been looking for something I guess ever since I left Eagleton. I don't think I found it. Had some fun along the way though." She began to tell Kate about funny experiences and her mood lightened. Kate watched the animation on her face and saw brief hints of the child she had known—quick to laugh, but just as quick to retreat into herself.

"You've grown up a lot but you're still the same Patty."

"Maybe not."

"What do you mean?"

Patty shrugged. As a child it had been easier for her to talk to her Aunt Kate than her parents. Even though Kate and her mother were the same age, in some ways Kate seemed to be closer in age to the Hoffmann children. "Nothing," she said quietly.

"You look the same except that you've gained some weight. It looks good on you though."

Patty folded her lips in, struggling with a reply.

Kate recognized the mannerism, and asked, "Something wrong, Patty?"

"Wrong? Yes, I mean no. You wouldn't understand."

"Maybe I would," Kate said softly. Patty's shoulders rose defensively.

"I don't think you will, Aunt Kate. I'm not as conventional as you. I'm different."

"We're all different. It's recognizing the differences and dealing with them that make for good relationships. I like to think we can always share anything with each other."

"Most things maybe, but not everything. But, then you're going to know soon enough."

"Know what?"

Patty turned to her. "Aunt Kate, I'm pregnant."

Kate reached for Patty, pulling her into her arms. "Oh, honey. That's wonderful. Why your mother will be so excited!"

"No, she won't." Patty couldn't stem the tears now that she'd allowed the confession, and her shoulders shook with emotion.

Pushing her away Kate looked into the emotion-torn face of the child she'd cared for since birth. "Of course she will."

"No, Aunt Kate." Patty wiped the sleeve of her jacket across her eyes. "No. She won't. Because there's no father in the picture and there never will be."

Kate sat very still.

"I'm a statistic. An unwed mother who's chosen to keep the baby. That's why I came home. Not because Mom wanted me to. I'm selfish, not…"

"Wait." Kate raised her hand. "Wait. Before you chastise yourself to death, think about it. You are going to have a child. The greatest gift God gives anyone."

Patty remembered Philip Branigan saying those very words to her. Her smile was feeble but it brightened her face. "Someone else just said that to me."

"Well whoever it was, they were right. "

"I've haven't told anyone."

"If you want to, I'll listen. If not, I'll understand. Maybe some other time would be better." She was thinking of the news she still had to impart.

"No. It doesn't matter anymore. I made my decisions. I'll live with them. He was older, a customer at the last place I worked. There was a party and Carlos, my boss, invited some of the waitresses to it. The man was one of his personal friends."

Patty hesitated, gathering old memories.

"It was very late, a perfect tropical night on the beach. We all had too much to drink. Everything was exciting and romantic. I wasn't usually so careless. It happened."

"Does he know about the child?" Kate whispered.

"No. He's married. I didn't want to be responsible for destroying a marriage. I saw them together not long afterwards. What happened on the beach that night was just circumstances of the moment."

Kate had no counsel. On top of her deep concern for Lily, now this. She shook her head.

"Disgusted with me?"

"Of course not. You're not the first one to make a mistake. If God can forgive, how can we do less?"

Patty laughed. "No matter what, you have a Sunday School lesson to apply, don't you?"

"Not always, or at least, not always right away. But this is different. You're not alone. You have your family. Me."

Patty squeezed Kate's hand. "You're something else. I was so afraid to tell anyone. I'm glad the first one to hear was you, Aunt Kate."

"I am too, dear." They sat quietly watching two waterfowl glide by making a double 'v' indentation in the smooth water. Somewhere a bird squawked loudly, the sound piercing the quiet of the forest that surrounded them.

"Your mother is going to need you very much, Patty."

Patty frowned. "You mean I'm going to need her."

"Well, I guess you're going to need each other."

"I don't understand."

"You will. I have something to tell you. At first your mother made me promise not to tell anyone, but I've convinced her that's not a good idea."

"What?"

Taking one of Patty's hands in hers, Kate looked directly into her face. "Life sometimes hands you more than you think you can handle, but then again, it makes up for the bad times with the good. I know that's something you don't understand right now. But think about it after I've told you what I have to say, okay?"

Patty nodded uncertainly.

Taking a deep breath, Kate continued. "You wanted to know the reason for the family gathering? After Christmas, your mother began to lose weight and became tired very easily. In January she made an appointment with Doctor Bob. You remember him?"

"Yes, but…"

"He did a lot of tests. At first he couldn't find a reason for the symptoms but in February he finished the tests and had the results. It's not good news, honey."

Patty's face began to crumple.

"Don't. Wait until I'm finished."

Patty looked away quickly and then back to Kate, searching her eyes for more information. "Tell me," she murmured.

"Your mother has cancer, she's dying."

Patty jerked her hand away, forming a fist. Stunned and reluctant to accept it, she cried out, "No! That can't be." She saw the truth in her mother's friend's eyes. Lowering her head to her arms on the table, she began to cry.

Kate patted her back. For several minutes the peaceful scene was violated by the sobs that escaped the young girl. When she looked up, her cheeks were wet, her eyes hollow and her mouth drawn into an ugly slit. Kate pulled her against her chest.

"It's been hard, honey—hard to understand, hard to watch. I couldn't let you come home and find your mother so ill without any warning. I had to do this."

"What kind of cancer? I thought that was all over five years ago. Isn't there something they can do?" the rapid-fire questions were blurred with emotion.

Kate shook her head. "Both lungs. Inoperable. That's why she needs you. And with your baby coming, you need each other. Think about it Patty. You'll need each other more than ever before."

Patty stood and walked away from the table, scuffing one toe in the moist rocks next to the water. She spoke into the breeze that rippled the wide expanse of water in front of her. "How long does she have?"

"The doctor gave her three to six months when he first diagnosed the cancer. Now she's on some new medicine, experimental medicine. She may have longer. She may be more comfortable but there's no guarantee. There's no cure, honey."

Kate moved to her side and slid her arm around the child now carrying a child. "You can't let this make you sick. You have the baby to think about."

Patty leaned her head on Kate's shoulder. "Right now I can't think about anything but Mom."

"I know."

"What about Dad?"

"He's being wonderful. I told Debbie there's been a big change in him."

"Debbie?" Patty jumped at the mention of her sister's name. "Does she know?"

Kate tugged Patty's arm and they moved back to the table. "I had to call her, honey. Your mother doesn't know that yet. Last night I argued with her that I couldn't keep this a secret from you and just dump you at the house to find out for yourself. She can be very stubborn sometimes."

"I know. What about Debbie?"

"She wasn't going to come home. Every August she spends a week with your parents. I couldn't let her put it off and not come home. I had to call her and tell her. She'll be here next week."

"What about Mike?"

"He doesn't know. He'll be here the end of next week, too."

"I can't take all of this in, Aunt Kate. I feel like I've been hit with a hammer."

"Let's get going. It'll take another hour to drive to Eagleton. We can talk in the car. Your mom's waiting for you."

"Is this why you came to meet me instead of them?"

"Partly, it would be very difficult for your mother to travel this distance, and your father has been taking quite a few days off work lately. It worked out better this way."

They gathered their things and walked back to the car along the sunny path. The quiet seemed different, deeper and more solemn than it did when they arrived.

CHAPTER TWENTY-FIVE

Patty shivered and pulled her jacket tighter.

Kate reached across the seat and patted her hand. “Still chilly?”

“No. Nerves I guess.”

“You’ve been quiet for the last ten minutes.”

“There’s so much to think about. I feel stupid. I was so annoyed because I didn’t understand the reason behind Mom’s letter.”

“You didn’t know. When your Mom first learned of the cancer, she was scared, then confused, then angry, she’s finally come to grips with this whole mess. I think she’s doing well, considering. It’s not easy finding out your time is limited. None of us are promised tomorrow but we always assume it’s going to be there.”

“But, why didn’t she just tell us?”

“She didn’t want you to come home because of pity. She’s a proud lady.”

“She always was.”

"Well, when she finally accepted the facts, she told your Dad."

"You mean he didn't know either?"

"Not at first."

"Wow. What happened then?"

Kate hesitated for a moment. She didn't want to vent her opinion that George had suddenly become attentive when he realized he was going to lose Lily. "He took it very hard. Your father loves your mother very much. He always has but emotions are not easy for him to share."

They were quiet for a few moments.

"I'm ashamed of some of the things I thought about him as a kid."

"Don't be. Rehashing old animosities is a waste of time. His mother influenced him. You didn't know her but she was a cold woman who never let herself feel anything."

"Still. Maybe if I'd been more understanding…"

"You were a child. Anyhow, after your Dad knew, he was devastated. He's been very understanding and comforting to your mother. But, getting back to the reunion, when she accepted the fact she didn't have a lot of time left," Kate's voice caught and she had to swallow before continuing, "she said the one thing she wanted was to have you kids all together again."

"But I still don't understand why she couldn't tell us and make sure we were all here when she wanted us to be. We aren't exactly the *Waltons,* and we live pretty far from each other."

"I know, and that bothered her. She told me 'I want them to be friends'."

"Friends," Patty moaned.

"Don't try to solve all the problems at once, honey."

"We don't have a hell of a lot of time."

As they neared Eagleton, the traffic became more congested and Patty noticed some changes. "Hey, that's a new shopping center isn't it?"

"Yes. You'll be surprised to see how the outskirts of Eagleton have changed. Downtown though, the city itself is the same, so you haven't been away that long."

"Over three years."

"I didn't realize it was that long."

After a few minutes Patty asked, "Doctor Bob doesn't have any hopes of prolonging her time with us?" Her voice cracked as she put her fears into words.

"No," Kate whispered.

"Oh, God, Aunt Kate. How am I going to act when I see her? I don't know if I can just say 'Hi, Mom, good to see you'."

Kate turned quickly to look at her passenger. Patty's cheeks were wet. She put the right turn signal on, looked into the mirror, pulled into the right-hand lane and took the next off ramp. Pulling into a gas station, she bypassed the pumps and stopped next to the convenience store.

"It's not going to be easy. Your mother has lost a lot of weight. She has to be on oxygen most of the time."

"Oxygen. Oh, damn. This isn't fair."

"She has a good attitude, Patty. You have to be strong, too. This new drug program Doctor Bob has her on is experimental with no promises but she has hopes it will make a difference—maybe add a little time."

Patty stared through the windshield, shaking her head. “I’ll try, Kate. I’ll try to be as strong as I need to be. But…”

“You can do it.” Kate glanced at her watch. “It’s almost four o’clock. We should be there in fifteen minutes. Your Dad won’t be home until after four-thirty so you’ll get to see your Mom alone. Do you want me to stay with you?”

Patty took the tissue she was offered and patted at her eyes. “I don’t know,” she moaned. “Maybe it would be best. Should I tell her about…?” She stroked her stomach.

“Why don’t you play it by ear? Don’t try to rehearse what’s going to happen. Your Mom’s going to be so excited to see you. Remember, she’s worrying about your reaction, too.”

“You’re right. Damn, this is going to be harder than I thought and I wasn’t planning on an easy time. I thought I might take a day or two to get the feel of things and then talk to them about the baby. What about Dad? Do you think he’s going to be…?”

“He’s going to be okay.” Kate started the car. “You all right now? Want to rest?”

“No, let’s get going. I want to see Mom. You’re right. I’ll play it by ear. After all, we don’t have a hell of a lot of time to start playacting, do we?”

Kate smiled. She was pleased to hear some spunk in Patty’s voice. She pulled across the side road and back onto the highway. In fifteen minutes they’d be home.

#

For the past thirty minutes, Lily hovered behind the lace curtains at the front window, anxiously watching for Kate's old car. For over an hour she had been pacing from the living room to the kitchen, stopping often to sit in one of the chairs in the converted sunroom.

George had fixed the room up nicely. Their bed filled the back corner, and a chest of drawers from the basement had been given a quick coat of white paint and placed along the wall. Two small, upholstered chairs were a gift from Kate. Reupholstered in a wild floral pattern Lily loved but would never have chosen, Kate had redeemed them from Mercy House Thrift Shop. They added a welcome bright spot to the room.

As she watched, Lily saw Kate pull her car to the curb. Her heart pulsed against her ribs. Patty was here. She looked around in panic. Where should she be when Patty came through the door? Darting toward her usual chair in the living room, she veered to the right and pulled the French doors to the sunroom closed, but not before she yanked the oxygen tube from her nose and threw it into the room. *No need to shock her with everything the first minute she steps into the house.* Panting from the exertion, and struggling to suppress her need for oxygen, she sat and waited. With trembling hands Lily patted her hair and straightened her blouse preparing for the long-awaited meeting.

The door opened and Patty thrust her duffle bag into the room and stood in the doorway clutching a small blue case. Lily saw Kate standing behind her. For a moment no one moved and no one spoke. Then Lily said, "Patty…" just as Patty said, "Mom…"

Patty rushed across the space between them, falling on her knees at the side of her mother's chair. She thrust her arms around her mother's bony, shaking shoulders. Lily's fingers combed through her daughter's hair, her hands finally resting on the back of her head as she pulled her child closer to her breast. Their mutual sobs were muffled by their closeness.

"Welcome home, Patty," Kate said softly. "You two have a lot of talking to do. I'll call later." She started to close the door.

"Wait. You don't have to go." Lily looked across her daughter's head at her best friend. "Stay, Kate."

"You don't need me right now. Call me later," she said and gently closed the door, leaving part of her heart with the two women. Slowly descending the stairs, she thumbed tears from her eyes. It took her several minutes to compose herself before she started her car. As she pulled away, she recognized George's car turning into the alley behind the house and quickly followed him. Before he could get out and open the garage door, she pulled up next to him, rolling down her passenger window.

He opened his door and stood next to her car. "What's wrong? Didn't Patty get here?"

"She's here. I just dropped her off. Get in George."

He opened the door and slid in. "What's the matter? Is Lily okay?"

"They're both okay. I just left them."

"Then what . . .?"

"You're home early, George. Maybe I shouldn't meddle but I don't think you should go in yet."

"I thought Lily might need me so I left work early."

"She'll need you in a little while. They both will. Why don't you give them a little time alone?" She bit her lower lip waiting for the explosion.

George stared at her and then turned and stared through the windshield. He didn't say anything and Kate's heart shrank as she watched his jaw tighten and release.

After a moment, he turned to her. "You're probably right, a girl thing—a mother and daughter thing. I should have thought. I'll go get a cup of coffee and wait until it's my usual time to go home. Thanks, Kate." He touched her shoulder and slid out of the car. She waited until he pulled down the alley and followed him.

Damn, she thought. *I'll be so glad when everyone is here and everything is out in the open. I'm sick of the intrigue and the manipulating. They're making it tougher than it should be and it's going to be tough enough.*

CHAPTER TWENTY-SIX

Michael stood facing the window in Kevin's office. At six-thirty the reception area was deserted, the quiet was a welcome comfort after a hectic day. He hitched up his trousers, remembering the necessity to punch another hole in his belt this morning. The past couple of weeks had been filled with new experiences for him, not the least of which was an unexpected loss of weight.

"I'm not used to intrigue and for two weeks I feel as if I've been the main character in a paperback thriller."

"It's going to be okay, Mike."

"Thanks to your help." He turned his back to the window and walked across the carpeted floor. Kevin's office was the same size as his and yet it appeared much smaller. Maybe it was a combination of Kevin's size and the accumulation of clutter that surrounded him. No neat stacks of files on his desktop and credenza, but disorderly piles of folders, books and spreadsheets that littered the area around the desk like so much jetsam following a barge along the river.

"Her lawyer is a real smart ass. He called this morning with a final demand. All Simone wants is cash—lots of it. Crazy. I knew I'd be taken for a lot but I wasn't born yesterday."

"Thank God you got in touch with Reichers when you did."

"Yeah—following your good advice."

#

The day following the final scene with Simone, Michael had swallowed his pride and revealed the whole unpleasant story to Kevin. He wasn't sure whether Kevin already knew some of it, or had surmised some of the problems, but he never questioned his friend. On Kevin's recommendation, Michael contacted Franklin L. Reichers, Attorney at Law, that morning, and met with him later the same day. After that meeting Michael followed a series of cloak and dagger directives that sent him along some strange paths.

Reichers, a man in his fifties, had silver hair, bushy black eyebrows and a pencil thin mustache. His complexion was mottled with tiny red veins, giving away a lifetime of serious drinking. Michael liked his listening abilities and his no-nonsense approach to the problem of separating from and divorcing Simone. Actually, Michael hadn't even thought of divorce, being interested only in ridding himself of Simone's presence and his responsibility for her.

"Get whatever you personally want out of the house immediately," Frank had told him.

"I don't really want much."

"The hell you don't. Think man. There are things in that house that mean a hell of a lot more to you than to her, but she'll want it all."

"I don't…"

"Do it. Go home tonight and look through every room. Take a mental inventory and then make arrangements to store whatever you want somewhere. Don't tell her what you want or where you're going to put it."

"But I thought we owned everything…"

"Jointly?" he finished for him. "Right. Still, you can keep "personal" things for yourself." He raised two fingers on each hand, describing the quotation marks.

"I still don't think there's much…"

"Do it. Now how about the car?"

"She won't want it. She rarely drives, prefers taking a cab."

"Is it in both names? Where do you keep it?"

"Actually, it's in my name. She didn't even want to come and look at it when I bought it last year. I keep it in a rented garage near the house. I don't drive to work every day either although I have a space in the firm's parking garage."

"Cancel the lease, move the car to another garage. Don't use it unless you have to."

"She won't…"

"Do it."

#

Michael laced his fingers behind his neck and smiled as he remembered his initial meeting with the feisty attorney. He'd followed Frank's instructions and was surprised to find there were things he wanted to keep. Things from his college days, special books that meant something to him, and the scale model of a Pennsylvania Railroad train that ran along the top of a bookshelf in the den.

The major problem at first was being in the house together. Simone adopted a superior attitude, even more apparent than prior to his ultimatum. She coldly announced, two days following their confrontation, that she'd retained an attorney. Solicitor was the term she used, and Michael winced at the falsely used foreign term.

"Fine, have him contact my attorney," Michael replied coldly as he passed her in the hallway going to the kitchen for a beer. When he was home, Simone usually remained in her room and he found himself wondering what she did during the day. Three weeks ago he hadn't really thought much about what she did. He didn't have long to wonder though because five days after the bedroom scene, he came home to find a note on the hall table.

Written on her cream stationery was a terse, "*I am gone. Contact me through Jeffrey Laughton, Esq.*" She had scrawled a bold "S" as a signature.

Michael frowned at the paper. Was she with Malcolm? She couldn't be. He couldn't see Malcolm taking her into his penthouse apartment permanently. Kay would be returning eventually, as she always did. He didn't want to admit his curiosity and yet the nagging thoughts kept returning to him all evening. After climbing the stairs, he looked into her room cautiously, as if he really had no right to be there. Tiptoeing across the carpet, he opened the closets and found a few abandoned hangers scattered along the rod. The empty bureau drawers put a note of finality to her leaving. He caught sight of himself in the triple mirror and scowled at his image. *Don't even think about feeling sorry for yourself. This is the smartest thing you've done in years.*

Even the bathroom had been stripped but she couldn't remove the lingering aroma of her perfume and cosmetics. It would be a long time before that cloying scent left the house. He closed the door firmly and climbed the stairs to his third floor bedroom.

He was surprised at the things she hadn't taken when he walked through the house. Most of the china and silver were still in the cabinets and drawers. Only the fine china she'd ordered from London during their first year of marriage had been packed and moved. Some crystal and most of the figurines were gone. Their supply of linens looked diminished but he couldn't be sure because it wasn't an area he was familiar with.

#

"You going to sell the house?" Kevin's voice brought him back to the present.

"Frank said I should and at first agreeing with him was difficult, but he's right. I can't be bothered maintaining that huge house and what do I need it for? Besides, I'll have to turn it into cash for the settlement. I'll find an apartment when I come back from Pennsylvania. "

Michael had also confided his concerns for his family to Kevin.

"You leaving Friday?"

"No. I decided to leave early Saturday morning and pick Debbie up in Philadelphia. We'll drive up together. Patty's already there. I talked to her last night."

"Everything okay?"

"No. Something is going on, but getting anything out of her was impossible and she seemed anxious to get off the telephone. Mom sounded tired so we didn't talk long." Michael's concern was obvious. He slumped into the clients' chair, stretched his legs in front of him, carefully avoiding a stack of papers. "It all seems to be coming down on me at once, Kev, and some of it I just don't understand."

Kevin stood. Three of the five drawers in his desk were partially opened and he shoved them closed, pushing the locks as he did. "One day at a time, friend, one day at a time. Let's get out of here. Want to come for dinner?"

"No thanks. I'm not very good company lately and I'm kind of getting used to being a bachelor. Quiet dinners at the kitchen table, eating out of Styrofoam containers; it's nicer than it sounds." He grinned at his friend and his face brightened with a hint of the old Michael.

"Well at least let's get a drink at The Brokers."

"Sure."

They left the office together, walking along the quiet upper hall to the elevator. "You know, you've been great. You're a good friend," Michael said, pushing the elevator button.

"Thanks but you'd do the same for me, if I needed help."

"Let's hope you never need this kind of help, but you're right. Just listening to me has been the best help you could give me. That and recommending Reichers."

The doors closed and the elevator descended with a soft swoosh. Outside, there was a definite hint of spring in the air and they left their topcoats unbuttoned, flapping at their sides like unfurled sails as they strode along the sidewalk toward The Brokers' at the corner

#

Michael was finishing his microwave dinner when the telephone rang. He stared at the wall telephone for a moment, then dashed down the hall to take the call in the den. Sliding behind the desk, he picked the phone up on the fourth ring.

"Hello."

"I thought you might be out. I was about to give up."

"Patty! I was in the kitchen when the phone rang and I wanted to take it in the den in case it was a client. All my papers and briefcase are in here."

"Is Simone home?"

Michael hadn't told anyone in his family about the separation or the problems. He grimaced at the mention of his wife's name. "No. She's not here. What's up? Are you having a good visit?"

"Yeah, it's okay."

He frowned. That didn't sound too positive.

"How's Mom? And, Dad?" he added.

"They're okay."

"So—what's up? I'll be there Saturday after I pick Deb up in Philadelphia. Her flight is due in at twelve forty-five our time so we should be there by four o'clock that afternoon."

"I know. Mike, I need to talk to you."

"Why are you whispering? Are you home?"

"No. I'm at Aunt Kate's."

"Oh?"

"Mike, I need to tell you something."

Michael didn't realize he was frowning as he listened to Patty, yet the crease in his brow deepened and he felt his stomach muscles tighten.

"What?"

"Okay, listen, before you say anything. Kate knows what I'm calling about. We thought it would be best if I used her telephone."

"Patty. What the hell are you talking about? You're not making any sense… "

"I wish you'd quit interrupting, this isn't easy."

Michael heard her take in a deep breath and a hundred and forty miles away he followed suit.

"Things here aren't what you think they are. I have two things to tell you. First, my news, which doesn't have anything to do with the other news, but it's easier for me to tell."

"For God's sake…"

"Mike, please!" she begged. The silence was thick for several moments and then she said, "I'm sorry. That wasn't how I wanted to start this conversation."

He waited quietly.

"I'm pregnant," she said softly.

His jaw dropped and his mind raced. Pregnant—his baby sister? "What? But, how…" he stuttered.

"The usual way you dope. And, before you ask, no husband, no father, and Mom, Dad and Kate are all okay with it."

Neither of them spoke for a long moment.

"Mike, you there?"

"Yeah, I'm here. It's such a surprise. Is that why you suddenly decided to go home?"

"Yes, and I'm so glad I did."

"Well, I guess so. I mean you're where you should be now with Mom and Dad. I'm not surprised it's okay with Mom. Well, you know what I mean, but what about Dad?"

"He's fine. He's changed."

"He must have."

"You'll see."

"I'll be there Saturday," he said, again.

"I know, but there's more and this is the tough one."

"What else?"

"Remember when we were talking last month and we couldn't figure out why it was so damned important for us all to be here?"

"Yeah. Got the answer to that mystery?"

"I do. And it's a shocker."

After a long silence, Michael said, "Well, are you going to tell me?"

"It's hard to put into words. Kate told me before I got home. We stopped at Hammock State Park. You remember that picnic area next to the lake?"

"Patty, I remember the park. What the hell has that got to do with the reason we're all getting together this weekend?"

"Please, Mike, just let me tell you."

Michael pushed himself back in the chair, wishing he'd poured himself a drink before he answered the telephone.

"Mom's sick."

"Sick? How sick?" He sat forward.

"Real sick. I've been here three days now and I'm still not really able to understand everything there is to think about."

"Patty…"

She recognized the desperation in his voice. "She's dying, Mike; she has cancer." He heard her sob.

"Oh my God!" The rest of his words caught in his throat.

"I know how you feel, Mike, but she's doing all right. I mean she's dealing with it and so is Dad. She's on oxygen so she has this big machine with a long tube and she's got to stay on the first floor. She can't go upstairs."

"Wait—oxygen? Cancer? I can't absorb all of this. What kind of cancer? Aren't there treatments, medicines, something? She had surgery before…"

"This is different. This time it's lung cancer. Inoperable. According to Doctor Bob there is no chance of her getting better. It's too far gone. She's on some kind of new experimental drugs but she's thin, Mike. Oh, God, she's so thin." Patty's voice trembled as she struggled to control her tears.

"Sweet Jesus, this is too much."

"Too much for who, Mike? We have to accept it. That's why she wanted us all here. She has some kind of crazy dream about us all becoming bosom buddies and living happily ever after in each other's pockets or something." She blotted her eyes with a rough paper towel. "That was snotty. I'm sorry."

"Patty, it's okay. I'm trying to understand. Just tell me what you know."

He heard her take a deep breath and tried to picture her but all he saw was the high school senior of six or seven years ago.

"She found out in February and didn't tell Dad right away but she did tell Kate. She decided she wanted us all to be together again before she…well, together again so we could become friends."

"Friends," he moaned and Patty remembered her similar feeling on a silent lakeshore that seemed like years ago but was only last week.

"Dad's moved their bed into the sunroom and made a nice room down there for them so she doesn't have to climb the stairs."

"How is he taking all this?"

"Pretty good. Boy, has he changed. He's so different."

"Listen, Patty. I can't get there any earlier. I promised to meet Deb in Philly. Does she know?"

"Yes. Kate had to tell her, too. Mom didn't…"

"Wait a minute. You mean you both knew and I didn't?"

"Mom didn't want any of us to know anything at all before we got here but Kate convinced her it wasn't fair for us to arrive and see her like she is. It's not a pretty sight, Mike."

"But…"

"Kate had to call Deb and tell her because she wasn't going to come home until August."

"I thought Deb sounded strange when I talked to her last week."

"She only learned because Kate told her on the *q.t.* Then when she picked me up in Wilkes-Barre, she thought I should know before I saw Mom. That's why I'm calling you. Mom doesn't know we know. Well, she knows I know, and she suspects Deb knows. Oh damn, does any of this make any sense?"

"Yes and no…" He choked.

"I'm really glad Kate told me because it would have been such a shock to see Mom like she is…" She broke down not even trying to hide her sobbing.

"Patty, it's okay. Don't make yourself sick. I'll be there Saturday." Mike twisted the telephone cord. "Are you all right?"

"I'm fine."

"Sure? You sound funny.

"I knew you had to know; I had to call you."

"And I'm glad you did."

Neither wanted to break the connection. The strained separation of the past years melted in the common trauma they now shared.

"I feel guilty for making Mom worry about us," Patty said, struggling to calm herself.

"Don't." Michael said, feeling the same guilt.

"We wasted so much time."

"We still have time. Time to be together. We'll work it out."

"What did we do that was so wrong?" she asked.

"I guess it wasn't what we did wrong so much as what we didn't do, kid."

Michael hadn't called her kid in a long time. Still sobbing softly, she said, "I'm the worst. Sometimes there were months between the times I wrote or called them."

"Don't blame yourself. You weren't alone. I lived closer to them than either of you and I rarely made an effort to go home or check on them."

"Was it because of Dad?"

"No." Michael's answer was quick and he wasn't sure it was honest but it was the answer he wanted to give. "Is Kate there now?"

"She's in the garage sorting through some tomato and pepper plants she's going to put in her garden tomorrow. I'm going to help her. It's like spring here. The trees are covered with little leaves already."

He was pleased to hear her voice leveling out to a more normal tone. "That's good. Listen, I've got to go. Do you want me to call you before I get there Saturday?"

"No. We'll look for you around four o'clock. Have a safe trip."

"Thanks. Be good, kid. God, I can't believe my baby sister is going to be a mother."

"Mom's excited."

"That's good. That's real good."

"Doctor Bob said so, too."

His hand cramped with the pressure of his grip on the telephone. "Patty, I have to go. I'll see you Saturday."

"Okay."

Michael dropped the phone onto the cradle, rose from his chair, and turned to the liquor cabinet at the side of the fireplace. He spilled almost as much brandy as he poured into the glass. Wiping the sticky spot with a paper napkin, he tossed it in the direction of the wastebasket and saw it fall short. With a trembling hand he put the glass to his lips and drank, feeling the liquid burn the back of his throat.

He sank into one of the chairs and closed his eyes but he couldn't stop the tears that seeped from deep within his soul. His failed marriage, his covert actions to protect possessions and attempts to guard his assets over the past two weeks paled as he thought about his family. Patty felt guilty? His own self-condemnation took on monumental proportions and he felt his chest constrict around his grief.

CHAPTER TWENTY-SEVEN

"Well, look at you. Talk about bright eyed and bushy tailed." Kate wiped her feet on the rug inside the kitchen door. "You look great."

Lily felt her cheeks warm. "Thanks."

"What happened? Feeling better?"

"Yes. And a touch of makeup and a huge portion of happy heart, doesn't hurt."

Lily sat at the kitchen table doing her nails, something Kate hadn't seen her do in months. The oxygen tube trailed across her shoulder and disappeared through the door to the dining room. Kate heard the faint hum of the motor as it pumped the lifesaving element into Lily's lungs.

"Patty up yet?"

"No. I thought I'd let her sleep. We were up until after eleven last night talking."

Kate filled the teakettle and took three mugs from the cabinet. "Had breakfast?"

"George made me toast before he left."

"Want eggs? Cereal?"

"No, thanks. Maybe I'll have something with Patty when she comes down."

Kate took the chair opposite her. "How is she?" she said, with a light toss of her head toward the second floor.

"Fine. Kate, she's fine. We had such a good time last night. George got us big dishes of ice cream and the three of us sat in the living room and talked about everything."

"Everything?"

"Not this," she said, touching the tube. "We talked about when the kids were young, remembering funny things. I think we were surprised at the number of happy times we could remember. I caught George and Patty exchanging curious glances."

"That's good. How's she feeling? I tried to ask her Wednesday, but she's kind of closemouthed about her pregnancy."

"It's still a little difficult for her to talk about it. Oh, but Kate, I'm so happy." Tears threatened and she blew on her nails to divert the emotion. "I didn't think I was going to get to see a grandchild."

You might not, my dear friend. It's April and the baby's due in August.

As if Lily could read Kate's thoughts, she said, "I know it's a stretch but somehow I'm not afraid anymore about not living long enough to see the baby. Something tells me I'll be okay."

The kettle whistled and Kate busied herself with the teapot. She put the mugs and spoons on the table and took the chair opposite Lily. "I can't get over how good you look today. The medicine must be working."

"Maybe. And maybe it's the medicine in here," she said, tapping her chest. "Patty's here and tomorrow Michael and Debra arrive."

"When will they get here?"

"Michael's meeting Deb in Philly sometime around noon. He called last night and said they should be here about four but not to worry if they're late." She raised her eyes to meet Kate's. "I think he knows, Kate. Did you tell him?"

"No."

"Patty must have then."

Kate didn't answer.

"I guess Deb knows too if Mike and Patty know. I don't care. You were right, my friend. Can't imagine what I was thinking of. How could they not notice?" Lily spread her fingers out on the table, scrutinizing her nails.

Kate saw her hands tremble and reached across the table to touch them. "It's okay now."

"I know. I'm feeling better and the kids will be here tomorrow. I knew my prayers would be answered."

"What prayers?" Patty asked from the doorway.

Lily raised her arms in greeting and Patty shuffled across the tile floor in slippers that looked like stuffed toy animals. She bent and kissed her mother's cheek.

#

Philadelphia International Airport, even with all the latest modern improvements, was a crowded jumble of people, baggage, transport trolleys, confusing signs, and unintelligible announcements.

Michael stopped in front of a bank of video screens to check the gate and concourse for his sister's flight. The clocks above the screens gave the time in ten different locations around the world. It was eleven-thirty in Philadelphia.

He stopped at the newsstand, bought a copy of *Business Week* and a candy bar, and started down Concourse "C" to the waiting area. He had an hour to kill.

The waiting area was crowded and he looked it over carefully before choosing a seat. Avoiding the milling noisy children smearing sticky hands across the windows overlooking the runways, he settled into an uncomfortable plastic chair attached to three similar seats and opened his magazine. It was difficult to concentrate even though he limited his reading to a quick scan of the lead articles.

Ten minutes later he checked his watch, stood and walked toward a coffee shop on the other side of the waiting area. At the counter he ordered black coffee. There were no tables available so he started to return to his seat when he noticed a dimly lit waiting room near an unattended check-in counter. An area designated for a small airline that apparently had no arrivals or departures scheduled for some time; the quiet room looked inviting. He took a seat away from the main aisle. It was too dim to read comfortably so he watched the constant flow of traffic.

"A good place to escape 'far from the madding crowd,' if you'll forgive a quote from Thomas Hardy."

Turning quickly, Michael saw he was not alone. A woman sat in the row behind him. She smiled

"You startled me. I thought I was alone."

"Finding any kind of solitude in this madhouse is almost too good to be true, isn't it?"

"You're right. You wonder where all these people are coming from and going to. Especially on a Saturday morning."

"It never ends. I think I spend half my life in airport terminals or taxies."

"Even weekends?"

"Weekends are the worst, finishing one job and going on to the next. Monday mornings in another location are the usual rule for me."

She spoke with a slight accent but Michael couldn't quite detect what it was. *Not French, thank God*, he thought. He twisted in his seat so that he could see his companion better. She was a large woman and he guessed her to be in her forties or fifties. Dressed in a well-cut suit and tailored all-weather coat, a beautiful leather bag lay on the seat next to her.

"I guess I don't know how lucky I am then. I rarely have to travel more than a few blocks to see my clients, the ones who don't come to the office, that is."

"You work in Philadelphia?"

"No. New York. I'm with a brokerage firm near Wall Street."

"Ah," she whispered, nodding her head knowingly. "The world of finance. Fascinating isn't it?"

"I've always loved it. Are you in the same field?"

"Almost. I work for the government and during the course of my assignments I often deal with various investments and funds. My diploma says I have a degree in law but I've never actually practiced as an attorney. I've been with the State Department for thirty-one years."

She didn't offer more information but Michael was intrigued. He still couldn't identify the accent and as he listened it became more pronounced.

"You're on your way to the next assignment?"

"Yes, this time in London. I'll be gone for three or four months."

"Months. That must be hard on your family."

"There is no family to speak of. It would indeed be difficult."

Michael didn't know how to respond to her lack of family and she didn't seem willing to expand on the subject.

Just then a large group of people, speaking in a foreign tongue and all talking at the same time, stopped in the concourse in front of them. With waving hands and faces filled with expressions that matched their raised voices, they were obviously having a difference of opinion. After a heated exchange, the matter must have been resolved because they resumed their journey through the terminal.

She smiled. "They were speaking Hindi. Something about the lack of directions someone had given them."

"Hindi? And you recognized it?"

"My family came to this country from India in the late forties. I was a toddler so I never really spoke the language fluently but I can pick up a word or two."

"Must be an asset to your career."

"Sometimes, and you, young man? Why are you hiding in a quiet little nook in this airport?"

"Meeting my sister, who's flying in from Chicago. We're going to our parents' home in upstate Pennsylvania for kind of a reunion. My sisters, I have two, and I haven't been together in about five years."

"Ah," she said quietly. "Most important to keep close to those who love you and whom you love."

"I know. I think we're all very sorry we haven't."

"It's never too late to mend fences."

Michael wondered briefly if his limited comments had hinted at broken fences or whether his companion was very astute.

"You seem troubled."

"It's not a happy reunion. We've just learned that our mother is dying of cancer." He sucked his upper lip between his teeth to muffle the crack in his voice.

"Mercy of God," she whispered, her fingertips lingering close to her lips as if in prayer.

Michael looked away, regretting he'd been so open with his trouble and wondering why he had been so quick to share the news.

"There are no easy answers to some of life's problems," she said quietly.

"I'm sure we're not alone. It's the first time we've all come together in over five years and I think we realize, with shame, that the reason for our getting together is our mutual guilt and sorrow."

"Sorrow yes, guilt no. No matter what has occurred in the past, what you do now is the only thing that needs your true concern."

"I guess you're right."

She inched forward, putting her hand on the back of the seat in front of her. “Every life has its sorrows and joys. They cause pain and happiness and the echoes of those emotions lodge in the heart. Echoes can be felt for a long time—perhaps forever. It is not necessary to fear them, however.” She paused.

He watched her with fascination.

“Pain recedes, and while there may be scars, the echoes in your heart serve as a reminder that one has faced a hard time and survived. There are always lessons to be learned.”

Michael couldn’t find the right words to acknowledge hers. He knew she was trying to be kind and he tried to smile.

The woman rose and picked up her bag. “I must leave and go to the other end of the terminal for my flight. I chose this place because it was the only quiet corner I could find and I am glad that we have met. Have a happy reunion young man, in spite of the circumstances.” She moved along the row of seats.

Michael stood, eyes focused on her back as she moved away. “Wait!” he shouted. Sidling along the row of seats between them he put out his hand. “I’m Michael. Michael Hoffmann. Thank you…”

She took his hand in hers and it was larger than he’d imagined. It felt warm and soft, like a comforter on a cold winter night. “Everyone calls me Singa. It’s the closest anyone can come to my name.”

“Thank you, Singa. I appreciate…”

“It will be all right, Michael Hoffmann. I will add my prayers to yours.”

He watched her disappear around the corner, blending into the crowd moving through the terminal. He looked at his watch. They had spent thirty minutes together.

The echoes in your heart, he thought. *What did that really mean?*

CHAPTER TWENTY-EIGHT

Michael jingled the change in his pocket and then stopped, remembering how annoying he'd found that habit in his father. His eyes darted from face to face as the passengers of flight 954 from Chicago streamed through the door to the waiting area.

Their eyes met at the same instant and he grinned as he recognized his sister. Her hair was several shades lighter and she looked smaller than he remembered. He pushed through the crowd and wrapped his arms around her.

"Hi Deb," he said into her hair.

"Mike, I couldn't see you at first. I was getting worried."

"You knew I'd be here," he said, steering her away from the flow of traffic.

They stood off to the side, identical hazel eyes assessing each other. "Your hair is lighter," he said.

"You seem taller."

"Let's get out of this crowd. Do you need to stop before we go to the parking lot?"

"No, I'm fine. I have one suitcase besides this, though." She held a small overnight case in her left hand. "We'll have to go to the baggage area."

As they walked down the passageway, Michael kept one hand protectively on her back. "You look great, Deb. A little thinner than I remember."

"Thank goodness. You look good, too. Where's Simone? Didn't she...?"

"She couldn't be with us this weekend. I've made arrangements to stay a couple of extra days. Might not go back to New York until Thursday or Friday. How about you?"

"I kind of left my return to Chicago open. They're very good at work. My ticket officially says Thursday but I can change it if I want to."

They watched luggage tumble around on the turntable and then Michael darted in and retrieved the suitcase Debbie pointed out.

He slammed the trunk shut after putting his sister's suitcase inside and saw her place the smaller case on the back seat, slid into the passenger side of his car, and snap the seat belt into place.

"Ready?" he asked.

"Ready as I'll be for this visit, I guess."

He saw her shiver and turned the heat on low. Pulling out of the huge airport complex, he signaled his turn onto the expressway, saying, "At least we have a nice day for the trip. I called Mom last night and told her we'd probably be there by four."

"I guess Patty got in early last week."

"Tuesday, I think."

For several minutes, they didn't speak while Michael maneuvered through some challenging lane changes as they fought the congestion leaving the airport.

"I'm anxious to get there and afraid of what we'll find." Michael's hands gripped the steering wheel and he waited for a response. "Have you spoken to anyone?"

He didn't see Debbie shrug her shoulders. "I spoke to Mom last week."

"Kate picked Patty up in Wilkes-Barre. I talked to her this week." Michael said, remembering the surprise telephone call from his sister.

"Kate?"

"No, Patty. She called me from Kate's house. I don't know how much you know, Deb, but Mom's not in good shape."

"Kate told me."

"Did you know she's on oxygen?"

"No."

"She is, and Dad's fixed up a bedroom downstairs. She's sleeping in the sunroom so she won't have to climb stairs."

"Oh darn, I didn't know that. Guess this *is* going to be tougher than I thought." She shivered again and pulled the sleeves of her leather jacket lower on her wrists. Michael noticed and asked, "Want more heat?"

"No. I'm okay. You'd think living in Chicago I'd be used to cold and damp."

"This is different. You're upset and anxious."

"When did you learn about Mom's cancer?" She turned in her seat slightly to watch Michael who was staring through the windshield. She noticed his white-knuckled grip on the steering wheel.

"Just this week."

They crossed a tall bridge over a railroad track, the tires making a high-pitched squeal as they sped over the metal grillwork in the roadway.

Michael looked at the dashboard, noticed the speedometer showed he was traveling at 60 miles an hour and eased his foot off the accelerator. "I understand you knew earlier."

"I wasn't going to come to Pennsylvania until August as I usually do so Kate had to tell me. Summer may have been too late."

"You don't know that," Michael answered quickly.

"It doesn't look good, does it?"

"No, but it's so hard to believe. Mom was always…"

"Until five years ago Mom was healthy."

"Right, but I was going to say 'always there.'"

They drove for several miles without speaking, lost in their own thoughts. The road became less crowded as they left the suburban areas. Fields, recently plowed for spring planting, rolled past the windows and the terrain became steeper. The sky, almost cloudless when Debbie landed in Philadelphia, had turned gray as heavy clouds appeared on the higher elevations ahead of them.

Debbie sighed. "I'm not looking forward to the reunion."

"Why?"

"I'm scared. We've never had to face a death in the family."

"Granny Steeb died two years ago."

"We'd left home by then and she was old and sick for a long time. It's not like your own mother. I'm not ready for any more bad times, I've had enough."

"Bad times? Oh, you mean your divorce? That was two years ago."

"Don't be so damned superior, Michael. It isn't attractive."

"Sorry, Deb. I didn't mean to be unfeeling. I guess I assumed you were over that." His mind briefly flashed to Simone and the divorce he was facing. *Not now,* he warned himself.

Debbie didn't answer, turning her head to stare fixedly at the scenery flashing by. "You don't get over some things," she said quietly. "They stay with you forever."

Michael didn't know what to say. Was that the kind of echo Singa meant? He took a quick look at his sister and noted her ashen face and the tight, hard line of her jaw as if she were biting down on something. "Want to stop for some lunch?"

"No, thanks."

"We could stop for coffee. I think we should talk before we get home," he said, slowing to read the signs for the next exit. "There's a diner ahead. We could stop there."

"What do you want to talk about that we can't discuss in the car?"

"I don't know, maybe it would be a bit more comfortable. Let's stop, okay?"

"If you'd like."

Michael signaled their turn at the next exit and stopped at the bottom of the access road. The diner was to the right and he turned and pulled into the parking lot. There were only three other cars outside the shiny building built to resemble a railroad dining car. "Come on, Sis. Let's try and relax a little before we get there."

Inside they slid across the red leatherette benches of a booth next to the front windows. Three men and a woman were seated on stools at the counter and they turned briefly to see who had come in. Muted country-western music drifted from overhead speakers. A waitress gave them menus, took their order for coffee and left.

"I don't know if I want anything, Mike."

"You probably haven't eaten anything all day. What did you have?"

"I had breakfast before I left," Debbie said, absently looking at the plastic coated menu.

"Well then, eat something. I'm having a burger and fries," Michael said, closing the menu and pushing it to the side of the table.

Debbie ordered a chicken salad sandwich and then turned to look out the surprisingly clean window.

"We've got to face it, Deb," Michael said softly.

"I know. It's such a shock and the closer we get to Eagleton the more I dread it."

"You don't think these things are going to happen in your family. We've all been so damn busy with our own lives."

Debbie didn't answer but Michael saw her fold her lips in as if stemming a reply.

"How are you, Deb?"

"I'm okay. I love my job and I have a beautiful apartment overlooking Lake Michigan."

"Friends?"

"Some. Enough."

"It's been two years since you divorced Jim. Any male friends?"

"No."

Her answer was too quick and not very convincing but her bitterness was unmistakable so Michael changed the subject. "I asked you before if you'd talked to Patty and you said you hadn't so I guess you don't know that news."

She looked up sharply. "What news?"

"Patty's pregnant."

Debbie's mouth dropped open and her eyes widened. "Pregnant?" she stammered. "Oh for God's sake, as if we don't have enough to worry about. What the hell is the matter with that idiot? She isn't married, is she?"

Michael reached across the table and took one of Debbie's hands, noting that it was icy cold. "No, but wait a minute, Deb. It's not such bad news."

"Not bad news? It couldn't be worse news. Mom doesn't need anyone else to worry about, another responsibility. She's…"

"Mom's delighted with the news."

"I don't believe it," Debbie said, pulling her hand free. "This is crazy. What else?"

"Patty's not married, and not going to be from what I gathered, but the baby is very much wanted."

"Oh, swell. Just what this family needs is an illegitimate kid. What's Patty going to do? Where's she going to live? Damn that brat…"

"Debbie, calm down. This might be the only bright spot on the horizon right now. Mom is delighted with the news. She's always wanted a grandchild."

"She wanted a grandchild she could fuss over, brag about. She's not going to be around." Debbie's voice rose with her exasperation and

Michael looked around to see if they were garnering the attention of the other occupants. They all seemed engrossed in their own conversations.

The waitress brought their meals, refilled the mugs with coffee and left. Debbie looked at the food in front of her and pushed the plate several inches away. "I can't eat. I'm too upset. It's not bad enough we have to rush home to watch our mother die, now we're going to be exposed to Patty's…" She couldn't find the words to express her disgust.

Michael picked up his hamburger, looked at it and then put it back on the plate. "Deb, this isn't going to help anything. What Patty has done has no effect on you. We can't bring our emotional baggage to Mom right now. If she's pleased…"

"Pleased," Debbie muttered.

"Stop it," Michael growled. "Dammit I thought you'd be glad to learn Mom was happy about something right now. We're going home not to watch her die but to visit with her and each other like she wanted us to. I won't stand for any upset." His hands were rolled into tight fists at either side of his plate.

"You won't stand for any upset?"

"You've got that right. Whatever goes on there while we are together is going to be as pleasant as any of us can make it. Is that understood?"

Debbie looked away. Her heart was an icy lump and her stomach had contracted into a tight knot.

"Can you understand that Deb? I know this is a shock to you but we're all in the same boat."

"Not Patty, evidently. She's found some favored position by screwing around with God-only-knows-who."

"Debbie!" Michael hissed. "The reason for this trip is to be with Mom and each other. It's what Mom wants and for now that's good enough for me. Forget what's happened in the past. Forget whatever personal problems we might have right now."

They stared across the shiny white Formica table, their eyes locking. Her shoulders, hunched in tight rebellion to the news she'd heard, relaxed a little and she sighed. "Okay. If that's what everyone wants, who am I to cause trouble. Let's get this damn visit over with and get on with it. There's nothing I can do about any of this." She reached for her purse.

"Aren't you going to eat anything?"

"No. Go ahead if you want to. I can wait. I'll find the Ladies Room and be back in a few minutes."

She slid out of the booth. Michael saw her ask the waitress for directions, then move along the long counter, turn to the right and disappear through some swinging doors.

He took a bite of his sandwich, made a face and pushed it away. Rising he put three singles under his plate and went to the cash register.

The waitress hurried behind the counter, noting the uneaten food on the table. "Was there a problem with your food?"

"No. The lady doesn't feel well. She'll be better once we get home."

He waited for Debbie at the door, his empty stomach sending an acid reminder of the coffee he'd swallowed to the back of his throat. When she rejoined him, her eyes were red and he knew she'd been crying.

"Come on, Sis. We're almost home." He held the door open for her and they left the shiny warm interior of the diner. The sky had become a dull gray and as they hurried across the parking lot, big sloppy raindrops slapped the roofs of the cars.

CHAPTER TWENTY-NINE

Following the excitement of Michael and Debbie's arrival, and the huge dinner Kate had prepared in honor of the reunion, the house was unusually quiet. Lily, exhausted, excused herself and went to rest.

Debbie offered to help Kate and Patty in the kitchen but they sent her upstairs to rest. "You look pooped," Kate said, shooing her toward the stairs. "It's been a long day for you. We'll have coffee and dessert when your mom wakes up."

George sat in the living room paging through the sports section of the evening paper. Michael, in Lily's chair, had the financial section of the paper across his lap. He could hear Kate and Patty giggling over something in the kitchen. He looked up as his father sighed and put the paper into the magazine rack at the side.

"Think I'll go out to the garage," George said softly. "I'll get some things done while Lily's sleeping."

"Need help?" Michael whispered.

"No, that's okay. You've had a long day and a tough drive. Take it easy." He touched Michael's shoulder as he walked past his chair.

For several minutes Michael sat in the quiet room alone, then stood and went to the kitchen. The door was closed.

"Hey. Need any help in here?" he said, re-closing the door behind him.

"Since when have you become domesticated?" Patty asked.

"You'd be surprised at what I've learned to do."

"You mean Simone isn't the *Betty Crocker* of New York City? How come she's not here?"

An icy silence settled over the room for a moment as Patty and Michael stared at each other. "That's enough, Patty," Kate said quietly. "Let's keep this on a pleasant level."

"I was just kidding," Patty sulked.

Kate turned to Michael. "We're all finished in here, but I saw your dad go into the garage. Maybe he needs a hand."

"I asked but he said he didn't. What's he doing out there anyway?"

"Who knows? He often goes out there if your mother's resting."

Michael stood uncertainly, facing the two women who seemed so comfortable with each other and with what they were doing. Women's things, he thought. Most women find contentment in such simple activities. Remembering the cold kitchen in New York where Simone found such little comfort, he shivered.

"We'll have coffee and dessert when your mom gets up, which should be in about..." Kate turned to look at the wall clock, "forty minutes or so."

"Well, I'm going upstairs and listen to the radio," Patty said before she closed the kitchen door. "Call me when Mom gets up."

"That's so strange," Michael said.

"What?"

"Seeing the kitchen door closed. When we were all home it was never closed."

"Things were too busy then. With your mother sleeping downstairs now, we close it so it's quieter for her."

"I know. Just seems strange."

"How are *you* Michael? We haven't had a chance to talk much yet, but we will before you leave.

"I'll be here until Thursday or Friday, I think."

"That's good. Lily was almost beside herself until you both got here earlier today." Kate frowned. "Debbie looks like she's taking this hard."

"Deb doesn't handle emotions well, I guess. I don't think she's over her divorce yet."

"Oh?"

"Just a feeling I got from a couple of things she said in the car. She'll be okay."

"I'm going into the living room to read. Want to come with me? There are some library books next to your mother's chair. Don't suppose they're your cup of tea, but you might find something."

"Thanks, but I think I'll go out and see what Dad's up to."

Kate watched him walk down the path toward the garage. She folded the towel she had been holding and put it on the counter. They're all wound tighter than a railroad watch, but it'll get better, she thought with forced optimism. She snapped off the overhead light; a soft glow from the range hood light cast eerie shadows across the room.

#

The familiar scent of dust, oil, bug spray, and old tires filled Michael's nostrils. He shook his head and looked around, marveling at the things he recognized and wondering why many of them had been saved.

When Michael entered the garage, the fluorescent lights over his father's workbench were on. George was seated on an ancient dining room chair tipped back against the wall.

"What's up?" Michael asked.

George leaned forward, the legs of the chair making a soft thud as they settled onto the concrete floor. "Just thinking."

Michael leaned against the workbench. His eyes scanned the tools hung neatly on the pegboard nailed to the wall. Nostalgia overwhelmed him. "How many times did I sit in that chair, Pop, while you fixed something I'd broken?"

"A good many, I guess."

"Probably too many."

"You didn't break much."

"Looks like you haven't thrown much away over the years."

"Your mother and I like to hang onto things I guess. Lot's of this old junk will have to be thrown out when she..."

Michael looked up sharply at the sob that escaped from his father's lips.

"Don't Dad."

George pulled a white handkerchief from his back pocket and wiped his eyes, then blew his nose loudly. "I try not to let your mother ever see this. That's why I come out here. To be alone."

"Want me to leave?"

"No." His reply was quick and would have been sharp if it wasn't tempered by his softened voice. "No, that's all right, Son."

Michael swallowed with difficulty and then scuffed the toe of his sneaker on the rough mat in front of the workbench. He waited until he was able to speak again. "Mom's..." He stumbled. "Mom's cancer has been a shock to us all, Pop, but I know how hard it must be for you. If I can..." *What the hell am I trying to say? Help? What help can any of us be? And, how dare I say I know how hard this is for him?*

He looked helplessly at his father; their eyes met and penetrated a distance that had been established long ago. He moved to his father's side and knelt on the dusty floor. His arm went around the body of the man who had fathered him, his head rested on the flannel shirt that smelled of *Old Spice Aftershave.* He gulped air into lungs that ached, and curled his fingers into the soft cloth. Sobs, from somewhere deep inside him, shook his shoulders. He felt his father's hands touch his hair and come to rest at the nape of his neck. For several minutes there was no stemming the flow of tears or the agony that had been imprisoned in the young man who now reverted to the little boy.

When he raised his head, he saw his father's face contorted with pain, cheeks wet with tears, his eyes squeezed into tight lines beneath brows drawn together in a shaggy line across his forehead. Michael struggled to his feet; unable to steady himself, he slowly sank back to the floor. He leaned back beside his father's chair, his head resting against the rough wall, one hand clutching the frayed flannel sleeve. For several minutes there were no sounds except the trembling gasps taken as both men fought to regain their composure.

"I'm sorry," George's voice was hoarse.

"Sorry for what? Crying? Don't be. I'm not."

"No, Son. I'm sorry for so goddamn many things I couldn't even begin to count them." Anger and regret gave strength to his words even though they were almost whispered.

Michael pulled his legs in and crossed them, sitting in a Yoga position. "I guess none of us have been…" He was lost. He wanted to say so much but was unsure of where to begin, where to go.

"Don't go blaming yourself, it was all my fault. I don't know where I failed but I know I did. You kids…"

"We always loved you. I did." Michael's voice was strained and thin. "You did your best."

"And God knows I loved you. But I was wrong. I wanted to fit you into patterns I was comfortable with, sports for you, girl things for your sisters. I missed out because I was so damn blind and now it takes this—this tragedy to make me realize what I missed and what I made you kids miss. Your mother is a saint."

Michael listened to his father's quiet sobs. He felt small and helpless and he didn't try to stem his tears. His tongue flicked out the corners of his lips and drew the salty drops into his mouth, savoring the anguish they represented. "None of us tried hard enough. I wanted to do my own thing instead of giving any thought to trying to please you. Just because we were different didn't mean we couldn't have been friends. I'm sorry. Sorry I learned that lesson too late. "

George jumped from the chair and strode to the end of the workbench. He turned suddenly, staring intently at his startled son. "Dammit, it's *not* too late. It's too late to be sorry. It's too late to change anything in the past. All the tears in the world ain't going to make a difference. But it sure as hell ain't too late to fix things." His hands were drawn into tight fists hanging close to his side as if waiting for a chance to flail at an enemy.

Michael rose slowly, keeping his back to the wall. For several seconds no one spoke. He extended one hand helplessly and then let it fall. "What can we do?"

George turned his back, his head falling forward as if he'd found something of great importance to study on the dusty floor. His quiet voice was strong as he spoke. "We can make every minute left to this family count for something. You mother's happiness and comfort are the only things I want." He turned and looked over his shoulder. "And by God that's what's going to happen. She's so damn happy right now that you kids are here, nothing and no one is going to spoil that. Do you understand?"

Michael nodded.

"She wanted you to be here together and you are. She wants you to be *friends* and that's what's going to happen." It was an ultimatum.

Michael crossed the space between them and put his hands out. Not in an effort to shake hands but palm up as if he was expecting to receive something. He stared into eyes the same color as his and his sisters and felt his father's work-roughened hands close over his. His mouth opened to speak but no words found their way to his lips.

George pulled his son to his chest and for the first time in over thirty years hugged, really hugged the young man he'd given life to.

For several moments it seemed as if there were no other souls on earth, then Patty called faintly from the back steps. "Mike, Dad, coffee's on."

George reached for the string to turn the lights out. He looked at his son. Signs of the emotional stress they had shared were plainly visible.

"We'll be there in a minute," he called through the open door and turned to Michael who was standing behind him in the darkened garage. "Let's wait a minute, okay?"

"Yeah," Michael said, taking a handkerchief from his back pocket.

Five minutes later they walked side by side up the narrow path. Through the window in the back door, they saw Patty, Kate and Lily moving around the brightly lit kitchen. Father and son's shaky, determined smiles were hidden by the darkness.

CHAPTER THIRTY

Lily sat at the kitchen table, the plastic lifeline trailing across the back of the chair and disappearing into the dining room. Her hands nervously moved the china and silver. Kate slid two folding chairs into place. A cool, damp gust of air entered the warm room with George and Michael.

"Where's Deb?" Michael asked, closing the door behind his father.

"She's still upstairs. I called a few minutes ago but she didn't answer. Maybe she fell asleep." Kate looked uncertainly toward the stairs between the living room and dining room. "She looked so tired when she arrived; and all through dinner."

"I'll get her," Michael said, hurrying from the room.

"Tell her it's chocolate cake, your mother's recipe," Kate called after him.

Michael took the stairs two at a time. Debbie's door was closed so he tapped gently on the wooden panels, leaning in toward the door to detect any sound from within.

"Come in."

He pushed the door open. A small nightlight next to the bed was lit and the room glowed in soft pink tones. Debbie sat on the side of the bed but it was obvious she'd been resting, the pillows were crumpled and her hair was mussed.

"You okay?"

"Sure."

"They're waiting in the kitchen. Chocolate cake and coffee."

"I heard you and Dad come in. Where were you?"

"In the garage."

"The garage?"

"It's Dad's sanctuary."

"Sanctuary?" Debbie parroted.

Michael crossed the soft carpet and sat next to his sister on the side of the bed. "He goes there when Mom's resting. He—he can cry there without her knowing it."

Debbie shivered. "Dad cry? God," she whispered.

"It's strange, isn't it?"

"Strange isn't the word. Everything is different, everything is such a mess."

"No, Deb, different, yes, but not a mess. Remember what I said in the car? We're going to make the very best of this for Mom's sake. And for Dad's, too. I need your help."

She shook her head. Michael defending their father?

"I know. That sounds strange coming from me. But, think about it, Deb. Why are we here?

Because Mom wants us to be. Because we're not going to have her with us for very long."

"I can't."

"You can! You're shocked by the way Mom looks, by the prognosis and what we all face. We can't change that or make it go away. The only thing we can do is make the best of things. And the best thing we can do is to salvage what Mom wants most. She wants us to be together and to be friends." He echoed his father's recent words.

Debbie quietly recalled Kate's message about being friends with her brother and sister. "That's easy for you to say."

"Easy?"

Her hand smoothed wrinkles in the bedspread. "Your life's easy. It's perfect." Her jaw was set in a hard line.

"No one's life is perfect."

"Well, yours seems to be, at least to me. Good job, wonderful home, so I hear. Beautiful wife. No worries."

Michael grimaced. *Perfect? Hardly.* "Isn't it more important to make Mom happy than to dwell on personal hurts right now?"

Debbie stared at the closed blinds. "I'm trying, Mike. I'm devastated by Mom's condition. Look at her. She's pitifully thin, pale, and hooked up to oxygen." She stared into her lap.

"It's just as hard for all of us."

"Not Patty, apparently. She's bubbling over with happiness."

"She's a source of joy for Mom, but she's hurting, too. This trip home wasn't easy for her. You know how Mom's always talked about grandchildren. You and I haven't been any help there."

"Stop it!" Pain flooded through her. Wasn't it her desire for a child of her own that had brought on the end of her marriage?

"Debbie I don't know what it is that haunts you because you've never shared your hurt with anyone that I know of. Is it your divorce?"

She pulled away from him, turning toward the blank wall behind the bed.

"Whatever it is, you have to put it aside for now. Please. Can't you help me, help us, make this a pleasant time for Mom?"

She rose, walked to the bureau and picked up her hairbrush. Staring into the mirror she saw the pale, ravaged face of a stranger. Waves of pain swept across the image. Put it aside? How? Michael was right. She couldn't share her pain with anyone. She had to get over this by herself just as she had all the other difficult times she'd faced. Staring past herself, she looked at her brother's image.

He stood, extending his hands to his sister. "Come on," Michael said.

"Let me brush my hair."

"I'll wait in the hall."

"You don't have to." She drew the brush through her hair in slow, rhythmic strokes. It was soothing to her, daunting to Michael. He watched the oh-so-familiar motion and immediately pictured Simone sitting at her vanity, the nightly ritual of her brush moving through the long strands of black hair. He shivered and moved toward the door.

"Ready?" he asked.

She shrugged. "Ready as I'll ever be, I guess."

Michael put one arm around her shoulder. He couldn't remember actually touching his sister for such a long time. How had they become such isolated islands? "We don't have a lot of time. Whatever baggage we carry with us has to take a back seat for now. Agree?"

She nodded, wanting to move closer and yet unable to. "You're different."

"Not really. Same old Mike." His humor was strained.

"No, you're different."

"How?"

"You were always smart, always organized, but isolated from all of us."

The same words he had just thought. "I'm sorry."

"Don't be. We're all guilty. All except Mom." Her words were stumbling from her lips and she squeezed her eyes closed. "You seem to be able to see things more clearly than I can. I want to be helpful. I want to make this time special for Mom."

"Well, together we can do that. What's the problem?"

"I don't know. Dad seems so different, you're different, even Patty is different. I don't remember her joining in like she did at dinner. Did you see them make a special kind of eye contact? I felt shut out, like I always do." She leaned against her brother, feeling his wooly vest against her cheek.

"It's okay, Deb. Those are natural feelings. You'll get through them. Trust me."

Trust him? Had she ever been able to trust any man? Charles' face flashed into her mind and she felt herself relax slightly. *Maybe he's right. Maybe it is time to trust but how do I learn that overnight?*

Michael opened the door and stood aside. "You said I was different? We're all different and we'll probably never be the same after this visit."

When had Michael become a leader? She shrugged her shoulders in confusion.

"Hey up there," Patty called from the foot of the stairs. "We're cutting the cake. If you don't hurry, you'll miss it."

He touched Debbie's arm and they descended the stairs, walking quickly through the darkened dining room into the kitchen, bright, warm, and filled with family. *Maybe the healing of the Hoffmann family has begun.*

CHAPTER THIRTY-ONE

During the night and very early hours of the morning, a soft, soaking April rain had drenched the garden and the young leaves of the lettuce and radishes glistened wetly. Patty looked up as she heard someone open the back door.

"You're out early," Michael called, starting down the steps.

"It's so nice today. I wanted to check the crops."

"Pretty wet in there, isn't it?" He walked down the path,

"Well, the plants are only ankle high so only my feet are getting soaked." She stepped over the row of bushy lettuce and joined her brother. "Kate gave me seeds for the lettuce, and radishes, and the onion sets. I plan to put cucumbers over in that area." Patty gestured with the small cultivator in her hand, dark, damp earth clinging to the curved tines.

He surveyed the freshly dug earth. "Who dug the garden?"

"Jackie Bolton, one of Kate's nephews." They stared at the neat rows of plants. "I'm going to plant tomatoes and peppers over there," she pointed, "but Kate says it's too early now."

"Quite an ambitious project, isn't it?"

"Not really. You mean because I'm pregnant? The baby's not due until August. Dad said he'd help me."

They stood in the early morning sunshine, contemplating the little garden that had provided a topic for them to talk about. Now there didn't seem to be anything further to say.

Michael linked his fingers together and stretched his arms above his head. "Thought I'd take a walk. Want to come along?"

"Where are you going?"

"Up to Indian Hills."

"Sure. I'll put this in the garage," she said, tapping the dirt from the cultivator.

The climb to Indian Hills Park was steep, the road changing from pavement to gravel at the top of the hill. The access road that surrounded the entire park curved to the right but they continued walking straight ahead on the footpath leading to the playground area and the small concession stand that opened at the beginning of every summer.

They walked past the baseball fields, tennis courts, and soccer fields, then started down one of the wooded nature trails to the picnic area.

"I hated this place when I was a kid." Michael kicked a small stone and watched it disappear into the ankle-high growth along the path.

"I loved it."

A wooden bridge spanned a gully with runoff water from the playing fields. The stream, fed by last night's rain, ran between lush green plants. They paused, leaning on the rough boards. "Why did you like it?" Michael asked.

"Oh, remember this is where the high school softball team played. Other times it was quiet and peaceful here. It was a nice place to be when you wanted to be alone."

"I hated it because it reminded me I wasn't interested in baseball and soccer and that was a disappointment to Dad."

She snorted. "He told me I should play tennis. 'That's a girl's sport,' he said."

Michael sighed and started walking again. Patty followed. This wasn't a subject either of them wanted to pursue.

Reaching one of the picnic areas, Michael brushed some twigs from one of the benches.

"Think it's too damp to sit?"

Patty pressed her palm against the rough board. "Not too damp. We've both got jeans on." She straddled the bench.

The woods around them were tinged with soft green spring growth. In the summer the foliage would limit visibility but now they could see from one area to the next. The underbrush, weeds, and wild flowers hadn't started to fill in the space between the trees. Two squirrels rushed around and around the rough bark of a huge oak tree in mad pursuit, either fun or a serious mating game.

"How are you, Patty?"

"I'm doing fine. Doctor Bob says I'm healthy as a horse. He's given me some vitamins and a suggested healthy diet."

"I'm glad you went to see him."

She grinned at him. "No more junk food, at least for a while."

"What are your plans? I'm not prying, just curious, and you don't have to answer if you don't want to."

"Plans? That's funny. I never made plans before. Just went from place to place, job to job. I know I can't do that any more." She bit her lower lip; her fingers traced the grain in the rough boards of the picnic table. "That's all changed now. Everything is changed."

"Life's full of changes." Michael remembered Debbie's words from the previous night. 'Everything is different,' she'd said.

"I know. Some of the changes are tougher to take than others."

"You mean Mom?"

The squirrels ran noisily through the carpet of dead leaves to another tree and began the ritual all over again.

"Yeah. All I can think of is how unhappy I've made her. I was so selfish." Patty pushed the heavy sweater sleeves up above her wrists.

"We've all made mistakes and we'll carry them with us. We can't let those thoughts dominate us, though. No one can do anything about the past except…"

"Except regret it?" Patty interrupted.

"No. Except remember and learn from it."

The sun was warm in the protected area and Patty slipped her arms from the bulky sweater she wore over her shirt and jeans. She took in a deep breath, smelling the earthy scent of the forest floor and the sun warmed air.

"Mom's happy about your baby." Michael concentrated on the activities of the squirrels.

"I know. I felt guilty about telling her after Kate told me how sick she was."

He searched her face. "Guilty? Why?"

"She's always wanted a grandchild. Now she might not get to see this one. It's so unfair." Patty pulled a crumpled tissue from her pocket and wiped her eyes.

"We don't know that. We have to be positive. You've made her happy, given her something to look forward to."

"And that makes me feel guilty, too."

"Why?"

She shrugged her shoulders. "Because…"

He waited.

"Because it's such short-term hope. She must be thinking of what she's going to miss."

"Maybe she's thinking of what she has right now. Mom always was an optimist."

"Damn, Mike," Patty shouted, standing up suddenly. "What the hell has she got to be optimistic about now?"

"I don't know. Maybe her family is enough for her."

She started to walk away, then returned to the bench. "Sorry I yelled at you."

"It's okay. We're all tense." He patted the bench. "Sit here. It might help if we talked."

She slid onto to the bench next to her brother and he noticed her shiver.

"Where's your sweater? The air is damp, you'll catch cold."

"It's on the bench over there," she said, pointing across the picnic table."

Michael reached across the table to retrieve the sweater. He hung it over her shoulders.

"Thanks."

"Talk to me, Patty. You've always been so quiet around me."

She sighed. "I don't know, Mike. I guess we're not the average American family. Growing up, you and Debbie seemed to have made a place in the family for yourselves. I always felt so…"

"Left out? God, I'm sorry if that's the way you felt."

"It wasn't you, you were eight years older than me, Debbie was five."

They listened to the forest sounds for a few moments.

Patty dug a dry twig from between the rough boards of the table. "Dad always acted as if I was just there, not important."

"He had a hard time being a father, I think. I talked to him for twenty minutes in the garage last night and I think I finally figured him out. He wanted to be a good father but he wanted children who fit into pre-designed packages. The son should be rough and tumble and the girls should be domestic."

"Dammit then he should have accepted us as we were." She clenched her jaw into a grim hard line.

"He should have, but he didn't and we can't change that. He realizes that now. He's changed. You must see how he's trying." Michael remembered the scene that took place in the garage.

"Why?"

"Because it's what Mom wants and he loves her."

"Because he feels guilty. Maybe that's what being a family is, feeling guilty." Her face echoed the bitterness of her words.

"I don't think so, Patty. That's too cynical to believe. We didn't try hard enough."

"Mom did."

"Yes, Mom did."

Patty stood and walked to the center of the clearing, pushing her arms into her sweater as she walked. She didn't move for several moments and then, throwing her arms out she whirled around. "I don't know if I can do this. I can handle being pregnant and alone but I don't think I can face Mom's death, and everything else…"

Michael rose and walked toward her, stopping a few feet away. "What's everything else?"

"This damn family healing she wants. Mike, I've been on my own for so long. When I got Mom's letter, I laughed. 'Family healing', I thought. 'What a joke.' Now we're together and I can see you've changed. But what's with Deb?"

He took her arm and they left the clearing, moving down another footpath. "You have to be patient with Debbie. She's gone through a tough divorce. She can't seem to get over it and she won't talk to anyone about it. At least not here, maybe she has in Chicago, but I doubt it."

"We've all had hard times. I know I have. I guess you haven't. Your life has always been perfect."

Those words again. If they only knew, he thought with a grimace.

"You were able to ignore Dad's pressures and do what you wanted. You were the one who inspired me to leave, really."

"I did?"

"Yeah, you did what you wanted to and I thought I could, too. The only problem was, you were focused on school and career and I really didn't give a damn what I wanted to do. I just started off anyhow."

"It must have been adventurous, moving around like you did."

She stopped and he turned to look at her. "Adventurous? Maybe. I wasn't afraid to take chances, some of them worked out and some didn't. I had no ties so it was easy to turn my back and move on."

They began to walk again, the path becoming less defined, moving deeper into the forest where the nature trails became more primitive.

"But that's changed now? Can you adjust to being in Eagleton again?"

"I didn't think I could at first. Something made me decide to come home. The baby, I guess. I didn't learn about Mom's illness until after Kate picked me up at Wilkes-Barre."

They came to a rickety wooden bridge across another small stream. The water was moving rapidly, coming from springs higher up the mountain. Again they stopped and leaned on the railing.

"I'm glad you're happy about the baby." Michael spoke softly, unsure of his sister's reaction to the mention of the child she was carrying.

"It was such a shock to learn I was pregnant. I thought I had the flu."

"No father in the picture? Just tell me to shut up and butt out if I'm being too nosy."

"No, Mike. No father and there never will be. That's all I want to say. I told Aunt Kate and she probably told Mom but nobody's digging for details and that's the way I want it. My decision to keep the baby was the right one. I'm happy about that. I can do this alone."

"You're going to be okay, Patty."

Suddenly she grinned at him. "You're like Mom. I thought she was the only Pollyanna in the family but you must have her genes."

He looked around and then up at the sky above them. The clouds had disappeared and the sky was a pale, clear blue. "Come on. Let's start back. We've walked a long way. It'll be lunch time before we get home."

They walked faster as they retraced their steps. When they came to the top of the hill and started down the paved road again, Patty pulled on her brother's sleeve.

"Thanks, Mike."

"Thanks for what?"

"For being the big brother. For talking to me." Is this the first time we've truly felt the sibling connection, she wondered? Patty grinned.

Michael patted her shoulder. "We're going to make it, Kid. You and I—and Dad—we'll have to help Debbie but it's going to have to be low-key help. She's fragile."

"I'm not good with fragile things. More used to thick diner dishes than fine china."

"You'll do okay. Dad will help, too."

They swung down the hill, their steps lighter than when they trudged up earlier.

When Michael and Patty turned the corner and entered the alley behind the house, they saw Kate's car pulled up close to the fence.

"What's Kate doing here?" Michael adjusted his pace to Patty's quickened steps.

"I don't know. Last night she said she wouldn't be over until evening. I thought she said you and Deb would have to cook dinner." They hurried along the narrow roadway.

As they rushed up the walkway, Kate opened the kitchen door. "Don't panic."

"What do you mean don't panic? What's going on? Where's Mom?"

Kate held the door open for them. "She's at the hospital."

The color drained from Michael's face. "Oh, God!"

Patty held the back of a chair for support. "What happened?"

"About forty-five minutes ago your mom felt very sick, dialed 911 and then called me. When I got here the paramedics were with her. They called Doctor Bob. He's meeting them at the hospital."

"Why didn't you go, too?"

"Because she insisted I wait here until you kids got back."

"Where's Debbie?" Patty sounded breathless.

"We don't know. This morning…"

"Don't know!" Michael shouted.

"Wait. Calm down, please. First of all, your dad is with your mother. I called him at work. Before she left in the ambulance she made me promise to wait here for you. She said Debbie got a long-distance telephone call this morning and right after that, left the house saying she was going out for a while."

Michael thumped his fist on the back of a chair. "Where'd she go? How? She doesn't even have a car. My car is down at Brownie's garage for an oil change before I drive back to the city." He paced across the room. "Wait. There's a bus stop three blocks away."

"There's no use in speculating, Michael, take my car and go to the hospital. Call me as soon as you know anything. I'll wait here for Debbie." Kate pressed her keys into Michael's hand. He jerked the door open and hurried out.

"What a stupid ass she is, leaving Mom alone," Patty snarled, as she followed her brother down the path to the alley.

CHAPTER THIRTY-TWO

The unmistakable smell of antiseptics greeted them as they entered Eagleton General Hospital and rushed to the reception desk.

"Lillian Hoffmann was brought in by ambulance about an hour ago. Where can we find her?" Michael rifled the words across the counter to the lady in the pink pinafore.

"Let's see, dear," she murmured, striking the keys on the computer keyboard. "She hasn't been admitted, so she must still be in the Emergency Room. Down that hall," she said, pointing to the back of the large reception area. "Follow the red footprints on the floor."

They were rushing across the room before she'd finished her sentence, oblivious to everything until they saw the Emergency Room sign with an arrow pointing to the hallway on the right.

In a minuscule triage office, a young woman in a wrinkled blue jacket and white pants, sat at a computer. She looked up as Michael and Patty filled the doorway.

"Missus Hoffmann?" Michael panted breathlessly, not from hurrying but from the panic.

"She's in one of the examining rooms. Let me check on her. Wait over there." She pointed to the dismal little room across the hallway.

Michael and Patty followed her directions but neither wanted to sit on the scarred, gray chairs bolted to the floor. An untidy pile of dog-eared magazines and newspapers covered a low table in a corner of the room.

Patty paced across the scarred tiles. "God, this place is depressing."

Michael kicked one of the battered legs of the nearest chair. "I don't give a damn right now what's wrong with this room; I want to see Mom. Where the hell is Dad?"

"Right behind you, Son. She's going to be okay. Doctor Bob and another specialist are with her now. They think it was a reaction to a new medicine."

"Thank God. Can we see her?" Michael put his arm around his father's shoulder. Funny, he hadn't noticed until now that he was taller than his father.

"Soon. They want to keep her overnight but she's making a big fuss about going home."

Patty stood a few feet away from the men. Fighting tears, she pressed her lips together, grimacing with the effort.

"She'll be okay, Patty," her father said, holding out his arms to her.

She cautiously moved into the offered embrace, unable to remember her father ever giving her a hug. Her efforts to contain her emotions failed and she broke into tears as she rested her face against his rough jacket.

"Michael. Patty." Doctor Willistein called from the doorway.

At the sight of his smiling face, the tension in the room eased.

Michael stepped forward as he asked, "How is she?"

"She's doing fine. We think it was a reaction to the last prescription. She took the first dose at six-thirty this morning. We have her on an IV and her vital signs are all back to normal."

"What happens now?" Patty's voice was as weak as her trembling knees and she wondered where the nearest bathroom was.

"I want her to stay overnight but she insists it will cut into the reunion you are having. If she's still stable after," he pushed his sleeve up and studied his watch, "say two o'clock, she can go home. Right now her attitude is crucial and having her children together is important."

Michael and Patty exchanged knowing glances.

"How long are you going to be in Eagleton, Michael?" Doctor Bob asked.

"Four or five days. Maybe I can extend it a day or two before going back to New York."

"Good. Patty, how are you?" The doctor took one of Patty's hands in his. "Can't have you getting too upset. You're going to be a big help to your mother when your brother and sister leave."

"I know. I'm fine. Just scared when we heard Mom was here."

Doctor Willistein's name was paged over the intercom. "Have to go. George, if Lily goes home this afternoon I'd like someone to be with her all the time for the next twenty-four hours. Call me anytime you need me, but I don't anticipate any more emergencies. We've put Lily back on the prescription she was taking up until this morning."

They watched him rush down the hall and disappear through double doors that flew open at his touch.

The dreary little room seemed to shrink around them and they moved into the brighter hallway.

"When can we see Mom?" Patty asked her father.

"Soon. I was with her when they told us you were here. A nurse will come and get us in a few minutes."

As he spoke, a young woman with blazing red hair swept through as the double doors opened again and said, "Mister Hoffmann, you can all go in to see Missus Hoffmann now. You know where she is?"

"Thanks. Yes, I'll find her."

Lily lay in a narrow bed behind drawn curtains. Her face was ashen but when they entered, her smile lit up the whole area. Michael and Patty took turns leaning over the bed to kiss their mother. George sat on the only chair in the enclosure.

"Gosh, you scared us," Michael said, stepping back from the bed.

"Sorry. I knew I needed help and no one was around so I called 911. Maybe I shouldn't have panicked."

"Where the heck was Debbie?" Patty tried to keep her tone less than as angry as she felt.

"I don't know. She left after the nurse came and was with me."

"She had no right to leave you alone. What a jerk."

"Don't, Patty. She didn't know. If you kids weren't here for this visit, I'd have been alone anyway."

"But we *are* here and one of us should have stayed in the house."

"Michael, that's not practical. Really it was a fluke. It never happened before and it will never happen again." Lily looked from one to the other. "Come on, cheer up. I'm fine. I'll be going home soon. We'll take up where we left off."

"Where did Debbie go?" George stood and moved to her side, taking one of her hands in his.

"I don't know. She got a telephone call this morning. I heard her answer the phone after the home healthcare aide came in. While we were in the bedroom, Debbie called through the door that she was going out for a while."

"Well, she couldn't have gone far, she had no car."

"And Kate hadn't planned on coming over…" Michael muttered.

"Oh, God, Kate. Mike, we promised to call Kate." Patty gripped her brother's arm.

"I'll find a telephone and call her," Michael pushed the heavy curtains aside and hurried away.

"And I'll find a bathroom," she said, following him through the curtains.

#

At two o'clock they brought Lily home, settling her in the living room since she refused to go to bed. "I've been lying down for hours. I'm okay. Don't hover over me," she said, as Kate, George and Michael crowded around her.

Patty thundered down the stairs. "She's not upstairs."

"Where the hell can she be?" Michael's fist slapped noisily into his open palm.

"She'll be back. Really, she's a grown woman. If she needed to get out for a little while, there's no harm done," Lily said softly.

"There was harm done. You needed help. She shouldn't have left you alone."

"Patty, what happened this morning was completely unexpected. The aide didn't notice anything wrong when she checked me and helped me bathe. Now let's drop it. I'm all right and Debbie will be home soon."

"How about tea?" Kate asked.

"Sounds good to me," Patty said, following Kate into the kitchen.

"I'm going to the garage," George said. "Sure you'll be okay now?" He touched Lily's shoulder.

"I'm fine. Patty, Kate, and Michael are right here." She smiled up at him, trying to will the worried furrow from his brow. "I'm fine," she repeated.

Michael sat in his father's chair, picked up the newspaper and tried to read, but his attention was on the pale woman in the chair next to him.

Lily leaned back, listened to the door close behind George and the sounds of Kate and Patty in the kitchen. It was good to be home, but where *was* Debbie?

CHAPTER THIRTY-THREE

When the telephone rang, Debbie was putting the last of the breakfast dishes in the dishwasher. It must be Kate, she thought as she picked up the receiver. When she recognized the voice, she sank into the nearest chair.

"You're not easy to find."

"Charles, how in the world did you find me?"

"As I said, it wasn't easy. You're the fourth Hoffmann in Eagleton I've spoken to this morning. The other three weren't nearly as nice."

She could hear his humor and grinned in spite of the tremors that rocked her heart. "I can't believe this. Really, how *did* you find me?"

"Process of elimination. I called three other Hoffmanns in Eagleton. The last one said, 'Oh you must want the Hoffmanns that live on Mountainview Terrace.' She even looked up the number for me. Is she a relative? I think her listing was for Harold Hoffmann."

"I don't think so. This is so weird. Why did you go to all this trouble? I was going to call you in a day or so."

"I missed you."

Until she heard his voice, she hadn't realized how much she missed him. "I miss you, too."

"I was worried about you. How's your mother?"

Debbie heard her mother and the aide talking in the bathroom. Panic filled her as she realized they would be finished with her mother's bathing soon. How could she explain a telephone call from Charles? It would raise questions—a new man in her life might prompt questions about her ex-husband and she certainly wasn't prepared to answer those.

The aide followed the same routine every morning; she checked Lily's vitals and helped her with her bath and getting dressed. Then she settled her into her favorite chair while she made the bed and straightened up the room. They would be coming through the kitchen any minute.

"Charles I want to talk to you but this isn't a good time. Give me a number where I can reach you later."

"I'm leaving in two hours for Denver. That means I have to leave for the airport in about an hour."

"I'll call you."

"Promise?"

"I promise."

"What's wrong, you sound upset?"

"I can't talk now."

He gave her the numbers for his home and his pager. "Call me, honey. I miss you."

She scribbled the numbers on a piece of paper next to the telephone. "I'll call...and thanks."

"For what?"

"For caring."

She put the receiver back in the cradle just as her mother and the aide came into the room.

"Who was that, dear?" Lily asked.

"Nothing important. Can I help?"

"You do what you have to, Miss Debbie. I'll tend to your mama." Charlene Wilson loved caring for Lily, who, unlike so many of her patients, made no demands and usually had a cheerful smile, especially for the past few days. She shared her patient's excitement about the children's visit. "She'll be ready for visiting in about twenty minutes and then I'll be out of here." Charlene's words were softened by her Jamaican accent and her face beamed as she trailed behind Lily, holding the oxygen line.

Debbie was on the verge of tears. Was it the call from Charles? Of course it was yet she knew she had to return his call out of her mother's hearing. Dashing up the stairs, she closed her bedroom door and took her cell phone from the pocket of her carry-on bag. Her fingers trembled as she punched in the number for Charles' home.

"Oh damn," she muttered as she saw the red light come on indicating the battery was too low. Her hands flew back to the pocket for the charger, but there was no charger. How could she have left Chicago with the phone and forgotten the charger? She sat on the side of the bed, vivid memories of her turmoil when she left Chicago sweeping over her.

Panic gripped her. She had to find a telephone outside the house because her mother would hear her if she used either the kitchen phone or the one next to Lily's bed in the converted sunroom.

Rising quickly, she took a jacket from the closet, picked up her purse and hurried back to the living room. She heard Charlene and Lily talking behind the closed double doors to the old sunroom.

"Mom, I'm going out for a while. I'll be back later."

"Okay, dear. Don't hurry."

Closing the front door, she stood on the top step, uncertain of which direction to take. Turning toward Union Boulevard, she hurried down the sidewalk. A bus ran along this avenue fairly regularly. She would find a telephone downtown.

She glanced at her watch. In about forty-five minutes Charles would be leaving home for the airport.

Twenty minutes later she stood on the pavement in front of Wilburn's Department Store. She tried to visualize the lounge area at the back of the second floor. Ladies' room, sitting area, was there a telephone booth? Telephone booths were almost nonexistent these days. She pushed the revolving doors, hurried past the familiar counters filled with jewelry and cosmetics and stepped onto the bottom step of the escalator. Another quick look at her watch showed she'd taken four minutes to make this decision.

It was early and no one was seated on the comfortable couches arranged in a U-shape in the Ladies' Lounge. The dignity of the old establishment was calming. Debbie scanned the area for a telephone. There! A long narrow table beneath an ornate mirror filled an alcove at the back of the room. An upholstered chair was pushed under the table that held a telephone. A large vase of silk flowers was doubled by the image in the mirror.

Seating herself, she slid a calling card from her wallet and picked up the receiver. The store operator asked if it was a local call she was making. Giving the Chicago number and her card number, she waited.

Charles answered on the first ring. "Where are you?"

"In a department store downtown."

"Why the cloak and dagger procedure?"

"Mom was busy with her healthcare aide and I didn't want to disturb her."

"You mean you didn't want to be overheard."

"That, too."

"Ashamed of me?"

"Of course not."

"Tell me, hon. How are you handling things?"

"Oh, Charles, it's so hard to see her like this," Debbie's voice quivered. "She's so thin and tired. She has to be hooked up to oxygen twenty-four hours a day now."

"Are your brother and sister there?"

"Yes. She's happy about that. Oh, damn, I don't know what to think, everything is so different. Michael's all resolved to the situation and being the happy leader of the group. My father has changed so much. And Patty is…"

Charles waited.

"Patty's pregnant. No husband, no father in the picture, and she's larking around like this is the best thing since sliced bread. It's disgusting and everyone seems to be so delighted with the whole thing."

"You sound as if you're dwelling on the wrong things, honey. Why not take them all as they are. You're not going to change them. Enjoy the time you have with your mother and who knows, maybe you'll all get to know each other a bit better. You admitted you were estranged."

"We were." She didn't notice the past tense.

Charles paused a moment, then said, "This reunion might be the answer to that problem. Want me to come there to be with you?"

"No!" She immediately regretted her sharp response. "I mean, it would be impossible, where would you stay? Besides, you're busy. I'll be home in a week."

"I'd stay at a hotel. I'd be there if you needed me, but I don't want to intrude. I'm just worried about you. You know how I feel." He hesitated, then said, "I love you."

The tears that had threatened earlier suddenly filled her eyes and she looked at her reflection in the mirror. A tired stranger stared back at her, face ashen, eyes sunken into shadowy circles above her cheekbones. She bit her lower lip to control the trembling. "I'm so confused and you're being kind. Why did this have to happen? Why now?"

"I don't have those answers, sweet. All I know is that you are a very special lady. You're hurting, and I feel helpless. I want to help."

"I know, but what can anyone do?"

"That's it. No one can change any of the things you're worried about. You'll find you need each other."

"That's what Mike said last night. He said we couldn't change anything that has happened and yet we'll never be the same."

"Wise fellow, I'd like to meet him someday. And Patty, too."

She wanted to see him, be in the same room with him, feel his arms around her. This was crazy. He was in Chicago, leaving for Denver. Next week she'd return to Chicago. "I miss you," she whispered.

"I can cancel this trip and be with you in a few hours."

"No," this time her response was soft. "I'd love to see you but that's not fair or practical. I'll be back next week."

"I meant what I said before."

"What?"

"I love you."

She clenched her jaw, "I think I love you, too, but I'm afraid."

Charles didn't respond immediately and Debbie waited anxiously. "I don't ever want you to be afraid again, Deb. We'll talk when you get home. In the meantime, you have my pager number. If anything—anything at all comes up, or if you want to talk, day or night, get in touch with me. If you need me, I'll be there as fast as a modern jet can make the trip."

She smiled. "Thanks."

"For what?"

"For caring."

"You said that before. I really do care, sweetheart."

"I know," she whispered.

For the next three hours Debbie visited the library, the museum and the park. Reluctant to go home, she wandered along the familiar streets of the city she'd called home for more than twenty years. The words Charles had spoken echoed in her mind, bringing her back time and time again to the real problem. He was right, there was nothing any of them could do about the past. They had to deal with what was happening in the family now.

At two o'clock she turned a corner and stood in front of Sacred Heart Church. The stone building nestled into the tall shrubs that had been small when she'd first attended Mass with her mother. She looked up at the steeple outlined against the pale sky.

Something compelled her to walk up the wide concrete walkway to the huge arched wooden doors. Were they locked? Tentatively, she pulled on the brass bar and felt the heavy door glide noiselessly toward her. She stepped inside and was immediately enveloped in the quiet, cool comfort of the sanctuary. How long had it been since she'd been here—or in any church? She couldn't remember. Tiptoeing down the center aisle she genuflected, slid into a pew, pulled the kneeler down with her toes, and knelt. For a while she stared at the statues that flanked the altar. The flickering candles to the right of the lectern drew her attention and she noticed she wasn't alone.

A woman knelt in prayer at the feet of the Blessed Mother. As Debbie watched, the woman rose, genuflected and walked up the aisle to the right. Debbie heard the soft sound of the heavy door closing behind her.

She bowed her head, folded her hands. Prayer didn't come easily and she stumbled through the words she remembered from long ago. When she raised her head the room looked brighter and she chastised herself for being melodramatic.

When she left the church, the sun had faded and a cool breeze blew off the river. Debbie shivered in the damp air, zipped her jacket and turned the collar up around her neck. A bus stop and bench were on the opposite corner. She walked toward it, noticing the same woman who had been praying in Sacred Heart sitting there. The woman looked up as Debbie approached.

"It's getting cooler. You should have a coat instead of that jacket."

"When I left home this morning I didn't think I'd need a coat."

"Never can tell this time of year," the older woman said.

"Is there a bus soon?"

"Which way are you going?"

"Mountainview Terrace and Union Boulevard."

"Number 27. Should be here in five minutes or so," the woman said, glancing up at a sign on the corner listing the buses and times. "That's the one I take; runs every half hour."

Debbie sat, shrinking into her collar, putting her hands in her pockets.

"You new in town?"

"Oh, no. I was born and raised here. I've been gone for a while though and forgot how the buses ran."

"They change anyhow. I noticed you in church."

"Yes, I saw you, too."

"I go almost every afternoon. Light a candle and say a few words. I lost my husband six months ago. We were married fifty-three years."

"I'm so sorry." Why did those words always sound so inadequate?

"Well, you have to go on. Never had any children so it's just me and the cat now."

Debbie looked at her, marveling at how calmly she related this sad news.

"Albert, that's my husband, he always wanted children but God didn't see fit to send us any. I made up for it by becoming a teacher. Helped lots of other people's kids get through third and fourth grade. Taught catechism, too. You go to public school?"

"No, I went to Sacred Heart. I don't remember seeing you."

"I taught catechism to the children who went to public school. You got your lessons from the sisters."

"Yes," Debbie smiled as she remembered her school days.

"Don't see many young people in church during the day anymore, just us old folks who have the time and the need to go there. I was surprised to see you. Everything okay?"

"Not really. I'm here because we recently got word my mother's dying of cancer."

The woman crossed herself quickly, her gloved thumb lingering at her lips a moment. "I'm sorry to hear that. It's hard to watch a loved one suffer. I know; Albert was sick for a little over a year. We had each other though."

Again Debbie marveled at the cheerful tone of her companion's voice.

"Nothing like family when trouble comes. Thank God I have a sister and three cousins, although the two boys weren't much comfort until the very end. Nevertheless, when you have difficult times, it's sharing those troubles that gets you through. That and prayers." She smiled smugly, pleased with her speech.

A bus labored up the hill and they turned to watch its progress. It was stopped at a traffic light a block away, but they both stood and moved toward the curb.

"You got family here?"

"A sister and brother. We've all left Eagleton but came home this week to be together for one more time."

The woman patted her arm. "Never lose sight of the blessings you have right here at home, dear. You may travel all over this world, but your heart is never away from your home and nothing and nobody is ever going to take the place of your family."

The bus pulled to the curb and the door opened with a whoosh of compressed air. They climbed the steps, dropped coins into the meter box and took seats on opposite sides of the bus. Debbie looked out the window as they traveled through town, turned onto Union Boulevard and moved toward the suburbs. The scenes were familiar and yet strangely different. The woman left the bus at a junction near a new mini-mall.

As Debbie road home to her parents, sister and brother, the words of the woman from church traveled with her. For the first time in her life she realized how much she needed her family. It was a strange revelation.

CHAPTER THIRTY-FOUR

The sky had turned a milky gray and it was chilly as Debbie hurried up Mountainview Terrace. She was anxious to get inside where it was warmer, where her family would be. For once she was looking forward to being with them. The day had had a profound effect on her attitude and she smiled as she climbed the steps to her parents' home. She didn't notice Kate's car at the curb. Pushing the door open she was greeted with a blast of warm air.

She closed the door behind her, and the soft click of the latch sounded loud in the empty living room. The doors to the sunroom were closed, so was the door to the kitchen. *Mom must be sleeping*, she thought.

In the kitchen Kate was peeling potatoes. She looked up when Debbie opened the door. "Hi."

"Hi. Where is everyone?"

"Your mother's sleeping. Michael and Patty are in the garage. Your Dad went down to the bowling alley. Just to see the guys, he'll be back for dinner."

"Michael and Patty are in the garage?"

"I think they wanted to talk and didn't want to disturb your mother." Kate ran cold water over the potatoes in the colander and put them in a large saucepan. "I started dinner."

"Thought you weren't coming over today."

"I wasn't but there was a little emergency."

"Emergency?" Debbie's heart constricted and she glanced at the closed kitchen door.

"Your Mom is okay now but there was a problem earlier. She called 911 and then me. The EMTs came and took her to the hospital. She's been home since around two o'clock."

"What happened? Are you sure…?"

"She's all right. Doctor Bob thinks it was a bad reaction to a new medicine she started this morning. He wants someone to be with her for the next twenty-four hours."

Debbie started toward the door.

"Wait. I just checked on her. She's sleeping."

Debbie slid into a chair at the table. "Oh, God. Why was she alone? Where was Michael or Patty?"

"They weren't here. Neither were you," Kate added.

For several minutes the only sounds in the kitchen was the pot of water hissing on the stove and the ticking of the wall clock. Glancing at the clock, Debbie was surprised to see it was after four o'clock. Where had the day gone? Why had she wasted so much time?

"Why don't you go out and see what they're doing in the garage?"

Debbie sighed and rose. On the ride home after visiting Sacred Heart she'd been so full of hope. Now what?

Kate patted her arm as she walked to the back door.

Outside she looked at the garage. She could see a light on but the door was closed. As she walked along the path to the back alley the sky seemed to descend and wrap clammy arms around her. She pulled her jacket closer to her body and reached for the doorknob.

Michael sat on a folding chair leaning against the garage wall. Patty perched on an upturned crate of some kind. They looked up as she entered.

Patty catapulted herself from the crate, sending it scraping across the concrete floor. She screamed, "How could you leave Mom alone?"

Debbie was stunned. "What?"

"Debbie where have you been?" Michael stood.

Patty glared angrily, her fists clenched at her side. "You left Mom alone."

The assault pushed Debbie back against the door. "Wait a minute, what's going on. Why are you blaming me?"

"You were gone a long time Debbie, where were you?" Michael stared intently into Debbie's face.

"Mom had to call 911!" shouted Patty. "She was so sick they had to take her to the hospital in an ambulance." She turned her back, unwilling to allow her sister to see her vulnerability.

"Kate said…" Debbie took several steps forward, then stopped. There was too much animosity in the room. She trembled. "I didn't know…"

Patty turned back to face her sister. "You *would* have known if you were here. You selfish little… "

"Patty! Debbie!" Michael barked.

"Look who's calling me selfish. The little brat who spent years wandering around God only knows where, worrying Mom."

"At least, I'm here now."

"Oh yeah? Where were you and Mike when this happened?"

"We went for a walk—up to Indian Hills Park." Michael spoke softly.

"Oh, so it's okay for you two to leave but not me. If anyone should have been here all day, it was you, Patty. You're the one who's going to live here and be with Mom. You're the favored little mother, aren't you?"

"You pigheaded spoiled brat "

Michael put a restraining hand on Patty's arm. "Let's all calm down. We were concerned, Deb. Anxious about Mom and then worried about you. We thought it was strange you'd disappeared for so many hours."

"Don't go sweet-talking her, Mike. She's being her typical arrogant self."

"Just who do you think you're calling names," Debbie spat back.

"You. How could you just take off like that?"

"I wasn't the only one. You say I'm selfish? You're trying to put fault on me because you're just as guilty. You think if you can make me feel responsible it will take all the blame away from you."

"Where were you Deb?" Michael, trying to remain calm, pressed the chair back against the wall.

"I had to think. I went downtown on the bus. Wandered around, doing nothing."

"Huh! You wandered around while Mom was being hauled to the hospital."

"She needed you. We thought you were here with her in the house all the time. She had to call 911 and then Kate." Michael struggled to keep his voice calm.

"So, you're both excused because you thought I was here? Well, I *thought* you were here."

"You didn't think."

"And so it's my fault? Dammit, we were all away from the house at the same time. And what if this had happened last week when none of us were here?"

"It didn't happen last week. It happened today." Patty's anger forced tears to her eyes. "Don't try and pass the blame back on us. Mike and I left, knowing you were with Mom."

"Don't lie, Patty. You didn't give a thought as to who was here and who wasn't. You just took off. If I'm to blame for anything, so are you." Debbie's eyes flashed from her brother to her sister.

"You were gone more than a few minutes. You were gone most of the day." Patty countered.

Outside, George stood frozen, his hand on the doorknob. He'd been listening to the shouting for several minutes. Grinding his teeth, he jerked the door open and stepped into the garage, pulling the door closed behind him.

"That's enough! All of you! You should hear yourselves! Fighting and blaming each other!

Well you're all guilty, guilty as hell of being inconsiderate." George faced his three children. His hands were clenched in front of him, fists with no one to strike. "Thank God Lily had the strength to call for help. No thanks to you." His voice crackled with emotion.

He looked at each of them, willing their eyes to meet and hold his. "You still don't get it, do you? Your mother's biggest wish was to have you all here with her. To have you together like the family she's always wanted." George's voice broke. "Like the family none of us cared enough about for way too long."

Pain gripped their hearts and forced them to take shallow breaths.

"This fighting and name calling is over. I won't have it. If you can't stop fighting with each other, maybe you shouldn't be here at all. As much as your mother wants to have you here, she doesn't need this. If you can't get along, you're no help to her."

Without another word he turned and walked away. They watched his trembling hand twist the knob and open the door. In their eyes he was suddenly older, smaller, defeated. Even after their father left the garage they were frozen, unable to make eye contact and unsure of what to do next.

"Look, I think we've all said things we regret," Michael turned to face his sisters. "We didn't come here to fight with each other. If there is any blame for what happened today, any blame at all, we share it equally."

Debbie looked furtively at her sister, Charles' soft words of encouragement echoing in her ears. "We have to remember, no matter what, we're here because Mom wanted us to be."

"She wanted us to forget the past and become friends again." Michael waited for a response.

"Friends?" Patty whispered.

"Friends," Michael repeated. He looked from one sister to the other. Their faces were pale, their heads bowed. "Can we make a new start?"

They nodded.

Debbie felt Patty's hand touch hers. She unclenched her fist and took her sister's hand, then reached for Michael's. Joined in a circle, the air thick with emotion, their anger began to recede, replaced with a strange feeling of togetherness.

"Let's go inside. Deb, Patty, you help Kate. Dinner tonight is going to be a pleasant, friendly gathering. Right?"

"I'm sorry." Debbie whispered to Patty.

"Me, too," Patty said.

He squeezed his sisters' hands. When he closed the garage door behind them it was as if they were stepping into a new world, still gray and chilled but even in the evening gloom it appeared a bit brighter than before.

When they entered the warm kitchen Kate looked at their faces, noting changes she couldn't readily identify. Something had happened.

Michael left the women alone. He glanced at the closed doors to the sunroom, and climbed the stairs, slowly, without enthusiasm, as if reluctant to leave yet unable to choose another option.

In the kitchen Kate faced the two young women, "Your Dad's in with your Mother. Debbie, you can make the salad and Patty, you can set the dining room table."

The directions lifted some of the weight from their shoulders. Cautiously exploring simple conversation, the sisters moved around the kitchen, doing things women had done since the beginning of time, preparing for their families, smoothing hurts, accepting responsibilities and facing uncertain futures. It was another start.

Lily noticed the forced humor, the careful glances and the undercurrent of managed stress at dinner that night. She smiled. Had they come to terms with each other, resolved things? Or had something happened during the day that she didn't know about? *Is it because of me, or is it something else?* It didn't matter. They were here. They were together. Tomorrow she wanted to talk to each of them. There was too much she didn't know about their lives and too little time to fill in the blanks.

CHAPTER THIRTY-FIVE

Lily watched George tiptoe into the room.

"You smell good," she whispered.

"Damn. I was trying not to wake you."

"I've been awake for about ten minutes."

George sat gingerly on the side of the bed and took one of her hands. He grimaced as he felt the bones roll around under the paper-thin skin. "How do you feel?"

"Tired."

"Go back to sleep. I'll get breakfast in the cafeteria so I don't make noise in the kitchen."

"Any of the kids up?"

"No."

For several moments they held hands. George leaned down and kissed Lily's cheek and she put her other hand around the back of his neck, her fingers sliding up through the silky hair above his collar. "I love to smell your face right after you've shaved."

"Don't let them upset you, Lil."

“They won’t.” She hesitated. “Yesterday was rough on everyone. We’re all walking a tight rope. I noticed the strain at dinner last night.”

George quietly remembered the real reason for the tension.

“This is hard for them. It isn’t what I wanted but I guess it’s what I should have expected.”

He watched her face crumple as she fought tears.

Sliding down onto the bed he put one arm under her shoulders and held her close. She was so light—too light. He sighed and stood.

“Go back to sleep. Call me if you need me.”

“I will. Go on. It’ll be all right. The girls will help and Kate will be over later.”

He left the room and she listened for the click of the back door. She could picture every movement because she knew him so well. In spite of everything she grinned as she leaned back on her pillows. The humming of the oxygen machine helped her to drift back to sleep. She was so tired.

#

Charlene patted the pillows into place and quickly looked around the room. Everything was in order.

“All done, Miz Lily,” she said coming into the living room.

Lily sat in her chair, a library book open on her lap. “Thanks for everything.”

“Now don’t you go getting everyone upset again today, you hear?”

"I promise. I was so surprised when you came in this morning and knew all about my joy ride to Eagleton General yesterday."

"I have my spies." Charlene's sister-in-law worked in the emergency room and was there when Lily arrived. She recognized the name and, on her afternoon break, called Charlene.

"You must."

"I'll go out the back. My car's in the alley."

"Bye."

"Bye."

Lily heard her speak to Patty who was sitting at the kitchen table. After the door closed Patty came into the room. Her slippers made scuffing noises as she crossed the dining room.

"How are you?"

"I feel much better, dear. Just a little tired."

"Can I get you anything?"

"You know what? I'd love a cup of tea."

"I'll bring you one."

"No. Let's have it together in the kitchen."

Seated at the kitchen table Lily watched her youngest daughter put the kettle on and get out the mugs. In her bulky flannel gown and robe she didn't look pregnant, just incredibly young.

"That Kate," Patty said. "She left the tea pot all primed. All I have to do is pour the water in."

"What are your plans today?"

"Nothing that'll take me away from you."

"Don't be silly. I won't have you become a prisoner here because of what happened yesterday."

"What happened yesterday was too scary to ignore, Mom."

"What can't be ignored?" Debbie said from the doorway.

"Good morning, honey. Sleep well?" Lily twisted in her chair, holding her lifeline up so it wouldn't become trapped between her back and the chair.

"I slept fine. How about you?"

"I don't have any trouble sleeping. Sometimes it's staying awake that's difficult." Lily smiled as she spoke.

"Want tea?" Patty asked.

"Thanks." Debbie sat next to her mother. She watched her sister in the bulky robe and gown take another mug from the cupboard and fill it with tea.

"Want anything with it?"

"No thanks. I'll get something later. I'm not an early morning eater." Debbie spooned sugar into her mug. "Do you have any maternity clothes, Patty?"

Patty was stunned, small talk from her sister? A mention of concern? An acknowledgment of her pregnancy? "Uh, no. Why do you ask?"

"I just wondered."

"That's it," Lily exclaimed. "You two girls can go shopping today. Wouldn't that be fun? You haven't done that in years."

More like ever, thought Debbie as she watched her sister struggle with a response. "I think that would be a great idea but we aren't going to leave you alone."

"Michael will be here. And if he has plans, I'll call Kate. I know I promised Doctor Bob and your father I wouldn't be alone again—for a while anyhow."

Patty looked at her sister. She was confused. This wasn't normal. "Do you want to?" she finally said softly.

"Sure why not? We can get the bus and go down to Wilburn's Department Store if Michael is going to be home this morning."

Patty looked uncertainly from her mother to her sister. She shrugged her shoulders, "If that's what you'd like to do." During the night she'd promised herself that while Michael and Debbie were here she would contain any anger or antagonistic feelings she had. After all she'd be here with her parents' until… She stopped there, not wanting to move toward the obvious and dreaded future they all awaited.

"Good morning," Michael said, stepping into the bright kitchen. With relief, he noted his two sisters calmly drinking tea and his mother looking happier than he'd seen her since his arrival. "What's up this bright and beautiful day?" he leaned down to kiss his mother's velvety soft cheek. "How's my favorite girl?"

"I'm fine. Did you sleep well?"

"Yep."

"Want breakfast?" Patty asked, starting to rise.

"Not yet, and I can fix it myself. You'd be surprised at how handy I've become in the kitchen. What's everyone up to?" he asked, reaching for a mug.

"The girls are going shopping for maternity clothes," Lily laughed and added, "for Patty."

"Only if you're going to be around. If you have plans, we can go another time. It's not…" Patty was going to say urgent, but that wouldn't be right. Everything had urgency now. How long was Debbie going to be in Eagleton? She realized she hadn't even asked.

"I have no plans at all. I'll be here with Mom. Shopping! Sounds like a great idea." He looked meaningfully at them, a grin lifting the corners of his mouth.

Later, as the two girls were leaving, the telephone rang. Debbie stopped in the doorway. Could it be Charles? She turned and watched Michael take the telephone from the wall fixture. She couldn't hear what he was saying but he continued to talk and waved, indicating the call was for neither of them. Debbie wasn't sure if she was disappointed or relieved.

"Can I get you anything?"

"No, thanks dear," Lily said. "Charlene was here earlier so I had breakfast." She didn't reveal that breakfast was a piece of toast and a promise to eat more later. "Patty and I had tea, too."

Michael perched on the edge of his father's chair. The newspaper was on the coffee table. He reached for the financial pages.

"Was that Simone on the telephone?"

He hesitated. No mention of his wife had been made except for a brief inquiry when he and Debbie had first arrived. "No," he said quietly, hoping his mother wouldn't pursue that topic of conversation. No such luck though.

"You've hardly mentioned her. Is she all right?"

"She's fine, Mom. We've…" He felt trapped. "We're having a problem."

"I was afraid of that."

"You were?"

"Well, you usually talk about her involvement in her charities and theater and this time you never mentioned her. A problem, son?"

Michael took a deep breath but it didn't relieve the tightness that suddenly squeezed his chest. "I don't want to talk about it Mom. You have enough troubles."

"Never too many to be able to overlook yours, dear."

He looked at his mother. The familiar small smile was there. The one that helped when you'd been left out of something at school, or gotten a lower grade than you thought you deserved. "It'll be all right. I think I can handle it okay."

Lily leaned back into the cushions of her chair. She didn't pry.

They listened to the soft murmur of the oxygen machine in the other room. Michael's eyes followed the plastic tubing snaking across the floor and disappearing behind the partially closed doors. The fear that had overtaken him when he heard Kevin's voice on the telephone earlier didn't lessen. Now his mother knew there was a problem with Simone. Damn he didn't need this now. The timing was wrong but then when did trouble know anything about good timing?

He looked at his mother again. Her eyes were closed.

"Do you want to go in and lie down for a while?"

"No dear, I'm just resting my eyes. I feel fine."

Michael squirmed in the chair. "That was my friend Kevin on the telephone before." Damn again. He didn't have to tell her that, she hadn't asked.

"Everything all right at work?"

"Oh, yes. I left a few things that needed follow up and Kevin is taking care of them for me. He's a good friend."

"That's good. Good friends are almost as valuable as family. Sometimes even more so, there's no old baggage, no intimate involvement."

Michael grinned. He read his mother and was amazed. When he was younger, he never knew what she was thinking. "You mean, you can count on friends but you can't always count on family?"

"Well, not exactly."

"You're right about the old baggage. But, don't worry, Mom. Patty, Debbie and I are working those old things out. We're all working at it."

The silence was comfortable and Michael felt himself relax.

"Tell me about Simone."

The words shocked him. His mother never pried.

As if reading his thoughts she said, "I know I've always made it a habit not to ask personal questions but it's different now. I don't have time to find out later."

"Jeez, Mom. Don't think about time, okay?"

"I have to. When something is limited, you can't ignore your need for it."

Her words sounded like an advertisement for a market commodity.

Before he could comment, she went on, "That's why I have to change my rules a little, I need to know what's in each of my children's lives. There are too many blank spaces, and too little time." She looked at her son intently.

"Simone is—was..." He didn't know how to start. Twisting his hands, he stared at the carpet between his feet. "Simone has left me." He heard her quick intake of breath. "But it's okay. I mean I wanted her to leave."

"Tell me."

"Where do I begin? I guess it was wrong from the beginning. Her beauty, her perfect manners, and her connections with the arts charmed me. I thought those characters were important—not only to me, but to my career. It was a stupid basis for a lifelong commitment. And now, I've come to realize I was the only one who made any commitment at all."

"I'm sorry, dear."

He looked at her. She seemed so small. Had both his parents shrunk while he was away, when he wasn't looking? "You have nothing to be sorry for, Mom. Nothing."

"Parents always feel responsible for the failings and hurts their children encounter."

"You and Dad had nothing to do with this."

"Maybe we didn't set a good example."

"Stop that." Michael almost shouted the words as he stood quickly and paced across the room. "Maybe Dad and I had our problems but they were normal growing up problems. Somehow, somewhere along the way, they got magnified and I'm the one who failed to see what was right in front of my eyes."

Lily didn't speak. She waited.

"Dad and I had trouble communicating. I can see that now. But he was always there for us and especially for you. I was the one that was blind." He sighed as he turned back to look at his mother.

"Sometimes your father had a difficult time letting down his guard with his children. He didn't want to see any faults so he didn't look closely at anything."

"I know I disappointed him."

"You really didn't."

"He wanted a jock. He's even admitted he wanted all of us to fit his preconceived molds."

This was a surprise to Lily and she tried to imagine George saying those things.

Michael grasped his hands together and then released them, shrugging the tension from his shoulders. He returned to his seat, leaning forward. "You asked about Simone. She's wrong in how she views what's right and wrong in a marriage but I can't be held blameless. I was blind and so she got away with…" He couldn't share the word adultery with his mother.

Lily waited. She guessed there was more than Michael was willing to volunteer. "How will you handle the separation?"

"I've seen a lawyer. That was what Kevin was calling about this morning. My lawyer wants me to call him about some details. We're getting a divorce, Mom." Michael's voice was apologetic. He knew how his mother felt about divorce. She had never said much about Debbie's but he knew her Catholic upbringing was bruised by her daughter's failed marriage. Now he was going to add to that burden.

Lily closed her eyes. "I always thought marriage was forever, and it should be. But should it be pain and sorrow? I don't think so. No loving parent wants a child to suffer."

Was this a dispensation? Michael doubted it, but it did sound like an acceptance on his mother's part.

"I'm sorry, Mom."

"For what? For making a bad choice? What is the penalty for that? Surely not lifelong misery. If you truly think there is no hope of reconciliation, no hope for a change of heart, then you have to do what will make you the happiest. I've learned that I can't change the facts, I can only accept them and adjust as best I can." The long speech drained her and she sucked deeply on the oxygen feeding her.

Michael slipped from his chair. Kneeling at her side, he took one thin hand in his. "You are an angel. No matter what came along, a tough exam, a fight with Dad, going away to school and not coming back to Eagleton, you took it all in stride. I wish I could erase all the bad times and leave you with…"

"With a perfect life? I think I've had a perfect life—a faithful husband, beautiful healthy children, and now a grandchild in the future. What more could a woman want?"

A longer life, Michael thought, *trouble-free time to spend with that husband, children and grandchild.* He felt hot tears boil against his eyelids. He rested his forehead against her hand, still in his.

For several minutes they remained joined by the bonds that only a parent and child can experience.

"You will do whatever you have to, Michael. And you will find happiness. I know that in my heart. I hope that I can share in some of that before I leave." She felt him jerk as she said those words and quickly went on, "But you can't dwell on the little things, like how much time you have. Kate told me I was lucky to know I was dying, that most people don't have the luxury of being able to fill those last months, days, and hours with what's important. And she was right."

"She always has something right to say. I envy her that ability."

Lily laughed quietly and Michael looked into his mother's face. "She said I could get run over by a truck and not enjoy the bonus of knowing ahead of time. I was furious with her when she said that but after awhile I knew what she meant. What a good friend she has been over the years."

"I'm glad you've had her and will have her. I wish I could be here."

Lily sat up straighter. "But you can't and you shouldn't. You'll know when to be here. This time together was a selfish wish of mine but I'm not apologizing for indulging in it."

"I'm glad you were selfish. I'm happy to be here sharing this time with you. It's made each of us a different—no *a better* person. Talk about selfish. You sure didn't get very generous kids, Lily Hoffmann."

"Hush. I got just the kids I wanted. I love you." This time she reached for his hand and squeezed it lightly. "You'd better call your attorney. Life goes on, Michael. Do whatever you have to, to make it the best you can."

He stood, his knees aching from the tension. "Did I ever tell you you're the best Mom in the world?"

"Often, dear, often." She remembered the crayoned Mother's Day cards. "Often," she repeated softly, watching her tall, handsome, oh-so-young son move across the room to the telephone.

CHAPTER THIRTY-SIX

"I think we should get this out in the open." Debbie sat next to Patty on the bus as it rumbled along Union Boulevard.

"What?"

"Don't act innocent. You know what I mean."

Patty stared out the window. "You mean us?"

"Yep. It'll make things easier. At least while we're here, together." She was strangely comfortable; she'd thought even starting the discussion would be difficult. It wasn't.

"I thought about this a lot last night." Patty turned to look directly into her sister's face. "I don't know how we got off on the wrong foot. Maybe it's a girl kind of thing, competition for attention. Whatever, it doesn't matter. As far as I'm concerned there won't be any more arguments or stuff like that."

"Good because that's what I decided, too."

For several moments the other passengers, and the frequent stops thc bus made, held their attention. When the bus pulled in at the curb in front of Wilburn's, they stepped onto the sidewalk, hesitating before entering.

"Wilburn's has a tea room on the first floor and a restaurant on the top floor. Want to get something to eat? I don't think you had breakfast, did you?" Patty clutched her light jacket to her neck. The early morning breeze blowing off the river was chilly.

"I don't feel like the tea room and the restaurant is only open for lunch and dinner. Is that old diner still on the corner of Ashton and Main?"

"I think so. Let's walk down and see. It's only about four blocks."

As they walked, Patty commented on the familiar stores and marveled at some of the newer additions to the main street in Eagleton "A lot has changed and a lot has stayed the same," she remarked.

"Guess that's the way it will always be. Some things never change and others are always new. I think that's the third or fourth little independent dress shop in that same location over the past five years." Debbie pointed to a small shop as they passed. "I check on it every year when I come home for a visit."

Dilly's Diner was still there. It was built in the forties or fifties and over the years so many additions had been added, it had lost its original appearance. Still, when they entered the main door they faced a long counter with a row of red leatherette topped stools. Along the front windows were booths, still with tall sugar dispenser, napkin holder, and tan and brown plastic salt and pepper shakers.

"Take any booth, ladies," the waitress behind the counter said as she topped off several coffee mugs. "I'll be right with you."

They slid across the red leatherette benches, took menus and were reading them when the same waitress arrived at the side of their table. A thick mug hung on one finger of each hand as she gripped two coffee pots. "Regular or Decaf?" she asked.

"Decaf," they both answered and ordered toasted English Muffins.

Patty watched her sister nibble her muffin as she slathered jam on hers. "Don't you want any jam? It's good."

"No, thanks."

"You're skinny."

"I am not."

"Well, you're skinnier than before, when we lived at home."

Debbie stirred her coffee. It was strong and she'd already added three creamers. "That was a long time ago. When we were all home, I mean."

"Yeah, it seems like a long time ago but you know, it really isn't. I left five years ago. How long has it been for you?"

"About eight years. Michael never did come home after college. I think he lived with a friend in Brooklyn before marrying Simone and moving to the city."

"You like Chicago?" Patty asked, sipping her coffee. "God, this stuff is strong. I can't get it light enough to drink."

"Neither can I. Don't drink it if you don't like it."

"I'm not," Patty caught the waitress's eye. "Could I have a glass of milk?"

Debbie smiled. It was strange to see Patty so unburdened. "Yes, to answer your question. I do like Chicago. In fact I really love it. I have a good job and a very nice apartment."

"I know you got a divorce, Mom told me. You want to talk about that?"

"No." Debbie retreated.

"Well don't get bent out of shape about it. I understand. There's plenty I don't want to talk about either." She smiled.

"Sorry. It's a touchy subject. I never even told Mom and Dad about it. Just that it happened. My marriage was a big mistake. Let's leave it at that."

"Okay."

"What about you? You traveled around so much. You must have some stories to tell."

"Not many I'd want to share. I guess you are referring to my pregnancy." Automatically her hands went to the bulge hidden by the oversized shirt and jacket she wore. "I told Mom a little about it but there's nothing really to tell. It was a dumb thing to do on my part."

"You weren't alone."

"I know. But it was still dumb. I was always so cautious, you know? It takes one slip up though."

"And you decided to keep the baby?"

"It's the right thing to do. It was what I wanted and I made that decision even before I realized it was what I wanted. Does that make any sense?"

Debbie looked around the diner. Talk about babies made her nervous and she couldn't help reflect on the time when she'd hoped to have a child. That, too, seemed so long ago and yet so painfully current.

They finished their breakfast, but remained in the booth. The early morning crowd had thinned out and there were only a few men left perched on the stools. She admitted to herself she was enjoying this time with Patty.

"I told Aunt Kate about the baby even before I told Mom," Patty continued, swirling the remaining milk in her glass. "She's easy to talk to."

"I know."

"You know, it doesn't make any difference what happened to your marriage, or what happened to me in Florida. What matters is now." Patty pushed her hair behind her ears. Debbie saw her hands tremble.

"You mean with Mom?"

"Yes, with Mom, but also with us. You and me and Michael."

Debbie reached for her purse. "I'm not sure I know what you mean?"

"You know damn well what I mean. When Mom found out she was dying, what was the one thing she wanted?" Patty waited.

Debbie shrugged her shoulders. At least they weren't talking about babies any longer.

"She wanted us to be together. Remember her letter? All about family and being friends with each other. I remember thinking she must have slipped a cog when I read all that but I didn't know the real reason behind her words. Now they don't seem so dumb."

"I never thought they were dumb."

"What did you think?"

Debbie hesitated. She'd been caught in a lie because she *had* thought they were dumb. Dumb, inconvenient and unnecessary. "I'm sorry. I lied. I thought they were dumb, too. And inconvenient. I didn't want things in my life to change. I was happy with my once-a-year visit and an occasional telephone call from Michael. I'd gotten used to not hearing from you."

"That wasn't right. I was wrong not to keep in touch." Patty looked at her hands folded on the table, closed her eyes and leaned against the back of the booth. "I remember when I got Mom's letter."

"So do I."

"There I was enjoying the best job and the greatest weather I'd ever had. Never mind that I was pregnant, unmarried and soon to lose this great job because I wouldn't fit into the uniform." Patty shrugged. "I guess I wasn't too smart."

Debbie didn't know how to respond. She tried to picture Patty as a waitress in Florida but the image was too dim, too distant.

"It suddenly hit me in that little dive I called home, that I was alone and lonely. I'd never thought of myself like that before."

Am I alone and lonely? Before Debbie could assess her status, Patty continued as if, now that the floodgates were lifted, she was compelled to divulge everything.

"I cried and didn't know why."

"What did you do then?"

"I called Michael and he sounded so practical that I was furious with him. I didn't want to admit that I was lonely. And, I guess, I didn't want to admit that I needed help."

"I'm glad you called Michael."

"So am I. I'm also glad I came home when I did because I never would have met Philip Branigan."

"Who's he?"

"A doctor I met on the plane coming home. A neonatal specialist. Takes care of babies who have serious problems at birth."

"And he helped you?"

"I guess in a way he did. I had already made up my mind to keep the baby," again her hands stroked her tummy. "I was on my way home so I'd made that decision, too. He kind of reinforced my decisions. Made them feel right." She grinned and nodded. "Yeah, he helped."

Debbie studied her younger sister. For the first time she realized the attitude she'd labeled as rebellion was really a sense of independence.

"I remember when I received Mom's letter, too. At first I dismissed the whole idea of coming home early. I always went home in late summer so I told Michael I wasn't coming in April. He didn't know the real reason for the invitations but he must have sensed something more than I did. He must have told Mom I wouldn't be able to make it."

"So Mom called you?"

"No, she must have told Aunt Kate because she called me and told me in no uncertain terms why I had to change my plans and come home. She told me the reason behind the letter."

"So you knew before you came home."

"Yes." Suddenly Debbie was transported back to her apartment, and her terror at the news, which prompted her frantic call to Charles. She remembered his tenderness, their kisses and the surprising strength she felt as she leaned against his chest.

"Kate told me about Mom when she picked me up in Wilkes Barre. I called Mike in New York and told him before he left to pick you up in Philadelphia. At least we all knew before we got to Eagleton."

"That's all in the past though, Patty. We have to deal with what's happening now."

"And how do we do that?"

"I did a lot of thinking last night after that..." Debbie hesitated, "after that shouting match in the garage. I'm ashamed of that."

"Me, too."

"But, after I was in bed last night I thought about everything we'd said and even hinted at. You're right, Patty. It was dumb not to keep in touch. We have separate lives, separate interests, but we're still family."

Patty saw Debbie reach for the check. She still had some of the money her parents' had sent her and her last paycheck but her financial future was uncertain. She'd never been one to plan ahead. As if reading her mind, Debbie's voice brought her back to the present. "What are you going to do, Patty? Are you going to stay in Eagleton?"

"I think so. After Mom goes—God isn't that hard to say?" she said as she wiped tears that had sprung to her eyes. "After Mom goes, Dad will be alone. I'm not sure, but I'd bet he'll want to keep the house and everything just like it is for a while. They've said I should stay, but I don't want to freeload. I'm not used to planning a future for myself and now I have a baby to think about."

"You could go to the new junior college that opened in the county a couple of years ago."

"And do what?"

"I don't know. After the baby is here, you could take some courses, learn a trade."

"You're trying to be helpful and I appreciate that. Maybe junior college might be the best thing. It's not something I thought of before, but then things are different. That word again. We talked about changes when we were walking here."

Debbie put a dollar beside her plate. "Ready to go?"

"Yeah."

They shrugged into their jackets and left the diner. While they had been eating and talking, the sun had become bolder and the air no longer held the chill it did earlier.

"I liked that," Patty said.

"The breakfast?"

"No, dummy. The chance to talk to you." Patty tucked her arm through her sister's for a moment then withdrew it and plunged her hands into her pockets.

Debbie grinned. Well, that was different. "Let's go buy you some fat clothes."

"Rat," Patty snorted.

CHAPTER THIRTY-SEVEN

Patty sat in the ancient rocking chair between the front windows. "I'm stuffed."

"You should be. You ate enough for three. Sure you're not having twins?" Michael stretched back against the sofa cushions.

Patty was going to scowl at him, and then noticed his eyes were shut.

Lily reached for her tea on the table between the two chairs she and George occupied. "It was a wonderful dinner. I wish Kate hadn't rushed off as soon as it was over."

"She had something to do at church," George's hand automatically moved toward the remote control, and then drew back. Not tonight. Tonight for the first time in longer than he could remember, the whole family was gathered in the living room after dinner. He turned to look at Debbie sitting next to Michael. "You're quiet, Deb."

"I'm full, too. I think Kate really enjoys cooking for a crowd. It must be frustrating for a good cook to have to deal with meals for one."

"What do you do?" Patty asked, turning to Debbie.

"About cooking? I usually get something from a gourmet deli on the way home from work. If it's not hot enough when I'm ready to eat, I can always zap it in the micro. Then, too, there's always the delicious, nutritious frozen meal in a box."

"Gourmet deli," Patty laughed quietly. "I always ate where I was working. Sometimes it was hamburger heaven; once in a while something good came along. It didn't matter." She left a lot unsaid. "How about you, Mike?"

Michael hesitated. His mind fast-forwarded through the elegant dinners Simone, with the aid of a caterer, had produced. The contrast when no company was being entertained was simple—canned soup and a salad if they were at home, or dinner out more often than not. "I—we eat out a lot, when we're not entertaining." His eyes went to his mother. Her eyes dared him to be honest. "Now I either eat before going home or do what you do, Deb. Eating from a plastic tray isn't all that bad."

The room was silent as they made eye contact with each other. Confused, they immediately looked away.

"Explanation—Mom knows and I guess Dad does, too. Simone and I are separated. We're getting a divorce." It was easier than he thought to confess and yet he felt his cheeks burn.

"What?" Debbie said, sitting up straight and turning to her brother.

"No way," Patty said, her hands gripping the arms of the rocker.

"It's true. I guess the easiest explanation would be to say it was not a good marriage and leave it at that. We've decided to go our separate ways."

"I was sorry to hear that, Son," George said, sounding genuinely remorseful.

"We don't need to know the details, dear," Lily said. She looked into the faces of Debbie and Patty. "Trouble isn't selective, is it? We all have our crosses to bear."

"Well, this seems to be confession time." Patty hesitated, then continued, "I've had my share of troubles, but I'm not counting this as trouble." She patted her tummy. "I'm not sorry."

"Never feel sorry about bringing another life into this world, Patty," Lily smiled at her youngest daughter.

"No. In fact, I envy you. Not having children . . ." Debbie choked.

"You'll find someone someday, Deb. You'll have a family. I always thought of you as a career girl but I was wrong. You'd be a great mother." Michael gripped her hand lying on the sofa between them.

"Maybe I have found someone." Debbie whispered but the words reached every ear.

"Oh, dear. I'm so happy for you." Lily leaned forward, her face glowing with anticipation. "Can you…?"

"Don't jump too far ahead, Mom. I've met a man who is the kindest, most patient guy in the world. Charles called me yesterday morning. That's why I went downtown. I needed to think."

Michael watched her, unwilling to say anything to break the mood or the flow of words. "That's why you weren't here?"

Debbie nodded, her eyes pleading for understanding. "I didn't realize I was away such a long time. I didn't know Mom was alone."

George nodded. "It's okay, Deb. We understand." He looked at each of them challenging them to forget the rift yesterday's emergency caused. "Your mother always said there was good in every situation. You know, she's usually right."

Debbie let a deep breath escape. She hadn't realized she'd been holding it. "I'm sorry about your divorce, Mike, but I understand. Probably better than anyone."

"You went through it and…" Michael didn't know how to finish. He knew he didn't want to air the details of his marital troubles, and understood why his sister had been so reluctant to reveal the specifics of her divorce.

For several moments the room was uncomfortably quiet. Patty pushed herself from the rocking chair, "Anyone ready for dessert? Kate made chocolate pudding and there's pound cake. Mom?"

"Not for me, honey. Maybe later." She smiled at Patty, knowing she was trying to jumpstart the conversation again.

"I'll have some later." George held out his empty cup, "with more coffee."

"Me, too," Debbie said. "Chocolate pudding. Do you remember when you dumped a dish of chocolate pudding into my purse, Patty?"

"It was an accident," she defended herself, and then laughed. The laughter was infectious as they all remembered the incident.

George shifted in his chair. "As I remember it you left your open purse on the floor next to you in the kitchen."

"Yes, I was finishing my lunch, getting ready to go back to school. Patty must have been what—four or five?"

"I must have been four because I wasn't in school yet."

"She tripped over nothing and fell forward, spilling the pudding into your open purse," Lily added, struggling to laugh and breathe at the same time. "I was at the sink when I heard your scream, Debbie."

"What a mess it was. There was pudding all over the place, the chairs, table, and the floor. Of course, I didn't know it was pudding at first. Just that everything was covered with brown stuff."

Michael was laughing so hard his eyes filled with tears and he noticed his father's face contorted with suppressed laughter. "Poor Mom. She didn't know what to do first, clean Patty and the kitchen, or get Debbie out of the room."

"I remember screaming at her, I could have killed her at the time. My new purse was sticky and disgusting, there was chocolate pudding in my socks!"

The room echoed with laughter. Lily leaned back in her chair and closed her eyes.

Michael suddenly realized she was quiet while the others were being so noisy. "Mom," he shouted. "You all right?" He bolted from the couch.

George pulled himself forward, locking the recliner in its upright position with a thud. "Lil…?"

"Mom?" Patty and Debbie said in unison.

"I'm all right. Really," Lily opened her eyes, sweeping each of them with a smile. "I was enjoying the sound of laughter again. It's been so long."

They crowded around her chair. "This is just the beginning, Mom," Michael said.

"You scared me."

"We're going to be okay, Mom."

"God, Lil, you scared us."

Their voices blended as they all joined in.

"I'm sorry. I wanted to keep those echoes in my heart."

"Echoes," Michael said. "That's funny. Someone once told me whatever happened in your life, each experience, was like an echo you stored in your heart. You could get over the troubles but you always had those memories to remind you that you'd succeeded in conquering the problems. I guess happy echoes are stored away, too."

"Whoever told you that was a wise person, Son. And, I'm a very lucky mother. I have so many more good echoes than bad ones." Lily closed her eyes again. "I'm tired. Maybe you should have dessert without me."

"I'll help you to bed, Lil." George put his arms around her, easing her from the chair.

Michael, Debbie and Patty watched their parents cross the room and disappear behind the closed doors to the sunroom.

"I'll put the kettle on," Patty whispered.

"I'll help," Debbie said.

Michael followed his sisters into the kitchen and closed the door behind them. "You know, it's going to be hard to leave."

"I know. I dread it. And to think I wasn't going to come home," Debbie's eyes filled with tears. "I was being so selfish, only thinking of myself again."

Michael patted her shoulder. "You weren't alone."

"I won't have to leave," Patty said quietly.

"You'll be here with her. For us," Michael gathered her close to him.

They stood closer to each other than any of them remembered but it wasn't the space between their bodies that had been reduced. It went far deeper than that.

Patty sighed and turned to fill the kettle. Debbie took mugs from the cupboard.

"What can I do?" Michael asked.

"You can cut the cake," Debbie said, gesturing with a knife she held out to him.

For several minutes they were busy with their chores. "Did someone really tell you about those echoes?" Debbie asked, turning to Michael.

"Yes. It was strange. I only met her for a few minutes in the airport in Philadelphia while I was waiting for you, Deb."

"Her?"

"An older lady. Indian. East Indian. Worked for the State Department. It was strange."

"Strange is right. I met a guy on the airplane. A doctor. He was neat. Not pushy, just kind of nice." Patty smiled as she remembered talking to him about her baby. "He made me think—really think."

Debbie was quiet. "I guess I was too busy feeling sorry for myself to let anyone tell me anything."

No one spoke for several moments, and then she added, "No that's not right. I listened to Charles when he told me I was dwelling on the wrong things. He was right."

"Things have changed for all of us," Michael said, putting slices of cake on a plate Patty held.

"You're right. Some things never change and some things are never going to be the same again."

Debbie put her arm around her sister. "You know, you're a lot smarter than I thought."

"You always were a rat," Patty said, laughing.

"And that's the last argument you two are ever going to have," Michael said, pushing his sisters apart.

"It isn't going to be easy," Debbie said, and then quickly added, "I mean losing Mom."

"No."

"I'll be here with her. I'll let you know when…"

"Let who know what, Patty," George said quietly entering the kitchen.

"Mike and Deb. I'll let them know whatever they need to know, Dad. They've just discovered how smart I am." She smiled at her father.

George shook his head, "I never thought she could pull it off."

"Pull what off?" Michael asked, pulling out a chair for his father.

"Your mother. She said you'd be friends and she was right."

In the converted sunroom, Lily lay against her pillows. The oxygen machine purred quietly. A streetlight in front of the house sent streaks of light through the slats of the window blinds. She looked at the framed pictures George had arranged on the windowsill next to her bed. In the quiet, she heard voices from the kitchen. Michael and Debbie would be here two more days. Patty would be with her until the end and then she, and later the baby, would be with George.

Lily smiled contentedly. She was happy. From the kitchen, the voices of her family sounded like echoes. She drifted into a deep peaceful sleep.

#

At three-thirty on the afternoon of the twentieth day of July, Lili Katherine Hoffmann was born at Eagleton General Hospital. Seven pounds seven ounces, loudly proclaiming her arrival, she was perfect. Her grandfather, uncle Mike, and aunt Debbie were with her mother. Her grandmother and namesake lay sleeping in a room several floors below the delivery room. Four days earlier she'd slipped into a state of semi-consciousness, rarely rousing, her breathing becoming ever more labored. Patty went into labor in her room and insisted on staying with her mother. The nurses and doctors allowed her to rest on a narrow cot in the same room until she had to leave for the delivery room.

Debbie touched the petal soft cheek of the infant sleeping in the bassinet. "She's beautiful, Patty

"I know. What a miracle, but then miracles do happen." Patty stretched her neck to look at her child. "Where's Mike and Dad?"

"They're downstairs with Mom."

"I want to take Lili to see Mom."

"I told Doctor Bob. He's going to make the arrangements."

"What arrangements? I can take her there. Is this a prison or a hospital?"

"Don't get testy. It won't help anyone. I was with Mom an hour ago. She's the same."

The same, Patty thought. *Not better. Not worse, thank God.* "I'm getting up." She pushed the sheets back and swung her legs over the side of the bed.

"Whoa. Where are you going?" Doctor Bob spoke from the doorway.

"To see Mom. To take Lili down to see her grandmother." Patty's voice was defiant.

"A nurse is bringing a wheelchair for you and an aide will push the basinet. We've cleared it with everyone. It's not easy getting permission to take a newborn off this floor." He grinned and patted the new mother's arm. "Wait five minutes, Mommy, okay?"

When Patty was wheeled into her mother's room, George, Michael, and Kate were there, seated in the stiff chairs next to the window. They stood and watched as the bassinet was pushed next to Patty.

"We'll be outside if you need us." The older nurse who accompanied them struggled with her own emotions as she viewed the family, turned and softly closed the door behind her.

Patty stood, pushed the wheelchair away and picked up her baby. A pink knitted hat was drawn down over the dark hair that covered the tiny head. A dark fringe of lashes made smudges above the silky cheeks; tight little fists guarded either side of a rosebud mouth. "Here's your granddaughter, Mom," Patty whispered holding the child for her mother to see.

Lily's eyelids fluttered. For the first time in several days her eyes opened and fixed on something. She appeared more aware of what and who was near her and everyone took in a small, quiet gasp of breath. "Isn't she perfect?" she whispered. "Oh, she's so beautiful."

Patty held the baby out to her mother's outstretched hand. They watched thin fingers touch the baby's face and stroke the tiny strand of hair that escaped the cap.

George stood at the side of Lily's bed. "Her name is Lili Katherine."

Lily smiled. "I know."

Lillian Hoffmann struggled for another ten days. None of the medical staff could explain her endurance. Perhaps it was the visits from the tiny infant and the family gathered around her bed every day. Whatever it was, it was a miracle but Lily had performed a miracle of her own; a miracle of faith. She had met and faced the greatest challenge of her life with dignity and peace; she had reunited her family, and she had passed along a legacy of love.

To order an autographed copy of this book, or any of the other books Sunny Serafino has written, fill in the form below and send check or money order to:

Sunny Serafino
Suite 1711
1225 NW 21st Street
Stuart FL 34994-9334

Echoes	**$17.95**
Nobody's Child	**$15.95**
Shadows in the Heart	**$15.95**
Pure Gold	**$17.95**

Please add $3.00 shipping and handling and 6% Florida State Tax (if ordering in Florida)

Questions? Call 772-692-5154

Send to:
Name: ____
Address: ______________________________________
City, State, Zip Code:____________________________
____
Phone No.(optional)(   )__________________________
Autograph to:___________________________________